Sailing Down the Mountain

Joan a. Nub,

B

1/15/15

Sailing Down the Mountain

A Costa Rican Adventure

Ben Harrison

**The New
Atlantian Library**

The New Atlantian Library
is an imprint of
ABSOLUTELY AMAZING eBOOKS

Published by Whiz Bang LLC, 926 Truman Avenue, Key West, Florida 33040, USA

Sailing Down the Mountain copyright © 2014 by Ben Harrison. Electronic compilation/ print editions copyright © 2014 by Whiz Bang LLC. Cover painting by Ben Harrison with a little help from artist, Cynthia Kulp, on the tail feathers. Cover design by Alisha Anisko and Helen Harrison. Title font: "Hand of Sean Pro" by Sean Johnson. Lyrics to the song, "Boats to Build" provided by Guy Clark.

This is an original work of non-fiction. While the author has made every effort to provide accurate information at the time of publication, neither the publisher nor the author assumes any responsibility for errors, or for changes that occur after publication. Further, the publisher does not have any control over and does not assume any responsibility for author or third-party websites or their contents.For information contact:

Publisher@AbsolutelyAmazingEbooks.com
ISBN-13: 978-0615985305

ISBN-10: 0615985300

LA DULCE MUJER

DEDICATED to my wife and boatbuilding partner, Helen, who was also editor-in-chief, and to the late Susan Mesker. Susan, after reading an early version, insisted that the book should be published—that I finish what, years ago, I'd begun. She was a force to be reckoned with, making those around her generally do what she thought they should be doing with a great amount of success. Periodically she would come by to have a glass of wine or two or three and sometimes stay for dinner. We'd sit outside under the covered part of Harrison Gallery (she was a big fan of Helen's work) and talk about all sorts of things. Occasionally, we would go out to dinner. Helen and I enjoyed her company and the twinkle in her eyes as much as she enjoyed Maine lobster.

Table of Contents

PART TWO

PREFACE

I BEGAN WRITING THIS BOOK in 1978 on a manual Remington typewriter while we were in Costa Rica. After banging out 400 pages and mailing off queries with self-addressed envelopes in which I received rejections, these papyrus relics were stored in a box where they languished for two decades. Without an agent or publisher there wasn't any alternative.

In 1986 when we bought our Key West storefront, which would become Harrison Gallery, and the house next door on the corner of White and Olivia Streets, the beginnings of the word processor were evolving in the form of typewriters with features that made corrections much easier. I needed this, so I enlisted my longtime friend Dan Simpson, who, in 1979, had begun recording my music on a Teac four track, to help me find the best one. Somehow we stumbled onto one of the original computer geeks who sold me an Amiga 500. It had no hard drive so I could regularly beat its spell check with a Webster's dictionary, but it could edit and spit out the results on a dot matrix printer. Previously, good authors were the ones who could write coherently in two or three drafts. It was these new innovations that let in the masses.

Mac was just happening, but it was expensive and had only a puny little green monitor while my Amiga had a large color screen and it could speak what I typed. I thought it was hilarious that I could make my computer say, "Fuck me."

I moved on to more sophisticated computers as I began putting together my first book, *Undying Love.* Eventually, I was drawn back to our Costa Rican adventure that I rewrote and rewrote and hope you enjoy the trip.

- Ben Harrison

Sailing Down the Mountain

PART ONE

1

BORDER CROSSING

WE WERE WEARING jackets so we could drive California's Highway One with the windows rolled down. Off to our right was the sheer rocky coast with seagulls soaring against the backdrop of the deep blue Pacific Ocean foaming and surging hundreds of feet below us. On our way to Carlsbad, near San Diego, this would be our final visit with marine architect W.I.B. "Bill" Crealock. Arriving later that afternoon, he was as charming as he had been the last time we had driven from San Francisco to meet with him. Conversing with an impeccable British accent, it was reassuring that he seemed to think that our idea – modifying a 36-foot fiberglass mid-ship cockpit ketch production sailboat into an aft-cockpit cutter with a hull extension of two feet – was conceptually sound. With Crealock's reputation and résumé of design achievements, it was flattering that he spent as much time with us as he did. At the end of our visit, we wrote him a check for $200 as a down payment for his services and left with a drawing of the side view of the boat we envisioned, as well as sectional blueprints of the hull he had designed.

Often we were asked when we told people of our plans to build a boat in Costa Rica, "Have you ever built a boat before?" Well, technically no we hadn't, but we had been studying hard. "Do you know how to sail?" Technically, yes, in small day sailboats. "Do you know how to speak Spanish?" Mine was mediocre and Helen would have to learn along the way. Such answers made it clear that, rationally speaking, there was no way to explain exactly why we would do what we were about to do. A grade school teacher once described me as a dreamer, and I suppose that's true. The best explanation I have to offer is that it was undoubtedly Helen's fault that we came up with this grand notion. When I was with her, I felt that anything was possible, and we wanted our lives to somehow be special.

From Crealock's office, we drove directly to a beach we had been told about near La Jolla. Even with all of the last minute things we needed to do before leaving the country, we still allowed ourselves a few hours to say goodbye to the magnificent coast of California and feel the cold saltwater on our bare feet. Unlike the first time, this boy from Texas and girl from Missouri uninhibitedly joined the clothes-less bodies sunbathing and walking along the surf's edge, enjoying the giddy feeling of being stark naked in the great outdoors. The incoming breakers created a haze along the coastline and made the tall green and purple sea vegetation sway mesmerizingly. It would be several hours before the sun fell below the horizon in a dazzling pink performance and we didn't plan to dress or leave until it did.

Two days later, on September 7th, 1974, filled with a wide range of emotions, in our used 1967 Pontiac Executive with 98,000 miles on the odometer, we began the drive to Nogales, a town that straddles the U.S./Mexican border. We were packed to the max with

Ralph, our Irish Setter, perched on an elevated bed we'd made for him in the back seat.

For over a year we had worked hard and saved every penny to augment the insurance payout we received when Dad unexpectedly died. We bought every book written on sailing and sailboat construction. By the time we were through with them, our nautical magazines looked as though they'd been in a doctor's office waiting room for months. In order to get wholesale discount prices of as much as 50% off marine hardware, we even established a business and obtained a California retail resale number. We had a letterhead printed reading: *Ben and Helen Harrison, Boatbuilding and Repairs.* It had a nice ring to it, though we had done neither.

All of the tools that our literature suggested we would need had been purchased brand new one afternoon from the Sears & Roebuck on Geary and Masonic Streets. Most of them, including the table saw, a pair of electric drills, a circular saw, screwdrivers, hammers and more, were crammed into the car along with thousands of screws, winches for trimming sails, clothes, a stereo, two bicycles, two guitars, a complete set of radiator hoses and any miscellaneous sailboat hardware we had room for in our large lumbering automobile, which was riding a little low.

We were homeless, and what was left of our earthly possessions were in two wooden crates that had been loaded aboard the *Cuidad Barranquilla*, a small rusty Colombian freighter headed for Central America. One crate contained a new thirty-six horsepower Volvo diesel engine that we bought for $2,300; the other: the clothing and tools we were unable to fit into the car.

In Nogales, we checked into a Motel 6, sneaking Ralph into our room before walking across the border for an introduction to life on the other side. As far as I could tell, we were the only "gringos" walking along a pair of railroad tracks where wood fires burned and unfamiliar foods cooked on grills made from fifty-five gallon steel drums cut in half sideways. The aromatic smell of meat and corn-on-the-cob was offset by the unpleasant odor of poverty. Nogales was a small town. Waiters wearing slacks with frayed pockets, carrying chipped, colorful porcelain coated metal trays advertising Cerveza Carta Blanca surrounded us, competing for our order. Filthy barefoot kids played with sticks and cans when they weren't begging for money or selling "chicle."

It being the night of a new moon, the only illumination came from the fluorescent light spilling out of the open doors of two one-room cantinas, and from the glow of outdoor fires. Loud Spanish music blared from speakers in front of one of the bars. Encircled by smiling Mexicans speaking rapidly trying to sell us something, I could imagine what was going through Helen's mind – because the same thoughts were going through mine. It's one thing to relax in a cozy California living room conjuring up exotic images of foreign lands and romantic Latin American moonlit nights.... It's quite another to experience it up close. Not far from us, a rat, almost as big as some of the scrawny dogs begging for food, waddled nonchalantly into a pile of garbage. With our big dog and old car on the U.S. side of the border, not knowing what lay ahead, I had a sinking feeling that maybe this wasn't such a glorious idea after all.

We'd had a nice, comfortable life in San Francisco. With our little nest egg of about $32,000, we could have spent some money on a skiing vacation at Lake Tahoe, used the rest as a down payment on a house, and even eaten out every now and then. If we needed to go boating, we could have taken the fucking ferry to Sausalito. This would not be the last time I would feel that what we were doing was just plain dumb, just like our parents had bluntly told us when we informed them over the phone that we were going to Costa Rica to build a sailboat.

But at the time there wasn't a whole hell of a lot we could do other than take a few deep breaths, order a couple of Dos Équis beers, and see what was cooking. It was grilled cabrito (goat). Was it even safe to eat? I gulped the first beer down quickly before buying some of the meat on a stick, which tasted good with lime squeezed on it.

Back at Motel 6, as promised in their advertisements, they had left the light on for us. Through our window, we could see the night manager, in a neatly pressed pale blue shirt and dark blue tie, doing paperwork. Inside our room with its bright, white sheet-rock walls and cling-wrapped Styrofoam drinking cups, there was a feeling of order. Things were written in English. At the side of the entrance to our room, there was a plan detailing how we should exit the building in case of fire. The price of the room and consumer protection laws were neatly posted behind Plexiglas screwed into the metal door.

Despite nightmarish thoughts of lawlessness, impending failure and lurking danger, one thing we couldn't do was go back to San Francisco – not now anyhow. We'd shared our dreams ad nauseam with our buddies and said our tearful goodbyes. If we had gone back, our friends would have been sorely disappointed. The people at the Cliff House, where I'd tended bar and Helen had waitressed, would have hurt themselves laughing if they found us knocking on the door. Tomorrow, September 8th would be my twenty-ninth birthday, which we had already celebrated at a farewell party with tequila and Mexican food at a friend's house in the company of some twenty-five well-wishers and co-workers.

Adding to the anxiety of leaving the United States, we were well aware that México, Guatemala, Honduras, El Salvador, Nicaragua and ultimately Costa Rica – every border we would pass through, would question what we were carrying and assume that we were trying to smuggle things into their country. We both woke up several times that night thinking about the momentous next morning when we would be making our first crossing into a foreign country.

The journey was about to begin.

2

THE WEDDING

BEFORE OUR COSTA RICAN adventure was even a twinkle in our eyes, Helen's and my courtship had been a complex and messy adventure in itself, with an ex-wife and a boyfriend muddying the water. There were a lot of pay-phone calls and secret rendezvous before she finally asked me to marry her.

"Well, no Mom, it's not Charles. You do remember Ben?" Helen had barely finished the sentence when her mother ran up the stairs crying. Henry, Helen's father, needed a drink. Not only did we want to get married, we were in a hurry. And once our hasty engagement became known, more than one of her relatives pulled me aside and said that if I ever did anything to hurt her again, they would kill me. Tongues were surely wagging because Helen's family was a prominent one within the community.

So how in the world did we get from Jefferson City, Missouri, and this soap opera to the Pan American Highway, driving south to Costa Rica to build a sailboat?

Helen graduated from Southern Methodist University with a Bachelor of Fine Arts the year before I finished law school in the spring of 1972. When I saw her for the first time, it was like Rodgers and Hammerstein's song from the musical, *South Pacific*, about falling for someone across a crowded room – "Somehow you'll know/You'll know even then." My immediate thought was that I could fall in love with someone like her – the way she laughed, and the way she moved. Why she initially agreed to go out with me is another one of life's inexplicable mysteries. I didn't even own a car, making me the only person in Dallas, Texas, over the age of twelve who rode a bicycle in 1970. The fact that she let me lock my three-speed Schwinn to her wood staircase so we could go out in her Pontiac, was telling.

Without going into the gruesome details, we fell in love and later broke up. It was my fault. My ex-wife decided that I wasn't so bad after all, and I screwed up. After a while, Helen found someone new.

But then, almost a year after that debacle, on an ordinary afternoon, I picked up the phone in my apartment and heard Helen's voice saying that she had seen me walking down the street and was wondering how I was doing. We talked for a while, confessing we'd been "okay." But that wasn't what made my heart flip. Her call *had* to mean that even after all we had been through, she was still, deep down inside, in love with me – it changed everything.

We soon began having an affair, sneaking around whenever we could. Not very long afterwards, I parted ways with my ex, who confessed that she too was having an affair – it was getting complicated. All I knew was that I wanted Helen to run away with me so we could begin again someplace new and exciting.

The idea that she and I could live wherever we wanted was mostly the result of a hiatus I had taken from law school during the winter of '69 and spring of '70. As an antidote to divorce, I became a ski bum in Aspen, Colorado, and the time I spent in the Rockies as a janitor, waiter, bartender and skier had been empowering. A good bartender can find work anywhere.

The emotional thermometer began rising rapidly the day her boyfriend left from a ten-day visit with Helen and her family at their home in Jefferson City. I drove through the night to nearby Columbia, Missouri, to meet her at Margie's house where she had surreptitiously arranged for me to stay.

I had never met Margie but, bless her heart, she instinctively thought Helen and I were meant for each other. So with her help, Helen made the decision that she wanted to be with me even though she knew that her parents would feel our marriage would be a disaster. One major negative for them was that I was once divorced, which was irrefutable evidence of a major character flaw. It was extremely uncomfortable for them to have all of this drama happening so suddenly. Early on, her mother often called me Charles.

On the other side of the aisle, my parents were cautiously optimistic since I had often left them confused. They felt that perhaps this was just what I needed to get my feet back on the ground.

Once we were married, our master plan was to move to San Francisco, unless we decided to stay in Aspen, and take it from there. But from the moment Helen decided that I was the one, she insisted that we leave under the right circumstances for her family's sake. That's why she asked me to marry her at Margie's in front of several of her friends and that I, without hesitation, agreed. It wouldn't have been right for her to say, "Mom, Dad, I'm leaving Charles and running away with Ben to San Francisco or maybe Aspen." This shocker was going to be difficult enough as it was.

Three weeks after the August 30, 1972 ceremony, we loaded up our dog, Ralph, who would be a companion for many years to come, and climbed into what was now *our* Volvo station wagon. Leaving the familiar behind, we drove north on Highway 63 to Columbia to pick up Interstate 70 west through the Missouri hills and across the great plains of Kansas. Giddy, we were on our way to wherever we were going – just the two of us. It had been an intense six weeks – three to organize a church wedding and three to prepare for the rest of our lives. Those we left behind were thoroughly and justifiably exhausted as we waved goodbye. Only days before my secret arrival in Columbia, Helen's parents had been introducing her new boyfriend, Charles, to their friends – eating at the Jefferson City Country Club and all of that. Two-and-a-half perplexing weeks later they were planning an elaborate church wedding and reception for their daughter and her old boyfriend, Ben.

The long drive through Missouri and Kansas took us straight to Denver and then up the Rocky Mountains, over Independence Pass and down to the Roaring Fork River on the outskirts of Aspen. After checking into the Hotel Jerome on Main Street, I showed Helen The Randy Tar Restaurant where I had worked while I lived on the third floor. Though the name had changed to Jake's, the antique Brunswick bar-back built during the Gold Rush was still there, and the general layout was the same. Originally, it had been a saloon with gambling in the basement and whoring upstairs.

I introduced her to several friends including the man who had broken me in as a bartender. What a disappointment he turned out to be. On cocaine, he wasn't the same person I had known. Hearing him incoherently brag about how much rich women were paying him for his services was pathetic.

Our best evening was at the Crystal Palace. They served a wonderful dinner, after which the waitresses, waiters and bartenders, accompanied by Mead and Joan Metcalf, performed songs and patter from Broadway sprinkled with political comedy.

Our hotel room had a pleasant view of the south side of town and the Roaring Fork River, so it was easy to spend an inordinate amount of time there doing what lovers do while taking black and white photographs of each other.

But, after several days we both decided that Colorado didn't click. So we packed, checked out, loaded the bags and drove north on Highway 82 through Carbondale and Glenwood Springs, passing the railroad station where the California Zephyr stops. The train tracks that follow the river bed are next to Interstate 70, which took us west, passing through Rifle and Grand Junction before connecting with Interstate 15 north to Salt Lake City. From there, we headed west on Interstate 80 through Reno, Sacramento and finally, to San Francisco. It is a wonder we didn't have a wreck as we couldn't keep our hands off of each other, even while driving. On a side road, at one particularly picturesque place, we put our blanket underneath a tree and made love in the middle of the afternoon beneath a blue sky with white puffy clouds lazily floating overhead.

Once there, we found a pleasant, one-bedroom unfurnished apartment in a residential area called Buena Vista, located between Haight/Ashbury and Market and Castro Streets.

It was cold getting up that first morning from the uncomfortable air mattress on the floor where we'd slept, so I turned on the wall heater and pulled up the blinds only to find a dense fog outside. In the chill, Helen stayed under our two comforters, her long golden brown hair in disarray on the white pillow that cradled her head while she waited for the temperature to rise. It was going to be a momentous day once we got up and going. After taking Ralph to the park around the corner and making breakfast in our iron skillet, we were going to buy a McRoskey Airflex queen-sized bed. Up until then we'd been making due with what we could carry with us in the car. Some furniture from back home would be arriving by truck, and we were anxious to turn our apartment at 280 States Street #2 into a home.

Part of the allure was that we saw more free-spirited human diversity in those first few days than we had seen in our entire lives. In Dallas in 1972, men with beards simply didn't wear make-up or lift their dresses in public, nor did men hold hands with men and women with women – or kiss one another as they shopped in the small stores, drank in the bars and did their banking at the Bank of America on the corner.

Driving a stick shift in San Francisco proved to be challenging for us flatlanders. On steep hills, to keep from rolling into the car behind us, we had to use our right foot to manipulate both the brake and the gas pedal, while the left let out the clutch. There were situations when the engine roared and the transmission burned. It took time (and one transmission) but we eventually got the hang of it.

Much to our relief, the McRoskey bed arrived on the same day as promised. After making it and messing it up, we dressed warmly for a walk down the hill to a small, dark Italian place on Castro Street where they let the multicolored candle wax drip onto the table all the way to the floor. The excitement of doing and seeing new things and the joy of being together alone in this strange and erotic city was doubly intoxicating in that this wasn't a honeymoon from which we had to return. Our new bed was just up the hill waiting for us – a tiny black and white television on some boxes by its side.

City-wise, San Francisco did click and we enthusiastically took in as much as we could. On one of our early day trips to the wine country, we met Juanita, the former madam of a Napa Valley house of ill repute who called me over, turned me around, and flopped her massive breasts over my shoulders for a photo opportunity.

Helen is a doer and what she did early on was set up a darkroom for developing film and making prints. First we built a plywood table along the wall of the kitchen for her new enlarger and developing trays. Then, after putting up curtains to keep out the light from the window and adjoining room, she began teaching herself how to develop black and white photographs including the ones we had taken in our hotel room in Aspen. All the while, in large part due to our new surroundings, we became – or at least tried to become – more sophisticated, educated and cultured. Inadvertently, we were off to a good start by driving a Volvo station wagon – the Californian's intellectual car of choice. It cracked me up that other people driving Volvos, who were complete strangers, would wave to us as they passed. I always waved back.

We visited museums and spent long periods of time in bookstores that had incense burning, classical music playing and people who looked like hippies working behind the counters. Back home, anyone with long hair was a hippie. Not so in California. San Francisco was so far ahead of the curve that people who looked like hippies said disparaging things about hippies, their point of reference being the Haight/Ashbury days filled with unemployed, broke, hygiene impaired, stoned disciples of free love. Not that the people of San Francisco were against love and for war. They were just over "spare change."

By the fall of 1972, Haight/Ashbury, the other side of our mountain, had changed quite a bit from the flower child days. Many of the old wood Victorian styled apartment houses and storefronts were being renovated. Though some of the head shops selling drug paraphernalia and *Mad* comic books were still around, new chic stores were moving in.

Helen took it all in with her Nikon camera the same year Paul Simon sang "Kodachrome" on our stereo turntable. Secluded in the darkroom, she developed some remarkable photographs.

"Buena vista" means "good view" in Spanish. In the middle of Buena Vista Park, located not one hundred feet from our front door, there was a rock formation that we would climb. If it wasn't foggy, we could see the rolling hills of the city and San Francisco Bay all the way to the Golden Gate Bridge.

We were on top of the world.

3

ROYAL IRISH RALPH

MEXICAN CUSTOMS AT NOGALES, where we officially entered the country on a clear sunny morning, couldn't have been more civilized, which somewhat calmed our worries about future borders and our undertaking in general. Dressed in a crumpled tan uniform, the Mexican guard explained the choice that we could unload the entire contents of the car so that he could thoroughly go through all of our possessions, or we could pay a ten-dollar fee which would make inspecting the contents unnecessary as long as we solemnly promised that we had no hidden guns. Within thirty minutes the necessary paperwork was completed, and we were on our way feeling a lot better about our "adventure" (defined in Webster's Dictionary as "an undertaking involving danger and unknown risks,") than we had the night before.

Ralph, our constant companion, couldn't sleep while he was riding in the car. In his dog mind he felt that it was his responsibility to see where we were going at all times. Over thousands of miles, and hundreds and hundreds of hours on our way to Costa Rica, not once did he close his eyes while we were on the road. We knew very well that there were people back home who thought that taking off as we did was not smart, especially with a big dog. But having him along turned out to be a good thing.

I grew up in south Texas near México and that is probably why I can roll my "r's" in Spanish. One of the problems I have had with the language is that my accent is better than my vocabulary, making people assume I understand more than I do. On our first night after clearing Customs, there was a comical amount of tongue slapping the roof of my mouth when I went to the manager's office of a small hotel in Guaymas and asked, "Queremos (we want) un cuarto (room) pero (but) tengo (I have) un perro (a dog) pero (but) es un buen perro (but he's a good dog)."

We had no idea how people would react to him, but not once throughout the entire trip were we denied a room or asked not to bring Ralph into a restaurant. It helped that he was well behaved and that he was an Irish Setter, very regal in his haughty demeanor. Though his front paws were a little slew footed, he had a well-proportioned head and shiny coat with impressive "feathers" on his legs, tail and chest. A handsome dog, he would obediently sit, stay and heel a good deal of the time.

"¿Cuánto cuesta?" ("How much did he cost?") was a question we were asked repeatedly. In Latin America everyone wants to know what everything costs.

"No tan mucho," or "Ochenta dólores," ("Not too much," or "Eighty dollars,"), which was the truth, were our standard answers.

"What kind of dog is he?" was easier, if more bewildering to the person hearing the answer: "Es un Seter Irlandés."

We soon discovered that having him along was like toting a six-shooter, albeit an unloaded one, since most Latin Americans not knowing that he wouldn't hurt a flea, were afraid of him. Dogs his size were intimidating and rare. It is quite possible that, at the time, Ralph was the only Irish Setter south of the border.

Gringos, who know what dorks Irish Setters are, were another story. They couldn't wait to pet and hug him because he reminded them of their dog back home.

"Where are you from?" was always the first gringo question. It's the way we North Americans begin conversations with each other in a foreign country. There is a thirst to meet and talk with one of your own.

"Well, San Francisco, but actually we're not from anywhere right now. We're on our way to Costa Rica to build a sailboat."

I don't think any of them believed us. I'm sure most thought we were nut cases or on some scam or drug deal.

One of the more extraordinary scenes in our travels was with Ralph riding in the smoke-belching buses in downtown México, sitting on my lap if the bus was crowded, looking out the window. People on the streets would point and some would even bark at him. He paid no attention as he sniffed the air, going with us almost everywhere except the ritzy Villa Fontana to hear the violins or the top floor of the Latin American Tower to see the astounding view. After a bus ride on the Reforma, he ran ahead of us up the long, gradual pathway that led to "Castillo Chapultepec" once inhabited by Maximilian and Charlotte, whose love for each other and reign together was tortured, brief, and tragic.

In 1855, Benito Juárez, who would become a national hero, caused widespread turmoil when he and the liberals who believed in the private ownership of land, took over. Under his leadership they were able to pass laws breaking up the large estates of the Roman Catholic Church and landed gentry, causing a bloody and expensive civil war with the conservatives. Juárez and the liberals prevailed, but the country was so bankrupt afterwards, it was forced to default on its debts to France. This gave Emperor Napoleon III an excuse to invade and conquer México, after which he appointed European Archduke Ferdinand Maximilian and Archduchess Maria Charlotte, Emperor and Empress. Upon their arrival they settled in the opulent Chapultepec Castle overlooking the Paseo de la Reforma and the city below. On a clear day they would have been able to see the majestic snow covered volcanoes, Popocatépetl and Iztaccíhuatl, named after another tragic couple.

After only a year, the political realities of the unstable social situation in which they found themselves in forced Carlota to return to Europe for the purpose of enlisting the financial aid and support of royal family members. There, without her husband, she suffered a complete mental and emotional collapse and never returned to México. Benito Juárez's army captured Ferdinand, killing him by firing squad on June 19, 1867. His final words reportedly were, "I hope that my blood flows for the good of this earth. ¡Viva México!"

During our visit to the nearby National Museum of Anthropology, another historical ghost, Montezuma, took his revenge on me. It's called "Montezuma's revenge" because he was the Aztec ruler who literally gave México to the Spaniard, Cortéz, rather than slit the conquistador's throat as he should have, or ceremoniously cut out his heart atop a blood stained pyramid to please the Gods, as they often did to captured enemies. Fortunately, I had my little accident near the "cuarto de baño." It didn't help that Helen was almost doubled over with laughter as I walked carefully, using only the lower part of my legs below the knees. Safely inside the polished, tan marble-walled stall, I had no choice but to pull out my Swiss Army Knife and cut off my soiled plaid boxer shorts with the little scissors. With a great whoosh of water from the powerful public toilet, my underwear went rapidly somewhere and my embarrassing problem was washed away.

By this time in our journey, we were used to eating inexpensive fish on a stick at the beach or tacos from street vendors. So was Ralph. There was no dog food in México or anyplace else along the way. The first time we asked a woman behind the counter of a grocery store for "comida por el perro," she laughed and looked at us as though we were crazy – special food for a dog? They also laughed and pointed when we fed him the same things we were eating. According to Ralph's tail, these were very exciting and aromatic times.

With varying degrees of regularity, we had begun keeping a journal to memorialize this epic.

9/16/74
The engine has been running rough on the Mexican gas so I adjusted the timing and it seems to be working better.

From Guadalajara we drove to Guanajuato only to find the hotels completely full due to the Fiesta de la Independencia, so we drove on to San Miguel de Allende.

In San Miguel we were faced with sleeping in the car again, which we were really tired of. Luckily, Ralph found us three girls with an extra room, which they loaned us for two nights. We all had a good time together and thoroughly enjoyed the fiesta and the magnificent fireworks, which at times would shoot at us or under our feet and literally kept us hopping and laughing to the point of tears.

Here again Ralph had come through. We met the girls because they too missed their pets. Good dog. Back at their place I pulled out my Martin D-28 guitar, and we sang and talked in English late into the evening.

Overall, the car performed well carrying us over the bumpy roads of México. Smaller cars bounced while the big Pontiac modulated smoothly sucking up tank after tank of gasoline. Our biggest malfunction occurred when a radiator hose blew in the middle of nowhere. Fortunately, Helen's dad had been so concerned about our safety that he had bought a complete set to take with us.

9/16/74

Upon leaving Puerto Vallarta, we encountered our first major car trouble, which is always a pain in the ass. The muffler and tail pipe worked loose and the car overheated. The muffler was finally repaired after jacking the car up four times and tying it up with a coat hanger. The worst problem proved to be the overheating.

A radiator hose broke and the radiator drained. Helen was frightened, grabbed Ralph and ran because she thought it was going to explode. There was a lot of steam and water. We had a spare hose and replacing it took about an hour. The problem of filling up the cooling system was solved by a very heavy thunderstorm. The cement gutters along the highway became full so I scooped up the water and strained it into the radiator.

Before the rains came, while I was working under the car, Ralph wandered off, winding up in mud up to his chest. Meanwhile, Helen got cactus thorns in her lips trying to smell one of the yellow flowers. With the smell of rain, thunder crashing around us, there was just enough time to extract the tiny hard-to-see thorns with tweezers. Then, using towels we got Ralph cleaned up enough to get him back into the car, and we were off again. Not a single car had passed.

We arrived in Guadalajara late after some incredible driving near the town of Tequila. Everyone had warned us about how dangerous driving at night there was. They were right.

From there we went to our last stop in México, San Cristóbal de las Casas, a city situated on top of an inactive volcano that can only be approached by a narrow road that winds around and around the mountain. From the top, there is a 360-degree view of the valley and from that vantage point, in the distant vastness, we could see the jagged mountains forming the Guatemalan border.

The marijuana we got in México City is almost gone; it will be tonight, as we will cross the border into Guatemala tomorrow. The excitement of the whole trip and the anticipation of building our own boat is extreme. The poverty of many and the impossibility of change for many others make us realize the opportunity we have. To dream and have the chance to succeed in our dreams is something few have and this seems to accentuate our need to succeed – to complete the boat. It is the dream of so many, and the fact that we have within our knowledge and skill the capability to do so, makes the completion of our boat and beyond, imperative.

I am writing from the bar beside a fire in the hotel here in San Cristóbal and the relief of the land and its beauty has raised our spirits, not that they had been low.

With late afternoon rain drops falling in the open part of the courtyard, I'd say it's fairly obvious that I'd burned through some of that remaining pot before I took beer and pen in hand.

The next day, just outside of town, Helen took a poignant photograph of a family of campesinos covering themselves with plastic as they stood in the rain waiting for a bus. Below the surface of this seemingly idyllic little town, festered the seeds of the fierce, deadly "Zapatista" social rebellion between Spanish descendants and the local Indians that resurfaced in the early 1990s.

From San Cristóbal we skirted the Pan American Highway and drove on a narrow road across a dry plain that brought us to a small Custom's office at Cuidad Cuauhtémoc late in the afternoon. We took the less traveled route thinking it would be better to avoid the main border crossing.

When asked if we had any animals or plants in the car, I replied, "Sí Señor, tenemos un perro." ("Yes, we have a dog.") Wanting to know his color, I told him "rojo" ("red") and was given a look of disbelief. "Rojo," he agreed as he approached our car filled to the brim. He was congenial and let us pass into Guatemala without any problems after we gave him two reflectors that he'd admired from our disassembled bicycles.

The night we spent afterwards in Huehuetenango was one of our worst. It was cold enough to turn the car heater on as the evening darkened and we tensely drove through a steady rain on a slick narrow road that wound through lush green mountainside. The number of men passed out drunk along the way steadily increased until there were some actually lying on the driving surface of the highway.

Arriving after dark, the town square was filled with even more drunk men. Off to the side of the road, two raunchy dogs were fucking, which was of particular interest to Ralph. There was only one six-room hotel and the beds in our room were damp, cold, and sagged a good four inches in the middle. Though there were two beds we slept together to keep warm, gravitating continuously toward the middle, tossing and turning as we tried to keep the thin damp wool blanket on top of us. Tired and sore, we left early the next morning. After getting back on the Pan American Highway, we drove through the mountain towns of Chimusinique, Machaquilaito and Chimaltenango on our way to Guatemala City where we had a so-so night in a so-so hotel.

The crossing into El Salvador was a lot harder than the two previous ones. Because we had so much in the car, Customs wanted a military guard carrying his rifle to ride with us to make sure we weren't smugglers disguised as two young idealistic gringos. Of course, we'd have to pay him for his time and buy his meals, plus the return trip bus fare. I argued our case as best I could, but a guard was summoned and was ready to get in the front seat with Helen and me when he saw Ralph and said something to the effect, "Son-of-a-bitch, there's a big dog in that car," to his superior.

"¿Muerde?" (Does he bite?)

To which I replied casually, "Sí, algunos veces. ¡Qué grande la boca! ("Sometimes. Look how big his mouth is!") I'll try to keep him in the back, but he's a big dog. You just never know if he likes you or not. Stay, Ralph!"

After a long discussion between the guard and the Custom's agent, they decided that perhaps we didn't need a guard after all – stamp, stamp, stamp, and we were off again through border number three.

Honduras was another hassle that had a lucky ending. At first, they were going to make us put everything in the car on tables inside for inspection. Knowing that that would be nothing but big trouble, I pulled out a letter we had received from the Honduran Embassy. Before leaving the States, I had written to the embassies of each country that we would be driving through explaining the purpose of our trip. Only Honduras had responded with a brief letter stating that we should be extended both military and civilian courtesies. After much debate among the men, the letter was shown to El Jefe, who ordered them to merely poke around the trunk a little and let us through.

It took us a full day of driving to reach the Nicaraguan border, which we easily crossed with help from Ralph who made "migración" nervous. Reaching the City of Managua next to Lake Managua at dusk, we kept driving around, trying to find the town. It was gone. The year before, most of the buildings had been ruined by a devastating earthquake and bulldozed away, leaving only streets.

It was one of our sleep-in-the-car-with-the-windows-down nights at the El Rancho Drive Inn. Not then, nor at any other time during the entire trip, were we worried about our security. We had good ol' Ralph and couldn't have been safer with a 300-pound gorilla or a brigade of cavalry. No one, but no one, was going to mess with big bad Ralphie who, to our knowledge, over a lifespan of fourteen years, never even considered biting anyone. His self-appointed job was simply to sniff, leave his scent, chase birds and female dogs – and keep his eyes on the road at all times. It mattered not whether there was the excitement of driving at night through Tequila, México, or the boredom of crossing a monotonous plain, ever-vigilant Ralph was there on the lookout to make sure everything was all right.

So far, so good.

4

SAN FRANCISCO

WHEN WE FIRST ARRIVED in San Francisco, Helen's and my future, though vague, had nothing to do with sailboats. Our first priority was to take time off and enjoy our new surroundings. The long-term plan was for me to take the California Bar Exam and once admitted, go from there. We weren't sure what we were going to do down the line, and we didn't dwell on it too much as we were really out there, floating on air.

For the time being we were unemployed but there was a lot to do that didn't cost much, if anything. Wearing our cool weather clothes (Helen usually wore her purple leather jacket and I a corduroy coat), one of our favorites was to walk down the hill to Market and Castro and catch the electric trolley to the Powell-Hyde cable car that ran up and down Nob Hill to Fisherman's Wharf. There, we might have a beer or an Irish coffee at the Buena Vista Cafe overlooking the water before buying a fresh Dungeness crab at one of the nearby seafood markets to eat back home with a fresh loaf of sourdough bread and California jug wine. At $2.75 a gallon, the wine was young but surprisingly good. We talked, listened to music and often made love in the late afternoon.

When the date to register for the bar exam arrived, I signed up to take the test as well as the Bay Area Review Course (BARC) that would help me prepare. Money-wise, we didn't have much in the way of reserves, but I had overly optimistic hopes that my Dallas booze bar, the very first "Hooters," would be sending me a monthly check.

In the beginning, turning the old automobile parts store into a bar had been a good way of supporting myself without having to work for someone else. After my stint as a bartender in Aspen and several places in Dallas, I knew the business well enough. My duties at the bar, located near the Southern Methodist University campus, included dropping by to keep an eye on things, counting money and closing up, but I had a partner who did half. If it was uninspired, it certainly wasn't dull. Every night was late and beer was free. Before I went to bed each evening, I would put an Alka-Seltzer and a glass of water on the nightstand to greet me when I woke up.

Our Hooters wasn't *the* Hooters of today. The full name of our place was "Jim, Martha, Oblio and Hooter's." But at that point in time "hooters" wasn't slang for breasts. In the early 70s, slang for bosoms was bazoombas or jugs, not hooters. Jim, Martha and Oblio were dogs. Kohoutek was the last name of my partner, and "Hooter" was his nickname. The name was meant to be a spoof on law firms like Bean, Barnhan, Tuttle and Turkey or stock brokerage firms like Merrill, Lynch, Pierce, Fenner and Smith.

Unfortunately, my original idea for naming the bar was vetoed by my partners, which in my opinion was a D-cup mistake as it could have translated into Hooters' size profit. Texas had just passed a law allowing liquor to be sold by the drink causing an unexpected surge in "titty" bars. In an effort to curb licentiousness, the state legislature passed a law allowing female exposure so long as the "discolored portion" of the breast was not visible – nipples had to be covered with "pasties."

"The Discolored Portion," would have been a great name and concept for a bar. I envisioned having the statute printed in large lettering on the wall surrounded by tastefully painted nudes. The staff would, of course, include buxom waitresses.

After I left Dallas, Hooter's went through some drastic changes and the bottom line was that the only check I received was $500 for my 40% interest. Without physically being there, I thought I'd better take what I could get. The bar is still in operation as a college hang out called the "Corner Bar and Grill."

On the bright side, I was in San Francisco with the woman I loved, riding real cable cars, sampling wine at the wineries in Napa Valley, sleeping late if we wanted and fixing meals from our new cookbook, *Cooking With Wine.* The fifty and sixty degree weather is so invigorating it made us want to go out and do things – if nothing else, take Ralph for a walk. As for our long-term future, we'd figure something out as we watched the boats sail past Alcatraz and the Golden Gate Bridge in San Francisco Bay, before the fog rolled in and made us snuggle closer together.

The California Bar Exam, one of the most difficult, is impossible to pass without taking a prep course because, not only is the amount of information that has to be ingested staggering, there are test taking techniques that have to be learned. While I studied, Helen began searching for a job. Her worst tryout was as a breakfast waitress at the Mark Hopkins Hotel, one of San Francisco's finest, located at Number One Nob Hill. After her interview, she was invited back the next morning for training. Up at 5:30, driving to the work in the dark, wearing borrowed white shoes that were too tight and a starched uniform provided by the hotel, she was a tired puppy that smelled like bacon and eggs when she returned home just before noon with $12.

For Helen, one morning was enough.

She soon landed a job as an evening cocktail waitress at Henry Africa's, one of the city's first "fern bars." That's what they were called because they were decorated with ferns and other vegetation hanging from the ceiling, visible from the street through large plate glass windows. She would wear an ankle length skirt with leather boots and a snug top. There weren't a lot of brassieres in California in the 70s, which made the landscape even more appealing in the cool weather. Waiting for her in the car after her shift, she looked awfully pretty with the ornate bar as a backdrop.

The bar exam is brutal. If ever a director wanted to make a horror film and needed realistic, life-like zombies, the people emerging from the final day of the exam would be perfect for the part. I was one of those numb, pale people with splotchy complexions and coffee stained teeth walking like a robot to the car – completely used up. I got drunk that night. So did one of the owners of Henry Africa's who fired Helen for stealing, which was ludicrous. She was beyond pissed off when she got home and kept trying to wake me up. Without someone to commiserate with, she had to be mad all by herself and that made her even madder. It was probably best for both of us that I didn't wake up.

The next day we went in and told the two brothers/owners that we thought they were major assholes, which they agreed they probably were. That night we celebrated with Boeuf Wellington and a bottle of St. Émilion at Ernie's, a swank restaurant with red patterned wallpaper and a décor reminiscent of California in the 1890s.

Since it would be two months before I received the results of the bar exam, now that neither of us had a job, we decided, "What the heck," and accepted my good friend Charles Knolle's invitation to accompany him and his girl, Debbie, on a sailing trip. They were going to take their Cal-32' sailboat from Corpus Christi to Florida and could use our help. I'd sailed with Charles before when he was in an offshore race, and it had been fun. His boat was a light displacement, fin keel that was small, but still large enough for the four of us to make the passage.

Why, after the trip, we had any further interest in sailing is another mystery.

The beginning was ominous. On the day of our intended departure, it was so foggy we had to postpone leaving until the next afternoon. Then, once past the jetties at Port Aransas, we rolled around in dark, sloppy seas until the wind picked up to 20 – 25 knots.

3/10/73

I took the helm at midnight and remained there for four hrs. and was extremely sore and tired. Debbie was ill the entire night. Sailed a course due south because the winds were unfavorable and from the east. Later that pm we were becalmed in rough seas.

Without wind, sails flapping, for a second time in even rougher seas, we tried to start the motor and found that the battery was too low to turn it over. The new back-up battery Charles had bought turned out to be a dud, meaning we had no choice but to flounder around until the wind picked up. Hours later, when it did, we headed north to Freeport where we had a dicey sail up the Intercostal Waterway, dodging barges. In three days we had gone approximately 120 miles. The bed at the marina hotel felt like a million dollars.

There was more fog the next morning as we again sailed a good ways southeast out into the Gulfo de México.

3/14/73
After daybreak a squall came in. It proved to be a long steady gale wind. Charles and I eventually pulled down all canvas and ran before the waves – south wind was in the area of 50 knots and seas were 35 – 40 feet. After a long day of bare poling Charles and I began one-hour shifts while the other slept. Helen stayed inside due to her bronchitis and Debbie was still unsure of herself. When we arose every hour, it was like getting up seven bad mornings in a row. Were blown 130 miles without any sails up.

3/15/73

Endured the storm and raised the jib. It had lasted 22 hours and was as fierce as anything I hope to ever see! We had strung rope from the stern in an effort to stabilize. Twice we had been caught by a breaking wave and were washed sideways. The girls took the helm this day while Chas. and I slept, cleaned up.

This was scary stuff. The "rope", which, nautically speaking, should have been called "line," that we were dragging from the stern, was an attempt to slow us so we wouldn't surf down one of the monster waves and "pitch-pole" – flip the boat over, bow first. Being washed sideways is called "broaching" and it isn't good either, but it's not nearly as bad as pitch poling. Fortunately, we had a bright moon, which made steering in between the oil platforms scattered throughout the Gulf south of Louisiana, a little easier. Otherwise, it would have been doubly scary.

3/16/73
Early the next morning Helen and I were up for sunrise. It was clear and we were becalmed. It was our first beautiful day and we dropped coins into the sea to see how far we could see them. The entire day was beautiful and when the wind picked up we saw what sailing could be. We had decided to head to New Orleans and the safety of the Intercostal Waterway.

We entered the Intercostal through the Berateria Waterway, a shallow poorly marked channel well known to pirate Jean LaFitte. He and other "freeboaters" operated in the bayous that were now inhabited by fishermen living in weathered wood frame houses with docks in various states of repair extending from the shore. Moss covered trees lined the shore where Helen took an especially moving photograph of a small dilapidated cemetery.

Harvey, Louisiana, is an industrial town on the west side of the Mississippi River. All along the inland channel there are signs saying how many miles it is to Harvey, and here we were at "mile zero." Rafted up alongside a tug, it was dusk when we went through the lock into the Mississippi. With the lights of New Orleans reflecting off the wide river, we motored across to another lock on the east side and then tied up for the evening at a government dock on the other side where a Custom's agent scared the crap out of us by boarding and searching us for drugs. Thankfully, he didn't find the pot or the bong I'd brought from California along with a case of Madeira wine.

Escaping that, we had a big time in New Orleans staying at a hotel, eating dinner at Felix's and drinking "Hurricanes" at Pat O'Brian's in the French Quarter where we had our glassy-eyed picture taken. With a little bit of the previous night on our tongues, breakfast at Brennan's the next morning was super.

Back on the boat, we then motored across Lake Pontchartrain to Gulfport, Mississippi, and docked at the yacht club just before...

3/21/73

A storm very near Hurricane force blew in, and we thanked our lucky stars we were not in the Gulf. Tides rose six ft. in a matter of hours. The rain stung as it hit our face and winds were as high as 60 knots. Late that evening it stopped as suddenly as it had begun.

3/23/73
Went only 30 mi to Hog Town Bayou where we spent the night anchored. It stormed like crazy. The lightning was loud and bright and the rain extremely heavy. The boat leaked in certain areas and was uncomfortable. The head has been broken for the past four or five days.

Crossing the Mississippi Sound, which was open water, we passed Horn Island and Petit Bois Island before entering Mobile Bay. Along the way the water had been chocolate in color until we crossed from Alabama into Florida where it abruptly became much clearer and absolutely beautiful.

3/24/73
Arrived in Panama City after only a mildly successful sail – but we were in one piece.

The reality of our passage was that the weather had kicked our asses while we dodged oil platforms without sails. We'd lost auxiliary power. Our asses were kicked again by horrible weather in the Gulf. We could have been busted for drugs, arrested, and sent to jail. The head broke. Mosquitoes bit. The boat leaked; the thunder rolled; the lightning flashed. In sixteen days we had traveled roughly 600 miles.

Just before leaving on the trip with Charles and Debbie, someone had asked Helen if she had ever been offshore. Indignantly, she replied that of course she had, not realizing that he meant really "offshore," not just off shore. Now she had.

We saw my dad for the last time the day we left Corpus Christi to go back to San Francisco. His coloring was worrisome, but he had that mischievous twinkle in his eye as he walked out of the house in a brown suit, smiling as he said goodbye.

Happily back in San Francisco and broke, I joined Helen in our search for work. In Dallas I'd had a taste of playing music professionally, so I first tried playing my guitar and singing on the streets. Economically, we soon learned that this was impossible unless you were one of the few musicians with a pass to play at retail complexes like The Cannery or Ghirardelli Square on the waterfront. One afternoon I made three dollars in tips while Helen gave five dollars to a blind man selling pencils.

Answering an ad in the newspaper, I also auditioned for a job singing at the Rusty Scupper Restaurant, which didn't go well, either. The musicians before me were professionals with a lot of experience. After I finished my set, the bartender asked me what it felt like to "really bomb out."

"Not good," I confided as he poured me a sympathy drink on the house.

I wasn't discouraged. Though I'd played a few Tuesdays at a bar in Dallas, this was my first real attempt at lounge singing and it was, after all, San Francisco.

5

THE CALL

THE CALL CAME ON APRIL 8, 1973, and the loud ring of our black rotary AT&T telephone awakened us from a deep sleep. Who could it be at this time of night?

"Hello?"

"Ben, this is Bob Morman. I have some bad news. Your father died tonight of a heart attack."

After I hung up and told Helen, we were unable to sleep. We talked for several hours in our robes, sitting on the corduroy couch with feather cushions overlooking States Street and the small houses illuminated by street lamps on the hill below us.

My first reaction was anger. I was furious. How could he not take care of himself? I saw him smoking too many cigarettes and drinking too much Scotch. I saw his bowling-ball belly, his skinny legs and then his mischievous smile.

Who was he? What was he really like? Absorbed with my own life, I hadn't thought about it that much. Though he had always been financially supportive as he tried to steer me in the right direction, we argued a lot and hadn't been terribly close.

Early photographs of my parents show a very handsome couple. One in particular is of Mother, pretty as a picture, standing next to him, rakish and fit in his military dress uniform. Another, taken at a Texas airfield near the end of the war, shows him and his crew looking cocky as they posed in front of their plane. I'm sure the image Dad had of himself was that of a dashing young World War II pilot, and it probably became part of his aura among his peers later in life. What I saw as he grew older was Dad in geeky Bermuda shorts worn high on his stomach playing golf with other dorky grown-ups.

It was hard for me to imagine him as a college kid doing the jitterbug at a fraternity party, drinking hooch from a flask, or trying to unhitch a bra strap so he could feel up the giggling girl (perhaps Mother) he had brought to the dance at Oklahoma A & M in Stillwater (now Oklahoma State University).

Helen and I flew out of San Francisco the next day with our dog, Ralph, and arrived in the afternoon at Corpus Christi International Airport. A Boeing 727 had flown us to Dallas where we boarded a piston driven, twin-engine Convair that brought us the rest of the way, with one stop in Austin. A blast of familiar hot air hit us as we exited the airplane door and descended the steps to the cement tarmac.

This was the same airport where years earlier I'd been told, in a condescending way, that Mexican women had punched holes in the turquoise and orange vinyl chair cushions with their high heels as they tried to get a glimpse of Lyndon B. Johnson, the presidential candidate who had given them free tamales during a campaign stop. Above us was the control tower that had once directed Dad as he landed and took off in our Beechcraft Bonanza, and me as I made touch-and-go landings learning to fly a Cessna 150.

Beside the main door of the terminal there was a plaque honoring those who had helped promote the need for a new international facility, and one of the names on it was "Frank Harrison." Outside and to the left was the private plane hangar where, thanks to Dad, I'd been a hangar boy – my first real job.

When we arrived at our house at 3140 Ocean Drive, we were warmly greeted by Mom and Dad's friends, the ones who went to the same parties and were members of the Corpus Christi Country Club. After living in California, it struck me how clean-shaven the men were, wearing coats and ties and smelling of after-shave. It was as though they had just stepped out of a barbershop. Their wives' hair, done at a beauty parlor, was the same style it had always been with make-up, perfume and shade of lipstick never wavering – no bra-burning lesbians, pink-haired queers or stoned out couples in this crowd. My shoulder length hair immediately irritated Mother.

As the day of the funeral wore on, I remembered tidbits, little flashbacks, of my growing up. I recalled Mom talking to me about an information sheet I had filled out during homeroom in Hamlin Junior High School. Beside "Father's Occupation," I wrote "Unemployed" because he didn't have a nine-to-five job like most. Not since I was five or six years old, had he gone to work at a set time and come home after a hard day at the office.

The school guidance counselor, worried about our social and economic welfare, called Mother to make sure we were okay and getting enough to eat. From then on I was told to list Dad's occupation as "independent oil operator."

Soon after graduating from college in 1940, Dad volunteered for the Army Air Corp and, unlike most, made it through flight school. Everyone wanted to be one of the flyboys and the pinnacle of becoming a bomber pilot was to sit in the left chair. Ultimately, he piloted a Boeing B-29 Flying Super-Fortress. Powered by four 18 cylinder 2,200 horsepower engines with duel super chargers, at the time it was the largest warplane ever built. With only a few hours in the new aircraft, he and his crew took off from California, headed for a top-secret Far Eastern destination via Guam. Before he left he and Mom had devised a code so she would know where he was—Tokyo Rose knew.

His mission, once they reached India, was to fly over the Himalayas, (nicknamed "Aluminum Alley" because so many planes crashed en route), refuel in China, and then continue on to bomb Japan. The first aircraft to have a pressurized cabin, the B-29 was designed to fly so high that it couldn't be attacked by Japanese fighter planes. Unfortunately, from that altitude they were unable to hit their targets. As a result they were ordered by General Curtis LeMay to fly these huge airplanes on night missions low to the ground where they had to defend themselves from enemy aircraft and hope that the flack exploding all around missed. It was a B-29 that ultimately dropped the atomic bomb and, though he never talked about it, Dad's plane had to have been one of those that firebombed Tokyo with devastating results as most of the structures were made of wood.

After the war and his discharge from the Army Air Corp, he took a job as pilot and accountant for La Gloria Oil and Gas, a small company located in Corpus Christi, Texas. The company prospered and, through stock options, he was soon able to go to work for himself, speculating during the oil boom when fortunes were made and lost.

Perhaps the biggest contributor to his untimely death was the financial bind he found himself in after investments in two Liberian registered oil tankers didn't work out. He gambled and lost, which forced him to get his stockbroker's license and work at Merrill Lynch as an account executive. After being an unemployed golfer/oil man running with the Corpus Christi big dogs, it was demeaning and ultimately deadly to have to take the job.

The funeral behind us, Helen and I stayed with Mother to help her out and handle his estate. As I sifted through his papers and possessions, I thought quite a bit about him and his cultural inclinations. He had a wonderful tenor voice and loved to sing, his favorite musical being *South Pacific*. He was proud of the fact that my sister, Julie, and I took music lessons and played musical instruments. It was Dad who flew us in one of several V-tail Beechcraft Bonanzas to Aspen each winter to ski and listen to the show tune music at the Crystal Palace. In San Francisco we saw *Applause* starring Lauren Bacall and went to a nightclub floorshow featuring choreographed routines with bare breasted dancers. In another of our adventures we touched down in México City where we stayed in El Hotel Presidente, dining twice at the Villa Fontana while listening to the soaring violins and twin pianos. In New York City he took us to see *Man of La Mancha* and *Evita*. Early on he strongly encouraged me to take commercial art lessons and later a class in painting from the legendary Corpus Christi artist, Mary Sloan. Without his financial support, I wouldn't have been able to spend a summer in Europe.

Perhaps unwittingly Dad was at least partially responsible for instilling in me a "go-for-it" attitude – he taught me too dramatically how short life is.

B. Frank, as he was known to his friends, the "B" coming from his first name Benjamin, hadn't been great at communicating with my sister and me, but he'd introduced us to a good part of the world. There is no question that he loved us immeasurably, perhaps so much that he had a hard time relating to us as people who were going to drink, screw, smoke pot, cuss, fall down, get up and live our own lives.

Was he a good guy? I think he was, and the people at the funeral seemed to think so, too.

6

FAREWELL

SAN FRANCISCO

IN CORPUS CHRISTI, it took a full six weeks to sort through the chaos left by a man who unexpectedly died too young. I had previously passed the Texas Bar, so with the help of an accountant, I was able to handle the estate, drafting and filing the necessary probate documents, which saved Mother a lot of money. In the process, I found that I had been left a $20,000 life insurance policy.

April '73
This money really put ideas in our heads. We are not sure what life's purpose is, but sailing seems to have some point. We looked at one boat, the Antonia K, *which seemed perfect but not for sale.*

During the depression of the 1930s, Franklin D. Roosevelt's Works Progress Administration, the WPA, built a functional harbor that drastically improved the waterfront of downtown Corpus Christi. Boulders of granite were put in place to form a breakwater that protected an area large enough to build two cement T-heads and one L-head that automobiles could drive on and boats tie up to. In one of the slips, the sailboat that caught our eye was an old 45-foot, wood-hull, gaff rigged sloop. Of course, it would take a lot of time and money to fix up, but it could be done, especially if we did the work ourselves. Our thinking was that if we could get a boat that we could live on without going into debt, we would be free to sail wherever we pleased and live on fresh fish.

After taking care of Mother's affairs, we were ecstatic to be back in California. The day after our return, we drove across the Golden Gate Bridge to warmer sunnier Sausalito. There, by happenstance, Helen and I met a couple that made a big impression on us.

Clint Hanger and his wife were in the finishing stages of building a classic Peterson-designed wood schooner that they had been working on nights and weekends for eight years. They were kind enough to take the time to show us around, and as they did, he wryly pointed out that since starting on his boat, his daughter had grown up, and he'd lost the tip of a finger on a band saw. Here was the realist trying to tell dreamers what they might be getting into. I called him shortly before we left for Costa Rica and told him about going there to build our own boat. He said, "You know, you have a lot of balls." Those were not the words of encouragement I wanted to hear from someone who knew what they were talking about.

What an amazing job they had done. Their boat was beautifully built and seemed structurally sound. I hope with all of my heart that it brought them joy because it was an inspiration to us. They'd had a dream and set about doing it, no matter what or how long it took. We reasoned, being initially impatient, that if we could do a portion of the work ourselves, our options would be greater and our construction time less consuming. But first, it became clear that we needed to get jobs so we could add to our capital.

We hit the streets and for several weeks I looked for work as a bartender, going from bar to bar, filling out applications, talking to bar managers. Moving into a new town like San Francisco is not the easiest of things because I didn't know anyone who could tell me that so-and-so had an opening. But eventually my luck changed. The bar manager at the Cliff House, overlooking the Pacific Ocean, said they might be able to use me. Located next to Seal Rock where the seals bark and frolic in the icy water, it had once been the elegant Redwood Room with large bark-covered redwood posts that separated the mirrors behind the original bar that was still there. Close by were the ruins of the famed Sutro Baths. Built of glass, wood and iron in 1896, it had had one freshwater and six saltwater swimming pools. It closed in 1966 and was destroyed by fire shortly afterwards. Within two weeks I had a full schedule at union scale – $37.50 a shift plus tips, which was a lot in those days.

The same people who owned the Cliff House also owned The Pub, a small fern bar with a local clientele located on the corner of Geary and Masonic Streets, across from the Sears & Roebuck where we would ultimately buy our tools to take to Costa Rica. When they hired Helen as a waitress, the money started rollin' in.

Our rent was $200 a month. I was averaging about ten dollars a day in tips in addition to union scale. Helen made anywhere from $25 to $50 a shift. In 1972, an Irish coffee cost 50 cents and well drinks (top drawer) were 75 cents. Together, we were taking home $80 to $100 a day, five days a week. If we were careful, we could live on $400 a month.

With good jobs and our expanding nest egg, the next hurdle was to figure what kind of boat we wanted and could afford. In our landlubber minds, the hardest part of making the move from land to sea would be diminished living space. Compared to a boat, our one-bedroom apartment was gigantic, so our natural inclination was to look for the biggest sailboat we could afford and handle while staying within our aesthetic parameters. The one we kept coming back to was a boat we had seen in Sausalito that was manufactured in Taiwan. With only slight variations, the Sea Wolf, Yankee Clipper, CT 41' and Imperial 41' were the same fiberglass boat with identical layouts. The cockpit was aft with the companionway ladder between the galley and a dining booth. Down two steps was the main saloon, which was in the widest part of the hull, while the head and a double berth were forward where the hull narrows. Ketch rigged, traditional in appearance with appealing lines, it was not very fast or terribly efficient to windward, but boats are a compromise. It looked as though it could get us from one place to another and would be comfortable to live on.

About this time the owner of the *Antonia K* called from Corpus Christi saying he was willing to sell her for $8,670. After thinking it over, we reluctantly declined because we were happy living in San Francisco, and it would take $3,000 to truck the boat to California with no guarantee a long road trip wouldn't hurt her.

This is when Jim Ryley, Sausalito yacht broker and entrepreneur, entered our lives. He came up with an intriguing proposition – a kit boat. For $14,200 we could buy a *Sea Wolf* that was finished on the outside yet unfinished on the inside. One evening he and his wife, Donna, took us out for a sail on a completed one that really sold us on the idea.

The sun had set by the time we motored from the dock into the Bay and hoisted the sails on a perfect evening with the moon reflecting off the water, silhouetting Alcatraz Island against the blanket of city lights draped over the hills of San Francisco. Bundled up in sweaters, it was too wonderful, quietly sailing in what could be our home – the warmth of the cabin lights radiating from below deck – hot buttered rum in mugs.

I managed to make a bit of a fool of myself by mishandling a line as I tried to cleat it off to the dock, but other than that minor embarrassment, the only way to describe the evening, especially when I was at the helm, was magical. Looking up at the moon-drenched sails as the ghosts of Al Capone and the Bird Man of Alcatraz looked on, we gently carved our way through the Bay. Afterwards, we sat in the main saloon talking with Jim and Donna, letting the experience soak in.

Bill Hardin was the man in Taipei, Taiwan, in charge of building the *Sea Wolf*.

After speaking with him over the phone and pondering the decision, we agreed to take the plunge and purchase a *Sea Wolf* kit.

10/8/73

Drove to Sausalito and paid $1,500 down. Signed the contract over a beer.

10/9/73
Established a letter of credit with Bank of America for the balance, $12,700.00 set to expire April 8, 1974.

11/8/73
After not enough research we decided on Perkins 4-107 engine. This one seemed to be the most reliable ... and the one that comes with the completed Sea Wolf. *The deposit was $230.*

The hard decisions are behind us as of this date while the hard work lies ahead. Currently we are working and saving money for the many expenses that will face us.

11/24/73
I found out last Saturday that I had flunked the California bar for a second time. Although the practice of law does not seem to be in our plans at this moment it was rather distressing. It seems as though I did not have my heart in it or that I am stupid. I hope it's the former. We have still not received a letter of confirmation and hope the boat is being built. The Nov. issue of Sea Magazine *calls it a seaworthy boat, and we would be really crushed if something went wrong.*

From this date forward I hope to keep a log of our progress.

We would soon find out our *Sea Wolf* dream was not to be. As much as we loathed and despised Bill Hardin for reneging on the agreement, unforeseen events shared the blame. Fiberglass resin is a petroleum byproduct and 1974 was the year of the "energy crisis." Oil prices soared as the country panicked. Cars waited in long lines for as little as five gallons of gasoline. In places that had little or inadequate public transportation, life slowed to a crawl. It wasn't very hard on Helen and me as the Divisidero bus transferring to the Geary Street bus took us within walking distance of the Cliff House where she had begun working because the money was better. Actually, it was hardest on Ralph who loved to come with us. It was cool enough that he could stay in the back of the station wagon until I took a break and let him run on the beach. The late, legendary social columnist Herb Caen of the *San Francisco Chronicle,* who came by the bar relatively often, even mentioned Ralph in one of his articles.

3/19/74

Last Wednesday Roger informed us that he would not be able to ship the Sea Wolf *to us. It was quite a disappointment since we had planned and worked for over five mo. with the* Sea Wolf *on order. It looks as though we are going to have to go to a smaller, lighter displacement boat, which will certainly be a compromise. The boat we are now considering is a 36' 10" boat designed by Crealock and scheduled to be built in Costa Rica. He designed the Westsail 42' and wrote a good article in* SAIL MAGAZINE *on yacht design – his credentials seem excellent and this is encouraging. Jim Ryley is giving us a good price on the hull. I cannot tolerate the mid-ship cockpit so we must custom design and build all but the hull. This is perhaps the most exciting aspect, and I feel certain we should be able to design a very comfortable boat. After the hull is completed, we must move the boat to a port city boatyard, where they would complete the remainder of the boat for us. I am apprehensive about this and will have to closely supervise every step to insure proper construction.*

If it works out we will move to Costa Rica in July or August of this year and hopefully have a completed boat four mo. later. Preparation must be extensive and will probably include brushing up on my Spanish.

We are very determined to fulfill our dream and I am confident we are going to be able to.

The biggest problem with this unrealistic scenario was that unbeknownst to us, there were no port city boatyards that were capable of doing the work. Four months? Once we got there, it would eventually take us two-and-a-half years to launch and another year to make the boat ready for blue water sailing, i.e. almost *four years*. Ah, but the longest journey begins with but a single, and more often than not, naïve step.

We did get family encouragement from a truly unlikely source – my mother. I had imagined her telling friends disapprovingly about what we were about to do, adding, "And they're taking that damn dog, too." Her surprising change of heart was because she had fallen in love with my late dad's college roommate who had always had a crush on her. Bill Caudill, a world-class architect and one of the co-founders of CAUDILL ROWLETT SCOTT, had gotten in touch with her and ... bingo! From darkness came light.

We flew out to meet him in Denver to bestow our blessings. If he was nervous that we might not like Mother running off with another man, he needn't have been. We were thrilled for them both.

In a letter dated 5 August '74:

Mr. and Mrs. Ben Harrison
280 States St. #2
San Francisco, California 94114

BEN AND HELEN, wonderful to be with you in Denver. You'll never know how much I appreciate your open attitude.

Building the boat and shaking it down sounds like a great project! Anticipation is sometimes as pleasant as the journey itself. The trip sounds exciting and very worthwhile. Through building and sailing with your own hands and heart, you'll learn much about life and its real values. It's an ego trip as well as a beautiful voyage.

From a gray-haired, hardnosed veteran who has failed many times, take this word of caution: Have reserved in your abundance of enthusiasm some room for doubt. Then if something does happen, you won't be completely frustrated. So much for the negative. <u>Have fun.</u>

Don't get seasick, but do get just a little homesick. If Aleen can convert my jungle house into a warm, cheerful home, which only she is capable of doing, it is yours to visit – if you don't stay too damn long.

Good luck! I'm glad I know both of you.

Bill

We did look at used boats, probably not enough, but none that we saw fit our imagination.

It will be truly sad to leave S.F. as it has been a wonderful two years for us. I am writing this in the park near our apartment that overlooks the city (the park that is). I feel certain that we will return to beautiful California. In August we move to Costa Rica.

The only obstacle at this point is import taxes. We would like to drive our dependable Volvo and sell it there but the tax on cars is 100%. The drive (4,000 miles) is exciting, and I hope we will not have to miss it and fly down. Our engine, we hope, will not be taxed twice and poses a possible problem. This whole thing is going to be a kick in the ass, and Helen and I cannot wait to get started on the construction.

Still, leaving was going to be emotionally tough. We had made good friends, both on and off the job, and were having a great, if risqué, time in San Francisco. By this time we had seen many of our fellow workers and friends undressed, and they us. Nobody sunbathed in a swimsuit on someone's deck, even if we were visible to neighbors. Everyone went to nude beaches. One evening at our place after smoking some particularly strong pot, we all just took our clothes off with Helen in the lead removing her top. We never did anything sexual. We just talked, giggled, wiggled, smoked, drank and listened to music – partied naked. It may have been voyeuristic, but this was San Francisco, California, in the early 1970s, and we were young and physically fit.

Our living room had a long wood coffee table in front of a very comfortable couch with soft, corduroy, down cushions. Overhead, on the wall, I had made a frame for a stained glass window we had shipped from Missouri with other assorted furniture. Behind the glass I had installed lighting that gave off a warm colored glow. Our KLH turntable and speakers sounded good. It was a pleasant place to live and have friends over.

Parting with most of our possessions and leaving the city was obviously a difficult decision, yet we had this feeling that there was even more spice to life.

7

FIBROTECNICA

9/28/74

Our last border crossing, the Costa Rican one, was the most important since we had to get the screws and winches we were carrying in undetected or be taxed on them. CR has no army and the police do not carry guns. An ideology that reeks of sanity.

At any rate we put them in the coolers because no border had checked our ice chests. The inspector was very courteous and although thorough, missed these items by a hair. He had his hand on one and had he been aware of the weight would have checked, but fate intervened, Ralph and I diverted him. We made it. So far things look great.

AFTER SLEEPING IN THE CAR in Managua, we were exhausted and checked into a little cottage on the beach at Playa del Coco. It was the kind of beautiful small town on the Pacific Ocean that we had envisioned. Happy that thus far Costa Rica was living up to its reputation, we rested and walked on the sand of the half-moon shaped bay. Ralph was a happy dog running up and down the beach, retrieving coconuts we threw for him into the water and chewing the outer fibers down to the hard shell. It had been a long trip for him, too.

Refreshed after a good night's sleep, and relieved that we had finally made it, we continued down the Pan American Highway through fertile farmland, taking the cut-off to Cuidad Puntarenas (Sandy Point), which was not what we had in mind at all.

Located on a long, thin peninsula, it was gritty. Driving around town during daylight, dodging potholes and poor people, we saw nothing that remotely resembled the quaint town we thought it would be. There wasn't much that was appealing in this, the only commercial port in Costa Rica that could handle large ships.

There were no streetlights. So other than the light coming from barrooms and windows, it was darkly reminiscent of the border town of Nogales – only bigger and badder. The typical saloon, and there were lots of them, had an open doorway with a partition set back several feet to shield those inside from view. Most were unkempt, two-story, wood frame buildings with an upstairs of presumably unmade beds and Puntarenas prostitutes who could be seen standing on the balconies, beckoning. There was no air conditioning and nothing had a fresh coat of paint.

Among the few good things, there were inexpensive outdoor restaurants on the beach where we ordered mussels steamed in onion and garlic with enough juice to sop up freshly baked La Selecta bread that came with the meal. Other than sodas, the drink menu was Imperial or Pilsen beer, rum or guaro liquor.

This was before bottled water, so like everyone else, we drank from the tap, as we had all the way down without thinking anything of it. We had no choice. As for beer,

Pilsen was the better of the two, but Imperial had by far the best label. On an oval yellow background with a silver border, there is a black, evil looking bird with a silver coat of arms. In the center are the letters, "CCR" – Cerveza Costa Rica. Below, boldly printed on a red background, is the word **"Imperial."**

It was only a two-hour drive up the mountains to San José, but due to our late start we arrived at sunset. As we looked for the apartment of a friend of a friend, who had agreed to put us up for our first few nights in his guest bedroom, we drove through parts of town that were upscale and others that were downscale. This was the capital of Costa Rica, the big city, with Puntarenas running a distant second in population. The weather was fantastically cool.

As with most apartments in San José, there was a two-way speaker by the side of a steel bar gate that led into the complex where ex-patriot John Johnson lived. Helen pushed the bell and heard a voice say, "Quien es?" ("Who is it?") Helen answered, "No this isn't Ken, it's Helen, Henry Andrae's daughter." Oh, boy. How little did we know about the long journey and how it would unfold.

We stayed at his place for two nights, but they were tense because Johnson, who was in his late 50's, collected valuable Mayan artifacts that he displayed on glass shelves throughout his fastidiously kept living room where his live-in maid cleaned and cooked daily. In the apartment, we had to follow Ralph's tail everywhere, as the last thing we wanted to be responsible for was shattering a priceless piece of history on a tile floor because our dog was happy or wanted something.

It didn't occur to us that he was a smuggler of indigenous artifacts who catered to North American collectors. We just thought he was a little kinky. The night we arrived he took us to a club filled with barely dressed young girls who knew him well and let him fondle them in front of us in exchange for money he put down their tops. It was uncomfortable sitting at a table with a strange older man in a whorehouse, not knowing what to do or say over the loud disco music. A foreboding introduction to the dark, expatriate undercurrent, Helen and I were completely out of place and Ralph was home alone. After the second night we happily moved to an inexpensive hotel.

10/8/74

Since Puntarenas we have slept in the car once – terrible. Stayed in the Pensión Costa Rica Inn – wonderful, and rented a weird little one room place for $90 a month. It is really nice to have our own place again even though it is not much. I almost forgot our stay with John Johnson, a nice but argumentative fellow who promises to be a great help to us in our venture.

Though the Apartamentos Miami #3, located underneath a stairwell, was like a cave, it was good not to be homeless as we had been for the past six weeks. The floors were red tile. In the front half of our one room flat, next to the only window, were two 1950s plastic covered metal chairs, a worn Formica table and a metal sink with a built-in two-burner stove. In the back half of the room was a double bed separated from the front by a planter containing real dirt and plastic vines.

But the big news for Helen and me was that we were able to let out a huge sigh of relief when we saw the boat factory for the first time. Unaware as we were of all the scams going on south of the border, it's a wonder we weren't the victims of one of them.

The most important thing is we have seen the mold, or plug I should say, for our boat and it is really wonderful. The size seems great and we are in good spirits about the project. We have seen Jim Ryley and Donna repeatedly – both socially and at the Ensabladora Automotritz where the hull is being made. We have visited it frequently and although slightly behind schedule, we are very pleased. We have also located a place to build the boat. Rather, two locations. One is on an old coffee bean plantation where Maury Campbell, who owns the teak plantations, does the finish work for his teak products that are exported to the States. It grows in Quépos and that is the other possible location for construction. The coffee plantation is about 20 min. out of San José in a town called Heredia. It is amazingly picturesque, and the site has a beautiful view of the mountains and the entire city of San José. There will be problems getting the hull there and back, but I hope they are not insurmountable.

Scottie and Bernie – Jim's two associates, the former the foreman and the latter the interpreter – should be of limited help to us as will Arturo's Bar. Art is the owner and Katie the barmaid.

Enough for now. I will catch up more later.

On our initial visit to the factory, we met Jim in the showroom where new fiberglass powerboats were displayed. It looked like something you might see in the United States – modern, polished floors, high ceiling, and florescent lighting. From there we followed him through a back door that led to an opening between two large metal buildings. In one of these airplane hangar-type structures, cars were being put together. In the other, there were boats in various stages of construction, the largest of which was the upside down "plug" of the TransAm 36' (soon to be re-named the Tiburon 36') sailboat hull. Though there was some overlap between the two companies, FibroTécnica manufactured boats and Ensambladora Automatriz assembled Land Rover automobiles. Both businesses were obviously legit. Things were looking good, but, man, there were a lot of unknowns out there that we had to figure out to pull this off.

In order to make production fiberglass hulls, a "plug" or form shaped exactly like the hull must be made. From this plug, a mold is made from which hulls can be mass-produced. What we were seeing was an exact replica, or mock up, of a hull the same exact shape and size ours would to be.

That afternoon we were formally introduced to Scottie, the gringo shipwright and Bernie, his translator, as well as the owner of the factory, "Don" Johnny Schofield. "Don" is the honorary title bestowed on the big chief. He turned out to be a great guy.

Everything just looked and felt right. From the beginning, we were allowed unrestricted access to the factory because we stayed out of the way, and I was able to help both Jim and Scottie with Spanish translations. Expatriated Americans with common goals, we began spending a lot of time together. Not all business, late one night Jim and I mooned a group of Mormon missionaries, which, at the time, even Helen and Donna thought was funny despite the immaturity of the gesture.

True, the factory was behind schedule, but we were assured it wouldn't be long before our hull was ready. Initially, the delays weren't troubling because we had more than enough to do logistically to get ready, including finding a place to do the construction. There was hardware and teak to order and important details to resolve – like designing the layout and figuring out how to build it. Bill Crealock was behind on his drawings, leaving us with the task of configuring the cabin from his rough drafts. Our original idea, to have someone else do the work under our supervision, had gone completely by the wayside. We would eventually become one of the extremely rarest of species – gringos who actually did physical labor in Latin America.

On a sailboat, everything is interrelated. The cabin sole becomes larger the higher up in the hull it is, which means more space for the water tanks underneath. But it can only go so high and still have headroom and a coach roof that isn't too tall for both aesthetic and performance reasons. It was a wacky, complex puzzle since nothing is square. Everything is curved and three-dimensional. The challenge was fitting the essentials: a double berth, functional galley, head, main cabin and dining area into the available space. The side decks, coach roof and cockpit had to be laid out topside. In a boat our size, an inch is a big deal.

Not only did we regularly go to the factory, watching the progress and fretting over the design, now that we were settled into our apartment and cooking our own meals (a lot of spaghetti), it was time to learn the Costa Rican ropes. There was no better place than a bar owned by a once rich American, Arturo, and his waitress girlfriend, Katie Bee. Arturo's, where mostly English was spoken, was Humphrey Bogart's *Rick's* without Sam the piano player.

There was a big difference between tourists and expats. Those on vacation went to the rainforest and the volcano; the others went to Arturo's.

As Steve Goodman wrote in his song, "Banana Republics":

> Some of them go for the sailing
> Caught by the lure of the sea
> Trying to find what is ailing
> Living in the land of the free
>
> Some of them are running from lovers
> Leaving no forward address
> Some of them are running marijuana
> Some are running from the IRS
>
> Late at night you will find them....

Late at night you would find them at Arturo's.

10/8/74

This area is like Casa Blanca in that everyone has a project. I expect to see Peter Lorre any day walk in with some gold scheme. It is really wild with all the promoters and fortune seekers hanging around – they are everywhere.

We knew why we were in Costa Rica – "caught by the lure of the sea," trying to build a sailboat – but what the others were doing was often shrouded in mystery. There were smugglers saying they were on vacation or trying to fit in with unbelievable cover stories – occupation: "entrepreneur." The guy would usually be in his twenties or early thirties, conservatively dressed (short hair), in good shape physically accompanied by a real good-looking girlfriend who waited on him. He would have plenty of money, ride in taxis, eat at the best restaurants and stay at the Gran Hotel Costa Rica. Their time of stay would usually be about two or three weeks before they disappeared for a while.

There were a few CIA types who worked for the U.S. Embassy doing who-knows-what. But most were get-rich-quick idea men stereotypically accompanied by an English-speaking Tico, whose job it was to take care of the language barrier, government problems and details. Tico (Tica for women) is what Costa Ricans are called because they have a quirky, endearing dialect. "Poquito," meaning "little" in Spanish, is pronounced "poquitico" – cerveza is cervecita, a glass of water is a vasito de agua.

One gringo we met had built oak barrels for export to France to be used for aging wine. The problem was, after spending considerable cash on the necessary equipment to make them, the wood turned out to be the wrong type of oak. As a last ditch effort to salvage the situation, he was going to try to use them to export pickles. He would soon be history.

There was always a something-for-nothing angle, using cheap labor and/or materials. Most of the scammers – they were all men – boasted of their friendship with some high-ranking governmental official or person of extreme importance that was the key to their success. Escorting unusually attractive women, usually Ticas with whom they could barely communicate, they invariably were full of shit.

It was only natural that, at first, our plans and aspirations were met with total skepticism. We weren't there to make a fortune or live in a large house in Escazu attended to by a very affordable staff. We were also unusual in that we were actually married ... to each other.

Arturo's was dark and smoky with Arturo, always the character, behind a long bar that had people two or three deep standing or sitting on stools. Katie Bee, the waitress, took care of the tables. Ironically, she and Helen were old hometown acquaintances so we found out about a lot of people fast. Compared to the local bars it was pricy unless Art got loaded and started giving everything away. When he found out that we were in Costa Rica to build a sailboat, he had to tell us the story of the 50-foot yacht he once owned and sailed to Hawaii. His favorite remembrance was about a high priced contraption that was supposed to throw the anchor out into the water. Disappointed with the way it worked, he turned it up side down and let it heave itself off of the bow.

It was in Arturo's that we learned about Joe Krumpsky's rental house in Santa Ana that was about to become vacant. Among expats it was easy to strike up a conversation.

The two locations we had first considered weren't going to work out due to bad roads. After driving out to Santa Ana, we knew immediately that this was perfect and sealed the deal with first month's rent. We would be able move in when the other tenants left in two weeks.

In these early days, as we watched the progress at the factory, we were unaware that we were witnessing a large-scale disaster in-the-making that would cost us, and everyone else, time and money – them much more than us.

Helen and I heard about everything going on at the factory at La Luz (The Light), the best bar in the world, which soon became our after-work meeting place. Close to the factory, not far from the Apartamentos Miami, there was a little cantina that we discovered one afternoon walking home from FibroTécnica. Beers were three colones, 35 cents, but the most wonderful thing was their "bocas." "Boca" in Spanish literally means mouth, and it is a tradition in Costa Rica for bars to serve something to eat along with drinks. With every round they would bring a large plate that had some variation of pejivalles (a small fruit) topped with a dab of mayonesa, cicharones (fried pig skin) covered with lime juice, slivers of aguacate (avocado), salchicha (sausage), yucca, sliced mango – all surrounded by thinly-sliced, hand-made deep-fried potato chips cooked on a stove behind the bar.

Behind saloon styled doors, the curly haired owner with a twinkle in his eye and a sparkle in his smile from his gold front tooth, was always glad to see us. Comparatively speaking, we were big spenders and good tippers who usually came early and never caused trouble. All we did was sit around a Formica table off to the side and talk about boats in English. Bars like this in Costa Rica were frequented by men. Never once in the hundreds of times that we went to La Luz was it crowded nor were there women other than Helen and the females who accompanied us. She was probably the real reason the owner was glad to see us.

The swinging doors, not two feet from the street, led into the medium lit room decorated with large posters of bathing beauties in provocative swimsuits on slightly greasy walls. In her famous bathing suit pin-up, Farrah Fawcett's big-hair, white teeth and hard nipples personally greeted us every time we went in. It was a nice touch as Farrah and I had gone to public school together in Corpus Christi, Texas, back when she was a somewhat shy girl with beautiful teeth – before fame and Ultrabrite toothpaste found her cheerleading at the University of Texas. Arturo's was fun every now and then when we needed to speak English and meet new people, but La Luz was the place we went almost every afternoon after work.

Jim is a good guy and a good salesman, perhaps too good. What he did, which turned out to be a big mistake, was convince Scottie, the shipwright, that rather than make the plug a throwaway, which is the usual way of building molds – why not turn it into a wood boat that he could sell? Scottie didn't like the idea, but reluctantly agreed. Not long after our arrival, Jim offered the wooden plug/hull to us, which we declined even though he made it sound attractive. Later, he offered us the completed boat made from the plug, which thank goodness we also refused. It was a bad idea in that it delayed the making of the mold, without which production could not begin, but even worse, a year after the wood version was launched, it rotted and fell apart, never to sail again.

At the factory, the blame game soon reared its ugly head and since we were neutral, all sides confided in us. No one was trying to screw up, do anything wrong or take advantage of anyone. It was just one of those ideas that sounded good at the time. Scottie blamed Jim for insisting that the plug be made into a boat. Jim blamed Scottie for everything because he was always behind schedule. It didn't help that Scottie was always overly optimistic about how long it would take to get something done.

In addition to making the hull mold, they also had to make a deck mold and, to make sure it fit the fiberglass hulls, Scottie built it on the plug itself. This was a good idea, but because the hull and deck plug were being made into a boat rather than being discarded, a lot of extra labor was required and a lot of deadlines weren't met. Things were getting uncomfortable as month after month went by, and delay after delay took place.

We weren't sure how dire Jim and their company's finances were, but it was obvious that things were getting dangerously close to the wire. To help him out, we agreed to pay the balance due on our hull in advance not long after we made the move from the cave-like Apartamentos Miami #3 to the little house in Santa Ana, about twelve kilometers from downtown San José.

Ralph thought he'd gone to heaven after living cramped up in the city. While in San José, we took him for walks and did as much for him as we could, but he still had to stay in the apartment more than he wanted to. We couldn't take him to the factory until after hours because he scared many of the workmen. That an Irish Setter, especially Ralph, would intimidate anyone was a joke to us, but it was very real to those who had never seen a dog his size. For the average Costa Rican laborer, owning a pet, much less a big pet, was financially out of the question. Veterinarians treated horses, pigs and cows, not dogs or cats.

Rent for our new place was $115 per month. The floor, walls and ceiling were all unfinished plywood and the tiny bathroom had only a cloth curtain, not a door. After moving in, the first thing we did was make two light fixtures out of yellow Kodak tin cans and hang them from the ceiling so we could read in bed. In the primary room, there was a kitchen, a double bed, a cheap 1950s style sofa, two chairs and a small table. In the bedroom, off to the left as you entered, were two single beds without headboards that doubled as our darkroom. In another small room on the right we built a workbench.

There was quite a contrast between the well-maintained grounds, which would have looked impressive in front of a millionaire's home, and the crude living space.

Virtually every aspect of lawn care in Costa Rica during the 1970s was done with one tool – a machete.

These guys were good, too. Leaning over at the waist, swinging it parallel to the ground, they could cut the grass so evenly it looked as though it had been done with a lawnmower. Trimming around the trees, planting the garden off to the side of the house or cutting back a hedge, were all second nature to our gardener Rico, who became a trusted friend.

On our red-tiled front porch were two metal chairs with bent steel frames that gave them some spring. In between was a matching circular three-legged metal table about two feet in diameter. Across the yard, on the other side of our barbed wire fence lined with trees and covered with flowering vines, was a dirt road where more ox-drawn carts carryings onions and coffee beans passed than did automobiles.

1/6/75

It is a funny little house that could not be better for the purposes intended. The yard is huge with an area 50' by 20' off to the side, just perfect for the boat. The rest of the yard is immaculately kept by a gardener that is part of the rent. On the boat side of the yard there is a two-foot ditch that winds through the yard and separates the beautiful part of the yard from the work side. The part left over from the boat area contains a hole for the garbage and a barrel for paper trash.

The other side of the yard looks like a small Disneyland sort of place with fruit trees, flowers and exotic garden areas. The grass is trimmed perfectly, and the trees are surrounded by flowers. Besides the four sweet orange trees, we have one sweet grapefruit tree. All in all we have a tremendous amount of fruit, which is not only economical but also healthy.

As the tension factor rose at the factory, when Jim and the U.S. investors were obviously financially stretched to the limit, teetering close to the edge, with rock star demeanor, into the picture walked drug dealer, Mike. We had met him through a mutual friend and took him to the factory. In a short period of time, he and a partner decided to buy the ill-fated wood boat made from the plug that would be named *Calma*.

Though I've known a few drug dealers, I have never been one myself. It would be too nerve wracking. But desperation and Costa Rican taxes turned Helen and me into marine part's smugglers. In the dark of the night, we met *Calma* at the dock behind the Hotel Colonial in Puntarenas for a shipment we had to have, tax free, if we were going to have any chance of completing the boat with the money we had.

Mother and Bill were unaware that they were accomplices.

8 October 75

BEN & HELEN, it's been a cliffhanger. Twenty-one packages are now down at Circle Airfreight, ready to go. They don't know the name of the airline and connections yet, but they'll let us know just as soon as they can. The packages will be prepaid and they're insured for $4,000.

Attached is your list plus our own numbering system and the approximate size of each of the 21 packages. Helen, you'll find the shoes in box #7.

> In haste,
> Bill

Under Costa Rican law a foreign boat in transit was legally entitled to import merchandise duty free. Since *Calma* was registered as a Panamanian vessel, it qualified for the exemption.

Smuggling was second nature to Mike and as a favor to us, he agreed to accept the twenty-one-box order of marine parts meant for our boat, claiming they were for his. The size of the order should have set off all kinds of alarms, but Mike, who was physically big even by gringo standards, used just the right amount of English audacity and moneyed charisma to get the goods released from the Custom's warehouse.

The shipment included our Paul E. Luke stainless steel three burner stove, a large spool of 5/16" stainless steel wire, a 36" bronze steering wheel with teak trim, our steering pedestal and quadrant, a chrome plated bronze Plath windless weighing at least 50 pounds, two brass dorade vents, nine heavy bronze Wilcox Crittendon turnbuckles, 12 lignum vitae blocks, hundreds of feet of line, two brass kerosene lamps, a Danforth compass, a 45 pound and a 35 pound CQR anchor and more – it barely fit into the Volkswagen van we had borrowed to bring the contraband back to Santa Ana. After midnight, driving through dense fog, we were hoping there wouldn't be any police checkpoints. Even though it was illegal, it was a chance that we had to take.

Mike, who would later spend several months in a Colombian jail after he and two female accomplices were arrested at the airport trying to smuggle cocaine out of the country in one of the girl's brassieres, had stuck his neck out for us, and we were gratefully in his debt.

10/27/74
We have parked the Pontiac because gas here is $1.00 per gallon and we simply cannot afford it. The way I see it we will be lucky if we have $500 in our pockets when the boat is completed. Hopefully that will last us for a couple of months until we can get someplace and scrape up some more.

When I found out that the import tax on foreign registered cars was calculated by weight and would cost about $5,000, we had no choice but to simply let the government have it or sell it to someone going back to the States. It had done its job.

3/21/75
Another great step was the disposal of our automobile, the "GOLDEN GROMMET." Joe and Peggy bought it in exchange for four leather rocking chairs.

The chairs are really nice and have added to our little house. We are enjoying them much more than we were the car, so it must have been a good deal.

1/6/75
The house is very secluded and cars rarely pass the front road, which is dirt. Oxen carts do pass frequently and their wheels ring like popcorn popping in a tin popper.

We are a curiosity, no doubt, walking up and down the road to town. At first, we couldn't figure out exactly what was being said to us as we passed people. It sounded like "Díos" which is God in Spanish, but that didn't sound right. We soon found out they were saying "Adios" or goodbye. Rather than say "Hello," people in Costa Rica say "Goodbye," which makes sense if you think about it.

The surrounding land is so fertile, the road to Santa Ana was partially shaded by trees that had sprouted from fence posts. There were so few cars, we all walked in the middle and rarely had to yield.

Down the hill from the house, there was a small grocery store that sold eggs (everyone had their own plastic egg carrier), bread, rice, beans, butter, onions (Santa Ana is the onion capital of Costa Rica), chickens (including the feet and head), coffee and other basic items. Next door, a dirty, fly-infested carnicería sold grass fed beef that was tough as leather and almost blue in color. Close to the carnicería was a dirt floor bar that sold beer and one type of liquor: guaro, which is a potent unrefined clear alcohol made by the government from sugar cane. Packing a powerful wallop that can result in a horrendous hangover, it left many a campesino red-eyed, staggering or passed out. I only went there once.

There was no trash pickup. Everyone had a compost where they threw waste produce like eggshells and onion skins. What remained, we periodically burned in a 55-gallon steel drum.

The buses that ran regularly from Santa Ana to central San José were individually owned and given names like "Jumbo Jet," which was the biggest and best. It was a Sultana with 16 forward gears. It got you to al Centro in a hurry, while some of the older Blue Bird, school-type buses, could take forever. I came close to becoming paperback literate reading on the trips back and forth to the factory. One bus that had a picture of Jesus painted above the windshield also had a sign that told passengers to throw their trash out of the window rather than on the floor.

For cheap thrills, there is nothing quite like riding a bus down a narrow street going way too fast with a wide-eyed, caffeinated driver maneuvering a steering wheel that has so much play in the linkage that he would be constantly turning it left and right. That, or sitting in the back seat of a small taxi whose shock absorbers are shot, hitting fifty miles per hour on a cobblestone road in a busy part of town. "Solo Díos sabe" – only God knows if something good or bad will happen to you, so why not put the pedal to the metal?

Cheap labor and raw materials were the primary reasons that Costa Rica was a good fit for boat manufacturing. In México and America Central, despite a growing middle class, wages were well below those in the States. A lot of the workers at the factory were earning three colones per hour, which was 35 cents. At the time, minimum wage in the States was $1.75 – more for skilled labor. Teak was one-third the price that it was in the U.S.

As for the other major boat ingredients like marine hardware, polyester resin, fiberglass cloth, mat and woven roven, there were laws that allowed companies to import materials tax-free so long as they left the country as a finished product.

Ensambladora Automotritz and FibroTécnica were prosperous enterprises that came about due to a shrewd manufacturing idea by Don Johnny, from England, who married Nora, an upper crust Tica. The government agreed to greatly reduce import taxes on Land Rovers if the parts were shipped from England and the assembly was done in Costa Rica. Understandably, when we arrived, almost all of the cars on the road were Land Rovers.

As a boating enthusiast, Don Johnny, a major player on the Costa Rican landscape, had expanded his automobile factory and added the fiberglass fabrication section. An unpretentious, pleasant person, he befriended us and one way or the other our trials and tribulations in dealing with problems always somehow worked out. We suspect Johnny had more to do with it than we knew. His son-in-law, Dañiel, a manager at the factory, also helped as his responsibilities gradually shifted from automobiles to boats.

The factory had its own Agente de Aduana (Customs agent) that helped us deal with importation. It also had contacts at all levels of society and government. When our visas were about to expire, not wanting to waste time and money by leaving the country only to return 48 hours later, it was suggested we go see so-and-so, who gave us an additional year as "students."

What set us apart from other gringos was that we ultimately decided to do the work ourselves, with our own hands. The normal expatriated American never did any actual labor, and virtually every huckster in Costa Rica had a sidekick who could speak both English and Español and made a living doing what we called "facilitating." If their gringo folded, which happened more often than not, it would be time to hang out at Arturo's Bar and hustle up a next one. If they were good at it, they could make money coming and going with kickbacks.

We met quite a few expatriated Americans during the six months we waited for the hull to be finished, including a nefarious ex-crop duster named Maurice Campbell and his right-hand man, Juan.

8

EXPATRIATED AMERICANS

Down to the Banana Republics
Down to the tropic sun
Expatriated Americans
Hoping to find some fun

First you learn a native custom
Then a word of Spanish or two
You know that you cannot trust them
'Cause they know they can't trust you...

-"Down to the Banana Republics"
by Steve Goodman

DOWN IN THE REPUBLIC of Costa Rica, the diesel engine for our unfinished hull continued to be our biggest tax problem with a potential tax liability of $1,200. So far we had been unable to find a long-term solution even though it would be leaving the country and legally should have been tax-exempt. Stuck in Customs, we hoped it was safer than our crate filled with clothes and tools had been. Somewhere between San Francisco and Puntarenas onboard the freighter, *Cuidad Barranquilla*, someone had pried open the wooden box and helped themselves to our cold weather clothes and a few of the tools inside. It was insured, so I made a claim detailing what had been taken and the approximate value. Silly me.

The insurance company replied that because all of the content wasn't taken, they weren't liable. No matter how many nasty letters I wrote on my Attorney at Law stationary, the clause allowing them to avoid liability was right there, plain as day, buried in fine print. We'd been had.

At the factory the mold was nearing completion, but until it was done they couldn't start laying up our hull, which was to be the first one manufactured. The weeklong Easter vacation that was upon us meant even more delay. Over budget, behind schedule, down and discouraged, nothing seemed to be working out very well. We didn't want to, but it was looking as though we might have to ship the hull to the States and do the work there. With the money we had, there were too many obstacles and import difficulties confronting us.

Still, we had no choice but to keep going forward. The importation demon was something that worried us constantly. But what caught us by surprise was the hassle of buying Costa Rican teak from gringo, Maurice Campbell. Our journals are peppered with expletives and frustrations.

6/6/75

Sorted through teak. About half was acceptable. We had to haggle with Juan who was threatening to quit. Sawmill in Quépos will not cut any more of Maury's without money. It's a big crisis for them. Hope we don't get burned.

Maurice owned several teak forests in Costa Rica that he had bought on the cheap from United Fruit Corporation, the largest banana producing empire in the history of the Banana Republics. With vast plantations around Quépos, a once bustling town not far from Manuel Antonio, a beautiful beach on the Pacific, the company was forced to pull out in the 1950s due to a disease that infected the banana trees. Before leaving, rather than let the land go to waste, they planted teak trees that would eventually make Maurice a small-time lumber baron.

Teak is a good wood for marine use as it can withstand the outdoors, finished or unfinished, and is the least likely to get dry rot that turns wood into mush. The Costa Rican trees, having never been properly pruned, which would have created a straighter grain, had a faint, swirling intricate gray/black pattern that, when varnished, came out as an appealing abstract Mother Nature creation. When our construction finally began, part of the creative fun was deciding aesthetically which piece should go where.

Soon after arriving in Costa Rica, before finding out about the place in Santa Ana, we decided to check out Quépos. We wanted to see the forests first hand and meet Howard Clark, a gringo we had heard about who was building a ferro-cement fishing boat in one of the abandoned United Fruit warehouses. Lots of people knew or had heard of Howard. We North Americans were a curiosity.

Thoughts of building our boat in Quépos were over soon after we began the drive west down the unpaved, deeply rutted road that would be impassible at times during the rainy season. No way could our hull make the trip and getting parts would be much more difficult. Still, we wanted to find Howard and learn all we could – and we wanted to go to the beach.

Once there, we had no trouble locating him and his boat that was nearing completion. Everyone in town knew who Howard was, just as everyone in Santa Ana would soon know who we were. A man of medium build with no body fat, he could not believe that there were any other gringos crazy enough to even think about building a boat in Costa Rica. It was a little unnerving to see him shaking his head and smiling with, "Good luck, amigos!" written all over his face. We did share a laugh when we found out that he too had stayed at the Apartamentos Miami #3 when he first arrived. We took that as a good omen.

After saying we would keep in touch, Helen, Ralph and I drove the short distance to Manuel Antonio. What is now an upscale beach resort, in 1974 there wasn't much of anything other than a small hotel and a single outdoor bar overlooking a jagged rock that forms part of the lagoon. To save money we decided to sleep in the car.

Waking up with the days first light, Ralph ran ahead of us, going in and out of the water while we walked the deserted crescent beach lined with tall coconut palms leaning out towards the water. About a mile down, with the sun rising behind the trees, we slipped out of our clothes, jumped into the chilly surf and swam for a while before coming back to the restaurant for a big breakfast. By noon, we felt it was time to head back up the dusty road to San José where in two days we would meet the nefarious Maurice Campbell in person.

Living in a modern, white apartment, we were shown into his sparsely furnished living room by a good-looking, well-proportioned, substantially younger Tica girlfriend who, we felt, did not look particularly happy. His ample-self, wearing white slacks and a white guayabera, was sitting on a cushioned living room chair smoking a Derby cigarette. In his fifties with white hair, salt and pepper beard and a white bandage on his right foot, he motioned distractedly for us to sit down and tell him what we were after.

Maurice, who appeared despondent, had recently lost his big toe in a boating accident and was not in good spirits. Nevertheless, he promised he could provide the teak and suggested we meet him the next day at his woodworking shop in Heredia, a mountainous coffee-growing area just outside of San José.

As directed, we drove up a rough, washed out road lined with coffee fields until we came upon the shell of a vacant colonial hacienda. It was overcast and drizzling when we got out of the car and walked to a shed that was originally built to house farm equipment. Inside the thick stucco walls of the compound covered with green algae and stained terra cotta tiled roofs, was Maurice's five-man operation.

We were immediately aware of the pungent sweet smell of teak coming from the sawdust and chips covering the floor.

When the rough-cut wood arrived from the lumber-mill in Quépos, it had to be run through a noisy industrial strength planer before a table saw cut it to width. Depending on what was being made, the drill press, table shaper and table sander were in constant use. Conversation had to be shouted over the loud whine of power tools.

There may be a perception that Latin America is the land of mañana workers, but this wasn't what Helen and I saw. The Ticos may not have had the latest machinery, and they may not have done things in the most efficient way, but these woodworkers, like those at FibroTécnica, were working their butts off, making good quality pieces for export to the United States.

The Costa Rican government, in an effort to preserve their forests, had laws restricting the export of raw lumber. Only finished products could be shipped out of the country, which forced this lazy Cajun into manufacturing parquet floors, boat handrails and other assorted products at his shop in the mountainous agricultural area overlooking San José. Juan and his men were obviously the ones who kept this little circus going – not Maury moving his heft with difficulty on crutches.

When Maurice was so inclined, he was a likeable Southern gentleman, but in the end he affirmed my father-in-law's law-and-order axiom – crooks don't look like crooks or they wouldn't be able to get away with stealing.

Maury has been getting started on our teak order. The only real progress has been my prepayment of $800, *but it should be cut in a few weeks. He has offered us a really good price due mainly to the tight pinch he is in and my prepayment.*

Before he saw a way to get into our pockets, Maurice was standoffish to the point of being rude. Then, abruptly, he decided he liked us so much that he took the trouble to drive his white Range Rover all the way out to Santa Ana, missing toe and all, to see how we were doing – just to say, "Hello."

Seeing our chessboard on a side table, he suggested we play a game or two. Not that I was any good, but he walloped me twice as we made small talk. All he wanted to do, he said in his heavy Cajun accent, was help because we looked like such fine young people. He was willing – he leaned toward me in a confidential way, making what he said sound sincere and generous – to sell us wood for $1 a board foot, cut and milled to our specifications – a fantastic deal – and all he wanted in return was a check in advance as he was temporarily in a bind. Payment from the States for his last shipment had not come through just yet.

He would help us if we would help him out of his unfortunate and embarrassing jam. "You can count on me," he said, shaking my hand, before hobbling off with our check in his guayabera shirt pocket. Eight hundred dollars doesn't sound like much, but it was a lot to us and went a long way in Costa Rica.

Maurice Campbell had made a great investment and would have been fine financially if he hadn't lived so large. Everything he owned was leveraged to the limit to support his big-shot ego and to buy the sailing yacht he intended to use for an escape from his difficulties.

A first attempt to flee the country and the ensuing tragedy that took place on a dark and stormy night happened aboard his newly purchased Morgan Out Island 41' named *CRUACHAN*. "Cruachan!!!" I would learn was the war cry of one of the oldest and largest clans in Western Scotland – Campbell of County of Argyll. No clan, it has been said by its members, can boast of purer, nobler Celtic blood than Campbell. "The Campbells are Coming," is their clan song.

Alone on his yacht, while trying to anchor in a howling thunderstorm, the line on its way out wrapped itself around his big toe cutting the darn thing off, depositing it on the ocean floor where it became part of the food chain. In a lot of pain, with a tourniquet around his foot, he struggled mightily to make it safely to a small seaport town. There, he hired a taxi to take him to the hospital in San José where the skin was sewed over his missing digit.

Unaware of Maurice's dishonest intentions, Helen and I felt so sorry for him that we took some homemade gazpacho to his apartment to cheer him up. I've wondered on occasion what was going on in his mind. Did he care at all about his very pretty girlfriend? Did he care about anything other than moving on to another lonely adventure in the same way he was alone in his bi-plane crop duster as he flew underneath power lines wearing goggles in an open cockpit?

People-wise, both Helen and I had come from relatively small hometowns where the more prosperous went to college. After returning home, they put on their coats and ties and went to work. They bought houses, had children, took an occasional junket to Vegas, played golf at the club, some had affairs, some were upstanding citizens, some caused scandals and some drank too much – *all in the same town.* But this was the Banana Republics, and from what we observed most of the expat schemers were loners who relished their anonymous outsider status. It wasn't hard to buy a girlfriend in Costa Rica, which apparently suited their disdain for emotional relationships.

Before leaving, Maurice had talked gringo Carl Ruggs, a self-proclaimed millionaire, into investing in his teak business. Maury's grand secret plan was to use the up front money to purchase a boat, liquidate what he could and sail away. Not only had the painful accident delayed his departure, it left him dangerously vulnerable to creditors who were beginning to discover his fudges and financial ineptitude. In such a hurry to leave, his foot was still bandaged when he successfully vanished.

6/6/75 [Helen]
Their company is folding because Maury has done nothing except spend. Ruggs invested $70,000 and Maury bought a yacht.

To my knowledge, no one ever tracked Maury down. Maybe he sailed to Scotland. *CRUACHAN!* Here Comes Maurice Campbell!!"

Now, Carl held our fate – and teak – in his hands, as he tried to sort out the mess he had been left with. The primary problem with the available teak was that the trees were small. Even so, we managed to find one rare piece big enough for the bowsprit and enough long two-by-twelves for the cap rail. Due to the tree size it became obvious that we were going to have to glue smaller boards together to make many of the larger structural components. I had always assumed that we would saw pieces that had curves from large, wide planks. Since there were not many, we were going to have to do a lot of lamination, which if done right, is stronger and better.

6/22/75 [Helen]

The circle never ends. I've just had it with a certain few. Sounds harsh but Ben and I have been blatantly lied to. A big cheat nearly happened concerning the ever-present TEAK scandal. Maury sailed away in his Tupperware boat which I hope sinks. Juan relayed Carl's message that we weren't getting but $500 of our $800 of TEAK. Carl on the phone said, "Yes, Ben, you'll just have to sue Maury for the three-hundred."

6/23/75 [Helen]

I was so angry and upset, I didn't finish writing last night. Today Ben is meeting Juan and Carl at five. Hopefully this will put an end to the dispute.

Maurice had apparently deposited $500 of our dollars into the corporate account and kept $300 for himself. Maybe some of our cash was in his pocket when he sailed away. At least the controversy was now over three, not eight hundred dollars. Meanwhile, the days leading up to the extraction of our hull from the mold were torture – one problem after another.

3/22/75 [Helen]

Today I can finally write that our hull has been started. Thursday, white and then green gel coats were sprayed on. Next a layer of black for the single purpose of detecting air bubbles on the glass lay up. From what I've seen, I feel sure we won't regret our color choice. Yesterday, Friday morning and afternoon was spent at the plant watching the first two layers of fiberglass being applied. It was done with a crew of four supervised by Scottie, Ben, me, Schofield, Jim and naturally Arcadio, when John Schofield was present.

Unlike the Westsail and most other sailboats being produced in the States, ours was going to have a balsa core that strengthens and insulates the fiberglass hull. Some production boats are so thin, light can actually pass through them. Not ours. Where there was no balsa, the fiberglass was a full inch thick. Where there was balsa, it was about an inch-and-a-half thick. It is very possible that *La Dulce* is the strongest fiberglass sailboat hull of her size ever built.

4/9/75 [Helen]

Our baby was born today. She is now in existence and beautiful. I started shaking when I first laid eyes on her. The sheen and color glow to perfection. Our waiting period has paid off. Scottie said this hull weighs 700 more pounds than their production model will. They plan to cut the lay-up down to four drums of resin instead of the five used on ours.

Ben is so charmed by his new woman and the old, too, of course.

What a beauty!

This afternoon the cradle will be built around her and then she'll relax a bit on padding while the ballast and engine are installed. Eight hundred lbs. of ballast delivered today. Too hot to touch and, of course, too heavy to manually move.

Must close and return to San José for the celebration at LA LUZ. Ben has arranged to treat the crew of workers to cervezas and bocas.

Everyone was happy that afternoon as we all congratulated each other.

4/13/75 [Helen]

The LA LUZ worker's celebration was something we wanted to do for the people who had made the hull. Everybody had 3 – 5 beers and platefuls of bocas and a good time. After the get-together, we were terribly tired and anxious to return home to re-live everything that has happened.

Ben believes, finally, we will need some sort of shelter to cover the boat while we work. I have wanted one all along. Another expense.

Now that the hull was made, all that remained to be done before delivery was installation of the ballast and the motor.

9

PIG ROAST

IN MAY OF 1975, Helen's sister, Jane, and brother-in-law, Tom, came to visit us in Santa Ana. Though the fiberglass hull had not yet been delivered when they arrived, it was out of the mold and almost ready to leave the factory.

With great pride we gave them a royal tour of FibroTécnica featuring our hull, the first one, big as a bus, majestically sitting center stage in the metal building. Even though months behind schedule, it was tangible, and it was magnificent. From the ground, it towered over us. From the top of the scaffolding, it looked like a large, empty swimming pool in the shape of a boat.

Helen was glad to see familiar faces, and we were overjoyed with the amount of good wine they had brought, one of those luxury items Costa Rica taxed to an unaffordable level. Having become devoted wine drinkers in California, we, especially I, over-indulged that night, and I would pay.

Our yard, about an acre in size, was splendid, but the house itself wasn't much and didn't have a hot water heater. In the mountains of Santa Ana there is no need for air conditioning or heating. The temperature stays in the high seventies during the day, cooling off at night.

Unfortunately, an ideal climate makes the water coming out of the tap cold enough to literally take your breath away. When we first moved in, there was a dangerous looking 110-volt coil showerhead that made the water a little warmer. From the beginning, I didn't like the looks of it and immediately disconnected it after it burst into flames while Helen was showering. From then on we braced ourselves, took a deep breath and stepped underneath cold water. Our showers were refreshing, to say the least, and short, especially for Jane and Tom who were staying in our guest bedroom.

Helen comes from a family that knows how to entertain, cook and appreciate well-prepared food, so in our guests' honor, she wanted to have a pig roast party. We had attended several where they dug a hole in the ground and built a fire in the bottom. The pig, shrouded in banana leaves, was then placed on the fire and covered with dirt. At one such get-together, the host, Arturo of Arturo's, got so loaded he couldn't remember where the pig was buried, so all of us, at the suggestion of one reveler, took off our shoes and began walking around the yard in the dark, some with flashlights, trying to find a warm piece of earth. It was a scene, but we eventually found it.

I had been told by several people, who certainly could have been more upfront about what to expect, that the best place to buy a pig was Puriscal, a town not too far away. With a throbbing wine hangover, early the next morning, I walked down the hill and boarded a crowded bus that would take me there. The luck-of-the-draw had me on an old Blue Bird school bus with gold balls hanging from the top of the front windshield that swayed as it pitched from side to side. "Jali! Jali!" the money collector shouted from the back of the bus when everyone was on board.

An agonizing hour-and-a-half later, standing the whole way watching the motion of the golden dingle berries, I got off at the town square with a gazebo bandstand in the center and wooden benches positioned underneath shade trees. It was surrounded by several agricultural feed stores, a small hardware store, a municipal building, a four-table restaurant with yellow plastic tablecloths, one pay phone, a pulpería (cantina), two little grocery stores and no hotels. Not seeing anyplace large enough to sell pigs, I asked a woman inside the closest grocery where I could buy one.

In Spanish, which I was getting a lot better at, she told me that the only way to buy a pig was to get in touch with the "pig man," who would soon be returning to the square in a maroon colored Land Rover. Not feeling good at all, I decided to wait for him at the restaurant where I, the only customer, ordered a beefsteak and an Imperial Beer, which briefly improved my spirits. After a second beer, just as the señora had predicted, a reddish-purple Land Rover rapidly approached trailing a cloud of dust that caught up with it as he stopped.

I explained my situation to Rodrigo and asked if he could help me. "¡Por su puesto!" (of course.) "¿Cuántas libras?" (How many pounds?)

"No sé," I replied. I had no idea how many pounds we would need because I assumed there would be one that looked about right hanging from a meat hook somewhere.

"No problema, vamos a ver," (No problem, let's go see.) said Rodrigo. "Podemos conseguir un puerco perfecto." (We can surely find one that will be perfect for the party.) With a flourish he motioned for me to hop into the Land Rover.

In Costa Rica, the seasons are the reverse of those in the States. Our summer is their rainy season and considered winter, while our winter is their dry season and considered summer, making the Christmas we had recently celebrated our first to take place in summer. It's such a beautiful country that even during the dry season I was day-dreaming, looking at the foliage when, about two miles from town, Rodrigo stopped and motioned for me to follow him down a narrow dirt path.

To the average Costa Rican, gringos are big and look different, so I was automatically a novelty in and around Puriscal, a town rarely visited by anyone, especially tourists. Three kids, mother and father, all squeezed their faces out of the front doorway as we approached their sun-bleached green farmhouse with worn wooden floors. Rodrigo told the owner that we were in the market for a pig and, based on the farmer's enthusiasm, this was good news. Grabbing his hat, he took us to a pigpen where a big, fat, fly-covered sow was lying in the mud. This is when my aching head belatedly realized that the pig we were looking for was not going to be dead yet. What I saw was a living, breathing animal, meaning we weren't going to go inside a store where they had pigs all dressed to choose from. This was not good.

Not wanting to look like a wimp and a total fool in front of everyone, all I could think of to do was pretend to evaluate the sow from behind the fence. After a few uneasy moments with all eyes on me, I explained that it was indeed a fine pig but not quite the right pig for me and, perhaps, I should call my wife and find out exactly how big it should be. "You know how women are," I joked. "I want to go home with one that is the right size." The farmer was disappointed but Rodrigo was undaunted. "¡No problema!" On the way back to the pay phone on the square, I asked if there wasn't one that was dead that I could buy. He thought I was nuts. Why would anyone have a dead pig lying around?

"Listen, Hon, I think we should have tenderloin or something like that. This pig thing is going to be a big deal." I proceeded to tell her about looking at a live pig and how uneasy I was about the whole thing, but she was insistent. If I hadn't been so "mal de goma" (hung-over), if I'd been firing on all cylinders, I probably would have put my foot down, but at this point the noon beer had turned sour in my stomach and the returning headache was relentless. Dejected, I trudged back to the Land Rover and off we went to yet another farm where there were more fly-covered pigs wallowing and oinking in mud and pig shit.

After making the gruesome choice, Rodrigo wheeled and dealed a price of two hundred colones ($25) for a white sow that looked about right as best I could tell. Feeling terrible about the fate of the animal, I walked back to the Land Rover to wait for them to do whatever they had to do.

When I heard squealing coming from the barnyard, I felt so bad for her that I had to look the other way knowing I was responsible for taking an otherwise happy pig's life.

What I couldn't figure out in my guilt-ridden stupor was why the squealing was going on for so long and seemed to be getting louder. As it turned out, all Rodrigo and the farmer had done was hog tie it, and they were carrying the smelly squealing animal to Rodrigo's Land Rover.

Even though this was not going well at all, from somewhere out of the blue, I recollected the face of my seventh grade science teacher and how much "pig face" really did resemble this animal that was now mine.

As we bounced along together, I assumed that we were driving someplace where they made live pigs into pigs suitable for roasting, I had no idea why Rodrigo slowed as we approached the bus stop at the town square.

What Rodrigo was about to do was drop Porky and me off. He had fulfilled his part of the bargain. This was a big hog, too. It had taken two men considerable effort to get the squealing, squirming animal into the car, but she was my responsibility now, and it was up to me, as Rodrigo saw it, to get her home to butcher and cook. It was something people in Costa Rica did all the time.

Looking back over my shoulder at the filthy, hog-tied grunting animal's bulging eyes, pink eyelids and long pig eyelashes, I felt so sorry for both of us, I wanted to cry.

"Rodrigo, tenemos que matar el puerco, aquí, en Puriscal. Puedo pagarse cien colones sí puede hacerlo." (Rodrigo, we have *got* to kill the pig here in Puriscal. I will pay you 100 colones if you can do it.) That brightened his day. The weenie gringo too pussy to kill his own pig was willing to pay half again what the whole hog cost so he wouldn't have to do the dirty work. Rodrigo, who worked hard for his money, put the car in gear, "¡Vámonos, amigo!"

With the pig still grunting and squirming in the back of the Land Rover, we set off to the slaughterhouse where she would meet her maker. I couldn't help but feel awful and fleetingly thought about setting the pig loose – "Puerco Libre," a rural, Latin American version of, *Free Willy*.

Rodrigo would have been amused.

It wasn't a big slaughterhouse. In fact it wasn't a house at all, only a round, fenced-in area with a tin roof. The problem was that the gate was chained and locked. While I was getting a sinking feeling, like the one I had had earlier at the bus stop, Rodrigo began looking for someone with the key.

Not being able to locate anyone who could unlock it didn't even slow Rodrigo down. With 100 colones riding on the slaughter, he went from door to door until he recruited two men to help us. I wasn't sure what the plan was until we began to lift the frightened pig over an eight-foot chain link fence as it squealed, squirmed and grunted loudly. Crime wise, we were breaking and entering a slaughterhouse with a filthy, noisy sow that I had grown attached to despite the short amount of time we had spent together.

My pig's demise took longer than I thought because a fire had to be built and water brought to a boil before they popped her over the head with a club and slit her throat. Still feeling the effects of the night before, waiting outside the fence I felt like throwing up as they gutted it and cleaned out the entrails, saving some parts and getting rid of others before submersing the body in hot water so they could scrape off the white fur. Now that the pig was dead, there wasn't anything I could do other than watch the process and help get the carcass back over the fence and into the car. I had to keep reminding myself that this wasn't barbaric. It was only the close-up reality of how food gets to the table. These were facts of life and death.

What I hadn't contemplated during the gore and murder was getting the damn thing home. Once again at the bus stop with a freshly slaughtered animal weighing a good 80 pounds, I was exhausted. I needed a drink and some aspirin. I didn't want to get on the bus with the pig and then wait at the bottom of the hill for the bus to Salitral to get up to our house. And that's when it dawned on me that this was way more pork than friends and relatives could possibly eat in one sitting so I propositioned Rodrigo. If he would drive me to Santa Ana, I would give him half.

We had a fine time driving through the countryside at twilight. We talked and laughed as I told him all about the sailboat we were going to build. He would occasionally look over and smile at the loco Norte Americano who had paid him 100 colones to kill a pig and then gave him half to drive him home.

At his own free pig roast party, I'll bet he and his buddies had a great time laughing at the wimpy gringo who said he was going to build a sailboat in the mountains of Santa Ana where they grow coffee and onions. Who did he think he was, Noah? I know for a fact that a lot of Costa Ricans thought we oversized people from the States were strange and grossly incompetent when it came to the simplest of everyday tasks. How stupid can you be to not even know how to handle a machete?

The following morning, feeling much, much better, I dug a hole in the ground off to the side of the house and started a fire with some gasoline, paper and logs cut from a dead tree across the road. There was no such thing as charcoal or charcoal lighter at Más X Menos (More for Less), the supermercado, just as there wasn't a butchered pig that I could have bought from the meat section. When the fire died down and the coals were red hot, we put the marinated pig in banana leaves from our banana tree, lowered her in and covered her with dirt just as we had been told.

As with most pig roasts, the meat wasn't cooked quite well enough when we dug it up, forcing me to relight a fire and get at least enough of the meat cooked so that our guests could eat before it got too late. All in all it was a social success as was their visit. But I have a feeling that our relatives were relieved when the taxi delivered them to the airport and they boarded a plane for home where they could take a long *hot* shower before crawling into their own soft bed.

10

THE HULL ARRIVES

AFTER HELEN'S FAMILY left, the next step before the hull delivery was installing the ballast.

According to Crealock, 7,800 pounds (almost four tons) would be needed at the bottom of the keel as a counter-balance to the force of the wind against the sails. This posed a problem for us and the factory. The original plan had been to melt down lead from old car batteries. For some reason, probably toxicity, this didn't work out, so we had to find an alternative.

The solution came about after consulting the owner of the foundry in San José that was casting the bronze portlights for FibroTécnica. He was an energetic, can-do fellow, who knew where to buy scrap steel railroad track that he could melt down, but the factory needed to supply him with molds whose shape had to conform to the bottom of the inside of the keel. Solving this problem was one of Scottie's finest moments.

First, he mathematically calculated how many square feet would be needed to achieve the right weight. Then, by pouring two liquid chemicals together in the keel of the wood plug, he created a polyurethane foam mold the shape of the inside of the keel. Extracting the foam, he cut it into eleven separate pieces that had to be shaved down enough to compensate for a layer of fiberglass that would allow them to be used over and over again. At the foundry, these molds were put in wet sand and then taken out, leaving an impression into which white-hot molten steel was dramatically poured in a flaming display of red-hot sparks that Helen and I watched from beginning to end.

Afterwards, these chunks of steel were transported to the factory and lowered into our hull.

5/20/75

The ballast took longer than expected, but what's new. It was installed and <u>was</u> it installed. Those turkeys at the plant bedded it with over 30 gallons of resin at nine lbs. a gallon and about $1 per gallon their cost – it should be there for good. Our bill at the plant was over $700 but we will get back some of that if we return the cradle. The bill also included a cutlass stern bearing for $110.

With the hull ready for delivery, the only thing remaining was some unanticipated last minute crisis. The God of Surprises did not let us down.

I received a one-year extension from the Aduana for the engine, which picked us up and was a great relief. All sorts of tension and deadlines, but we got it. The other hassle was with FibroTécnica, which was totally unexpected. The hull was to arrive early Sat. morning so, after rushing around and exhausting ourselves Friday we had dinner and were about to retire early when the phone rang and Jim told us they could not deliver it because: 1) he had to pay $3,000 to FibroTécnica and 2) there was the possibility of a $2,500 tax. Needless to say *we were flabbergasted and had to wait until Mon. to work it out or get burned – the big burn.*

We had been ever-present at the factory for six months and in daily contact with everyone, so we understandably felt this was over the top. The worst part was that we had to brood over the possibility of the big burn for the entire weekend. By Monday we were both livid.

I had to talk to a man named Luis who works for John. After he told me nothing could be done and that I must pay a 30% tax, I blew my stack. Told him he didn't know what the shit he was doing, and he called me a clown. We were both furious. Anyhow, after a day of suspense, if I would sign a few papers saying I must leave with the boat in one year and that I could not use or sell the boat during that time, there would be no need to pay the tax. Jim took care of his responsibilities.

Nothing had come easy, nor would it now that a new chapter in our lives was about to begin.

5/14/75
Driver was a mad man.

5/20/75
Much has happened since the last entry, and things are in good shape for a change. The boat has arrived!!! The hull was driven out early Wed. morning. The driver was late, and I was worried until I heard this car screech

around the corner, hit all four gears in the drive and slide to a stop. I knew this must be our driver, and he was.

The hull, sitting on a cradle made of large square timbers, had been loaded onto a lowboy trailer and coupled to a diesel truck. It was still dark outside when we arrived at the factory, where, along with Jim, Scottie and two workers, we nervously waited for the driver. Since we were anxious to get started before the morning traffic, when he skidded to a halt, one worker and I quickly got into the cab of the truck, while another worker climbed inside the hull. Helen, Scottie and Jim jumped into a Land Rover that was to follow.

I thought I was going to put my foot through the floorboard as my pleas of "¡Más despacio!" (Slow down) and "¡Cuidado!" (Careful) were laughed off by the driver and his sidekick. The truck was actually passing cars on our way out of town. The third helper, an integral part of the procession who had stationed himself at the bow of the boat, held a crudely made wooden "T." His job was to push up electrical wires that were too low for the hull to pass underneath. The driver obviously had tremendous faith in his ability to anticipate and judge distance at the speed we were driving.

The roads of San José are haphazard and often narrow. Finding the location of a building or home was archaic as, typically, the address referred to its distance from some monument or landmark. Our address in Santa Ana, where we were rapidly heading with our hull in tow, was "800 Vares Sur de la Bomba Chevron" or 800 vares (slightly more than 1,000 yards as best we could figure) south of the Chevron Station. In many cases, including ours – the Chevron Station had closed years earlier – the landmarks no longer existed, adding to the confusion.

The facial expressions of the men standing around, having early morning coffee in front of the street side vendors that lined the industrial part of town, was one of utter astonishment. No one in mountainous San José had ever seen anything even resembling what was passing before them. Helen got their reactions on film.

Unloading the hull and cradle from the trailer was a nerve-wracking event in itself. If something bad were to happen, well, that's the way it goes. ¡Qué lástima! (what a shame). The first obstacle was the narrow entrance to the yard. This was quickly solved when one of the workers took a chainsaw from the truck and, without hesitation, sawed down ten feet of our landlord's fence. No problem, but once the driver was able to back the trailer into the yard, we were confronted with a more serious and critical task.

To unload the boat, we had to manhandle long hardwood timbers about eight inches square, weighing over two-hundred pounds each, and put them underneath the wood cradle so that the boat – weighing at this time roughly 16,000 pounds or eight tons – could be jacked up off of the lowboy. But even after our hand-operated hydraulic jacks had lifted the hull inch by inch, dangerously high off of the ground, due to the slope of the yard, we still couldn't quite get the trailer out from underneath it. Afraid to go up any more, we all took turns digging trenches below the tires. Five hours later, once the trailer was free, we slowly lowered the boat as close to the ground as we could.

At one anxious moment on its decent, the hull listed precariously to one side. To this day I believe Jim thinks that he kept it from falling over by pushing against its side. Maybe he did, but I suspect we were just plain lucky that it didn't fall and crush our friend. Helen succinctly described it in our journal as *a painfully tense operation.*

That evening, before the people we had invited to celebrate arrived, I wrote:

I don't know if we will ever get her out now, but I'll wait a while to worry about that.

Around six, Jim, Donna, Harold Rolfdoll and his new Tica wife brought us our ten bronze portlights and stayed for some celebrating. They left, and Helen and I toured the boat, drinks in hand, and talked for hours.

Even though we had stared at the silhouette until late into the night, it was hard to sleep. Out of bed with the first morning light, we again marveled at the hull sitting in our backyard in Santa Ana. The chill of the morning gave way to the rising sun, filtered through the leaves and fruit of the large mango tree next door, reflecting off our very own sailboat.

At this point we couldn't even get inside the hull until I made a wood ladder. Since we could walk around it only so often, it was time to get started. With the exception of the Volvo diesel sitting on the motor mounts, the hull was completely empty – no deck, no cabin, no nothing. This was what we were going to build using traditional woodworking techniques, and it was going to be quite different in design and appearance from the production boats being built at the factory.

According to our how-to books, the first step was to level her. Otherwise, everything would be out of kilter once she was actually sitting in the water. As instructed, we took a long piece of clear plastic tubing filled with water and taped one end to a spot along the waterline. The other end we took to other points around the hull, meticulously jacking and shimming, until the water levels matched.

As yet, we hadn't bought wood or tin to make a shed over the boat, which was going to be a challenge in itself as the hull was really high off the ground. With the cradle sitting well off of the ground in the aft due to the slope of the yard, the shed was going to have to be approximately twenty feet high at the stern, fourteen feet high at the bow, and fifteen feet wide with a stairway alongside. Twenty feet is two stories tall.

To begin with, we built six stairs and a platform from which we put a homemade ladder against the side of the hull so we could get inside. Later that afternoon, we walked down the hill to the local lumberyard and bought the least expensive materials available – reddish hardwood studs in odd sizes and the cheapest grade of corrugated tin for the roof. A truck-for-hire hauled it up the mountain and helped us unload.

5/17/75
Erected tallest members of shed after one mishap in which Helen was almost beaned. They were awfully awkward, but managed after a bit of a struggle.

Screwed up and did not begin the metal roofing aft. Am afraid we will have to live with a leak over work area as I cannot put the two pieces in without tearing up the ones installed.

5/18/75 [Helen]

We had planned not to work on Sundays out of respect for our neighbors on the left of us. I can tell already it won't be a work free day because there were a million other projects (laundry, house cleaning, letter writing, gardening) to do. Still quite anxious to show off the boat, we also had to prepare for the guests we had invited. The first one to arrive was John Johnson, the artifact dealer.

He had come to propose that we help him smuggle artifacts into the States. I had to tell him we couldn't despite his zeal for the idea. The biggest reason we declined was, unless we were going directly to the U.S., how would we explain our illegal cargo to Customs in the countries we planned on sailing to? A close second was that we didn't like him, trust him or want to be around him.

Construction-wise we began with a blunder. Had we done a more thorough job setting up the work area with scaffolding and a better shed, we could have saved months in construction time. But, lacking experience and discipline, we were in a rush to get started on the actual boat building, and having never built anything much before, we had no idea how long it would take. What we had originally thought could be done in four months and later revised to six months, ended up taking us years. A big part of the reason: the only outside help we would eventually get – a wonderful luxury – was the maid we hired who cleaned and did the laundry.

We tried limiting trips to San José to once a week, spending the rest of the time working alone until we walked down the hill for supplies or caught the bus to Mas X Menos.

5/16/75 [Helen]

Reinforced the STAIRWAY TO HEAVEN. Finding out about the pleasures of constructing and being exhausted at end of day's work.

Platform is about four foot by five foot and stairs are fairly sturdy.

I am truly loving every second of life. An amazing amount of work has already taken place. Ben and I are close and loving while we work – almost unbelievable it's true because nobody else is pulling this type of life off. I'm proud however selfish as that may sound. Time to feed Ralph.

What we had done thus far looked awful, but what we would do later on would not.

11

GETTING STARTED

TWO PHASES OF CONSTRUCTION would take place in our yard in Santa Ana.

Phase One began in 1975 and was peaceful and productive. Most days we worked hard before going to bed early. Though we had occasional friends over, it was nothing like a year later, during Phase Two in 1976, when I started working at the factory. The final phase was to become a super-human effort where we relied on youth and raw stamina to do what we had to get done despite all of the social interruptions, many of our own making.

During Phase One, there wasn't much to see other than a bare hull with plywood bulkheads being fiberglassed into place, built-in water tanks being fabricated and the carline being completed with deck half-beams. Phase One was mundane. Looking at the foundation of a house isn't nearly as fun as seeing it framed in. It was during Phase Two that the boat began to take shape and became of interest to friends, future bosses and even friends of friends. Word was getting around and people were anxious to meet us and see what we were doing.

We had seen how to fiberglass bulkheads to a hull by watching the workers at the factory. The hardest part was determining exactly where they should go due to the interconnectedness of everything. This weighed heavily on us because the design work done by Mr. Crealock was not detailed – he painted with broad strokes. He would send rough drawings with, "Details will follow in 48 hours," written on the envelope. They never did.

What kept me rattled was the importance of these early decisions. How high up in the hull we put the floor dictated how high the coach roof would be above the deck to give us the headroom we needed. The cabin roof has to be in proportion to the rest of the hull or the boat would look ugly and have too much windage (the portion of the vessel's surface upon which the wind acts). Like the old song, "Dem Bones": "the thigh bone's connected to the hip bone, the hip bone's connected to the back bone" ... and so on.[1]

Physically putting in the bulkheads was messy but not too difficult once we got over the jitters. We'd witnessed a lot of boat building at the factory, but until the hull arrived in our yard, we had not done a lick of actual work. Our shiny tools, which we had bought based on lists provided by "how-to-build-a-boat" books, were virgins. Our work clothes were clean. After quickly getting the leaky shed up, we cautiously but enthusiastically began.

Our overall task would be to build the cabin, decks, and cockpit as well as the furniture inside the cabin. Nervously, we again leveled the hull several times just to make sure it wasn't listing one way or the other.

Just as the floor dictates the cabin height, the bulkheads do the same thing for the linear layout. The bed

---

[1] "Dem Bones" by James Weldon Johnson (1871-1938).

can't be too short nor the galley too narrow. The table had to be placed where people wouldn't hit their head on the deck beams as they rose from a seated position – compromise is a constant.

Two o'clock in the morning was a wonderful time to wake up and worry about some aspect that lay ahead of us. Even after we felt we had a grip on the layout, it was one thing to draw it to scale on a flat piece of paper and another to transpose the lines with Magic Marker to the inside of a three-dimensional empty hull. That first day we couldn't even start drawing where the bulkheads should go until we gave the inside of the hull a washdown.

5/15/75 [Helen]
I took it upon myself to clean the inside of the boat, WD-40 the Volvo diesel and cover it with plastic. By mid-afternoon I had a case of glassitus – itching horribly.

"Pica" is the Spanish word for it, and it best describes the torment of invisible glass particles imbedded in the pores of your skin. We learned to live with the sensation and minimize it, but it was always uncomfortable.

At first, we could only stand upright on the narrow ballast running down the center of the hull. Wearing tennis shoes we could move a bit from side to side, but for the next several months much of the work would be done in awkward positions, lying and semi-sitting against the sides of the hull.

As a point of reference, the first thing we needed to do, before we cut any wood, was to mark the waterline on the inside of the hull. Then we began drawing the layout. It took days of holding up pieces of wood, and measuring and re-measuring in every which way. There isn't much that can't be corrected in construction, but mistakes tend to multiply themselves if they aren't fixed as they come up.

5/22/75
Cut first bulkhead. Made second template. Worked on design problems.

Chain locker bulkhead fit perfectly. It is waiting for installation. Cut template for sail bin. Upon checking, found a three-inch difference in Bill Crealock's drawings and went crazy trying to design adequate galley and locate fireplace. Failed and called Scottie.

We made templates from scrap wood to help us fit the plywood to the curve of the hull at the specific spot where it would be glassed in.

5/23/75
Solved design problems. Made sure boat not sitting on saddles that might distort the shape. Re-leveled completely. Made prelim. markings.

Positioned fireplace in front of settee and recessed under double berth. We are pleased with this arrangement and think it is better than previous location. This allows us the room in the galley thanks to luck. We had changed our stove from model H5 to model 5 because the latter can be vented. This stove is much wider but also shorter and not as deep which will enable us to move the stove closer to the hull and compensate for motor size.

Marked approx. location of stateroom and main saloon as well as cabin sole level. Appears to be good tank space. Rain began. Must fix shed leaks tomorrow.

Rainy season slowed us down a lot because we had to stop work when the sky darkened and the raindrops began to fall. We didn't have a large enough area that was covered to operate power tools outdoors, and there was too much moisture in the air to work with fiberglass inside the hull. Usually it began about the same time each afternoon and the run-off from the mountain went down a gully that cut through our yard and led to a cast iron drain next to our back fence.

7/14/75 [Helen]
Had a terrible FLOOD in the yard and washed away 1/2 my garden and all tomatoes on Sat. God, was it awful. Trying to clear the drain, Ben was standing in the middle of 5 feet of muddy, mucky water that had backed up.

Okra ready and gigantic. Broccoli every night.

Normally it was calm and quiet where we were, but every now and then there was action.

7/23/75 [Helen]
Today we saw a runaway ox cart. Made me cry. Ben got a bit choked up himself. The oxen were blazing down the road. I knew immediately the frantic sound, but not until we heard a cry from the ditch did we rush down the stairs and out of the gate. One of the three little boys had been pushed aside – hurt feelings seemed to be

predominant over broken bones. To think of the poorness of their lives. The old man finally caught up to and stopped oxen and fixed cart. All barefoot running on rocks. You ain't gonna find me bitching anymore.

We took turns holding the saber saw while the other took pictures of our very first cuts. We were delighted when the bulkhead actually fit. These were big pieces of plywood three quarters of an inch thick that took both of us to carry.

It doesn't take long to become a fiberglass expert. Still, those first few times are awkward, causing bad words to come out of even the loveliest of mouths. It's nasty, smelly, messy, toxic, unstable, sticky and hard to clean up afterwards.

Once we had cut a bulkhead, it was carried up the "stairway to heaven" and into the boat, where we clamped and cajoled it into place. Then, after checking it with the level all the way around, we were ready to "tack" it to the hull. Into a bucket we poured the amount of syrupy, faintly blue tinted resin that we thought we would need from a five-gallon square tin container. Then, after cutting about ten pieces of fiberglass mat into strips approximately two inches by six inches, we added the catalyst (MEK) that makes the liquid harden. "Mat" is random fibers of glass, while "woven roven" is loosely woven glass fibers. By alternating layers, mat provides rigidity and woven roven gives a certain amount of flexibility. Once the catalyst is thoroughly stirred into the resin, it's time to go – the clock is ticking.

Using a throwaway paintbrush, the small strips placed half against the bulkhead and half to the hull were saturated. When the resin hardens, these strips are strong enough to hold the bulkhead in place until it can be permanently glassed to the hull.

No matter how neat or careful a person is, it doesn't take long for his or her hands to get sticky. Soon, both look like big balls of white fibers sticking out every which way. Try to get it off one hand and it sticks to the other. It sticks to the bucket, to your clothes, to everything. Acetone, which is industrial-grade fingernail polish remover, is the only thing that dilutes the stuff that is now even in your hair. After enough acetone rinses, it does become soluble in soap and water, though your hands remain a little tacky for a while. But, if all goes well, it is strong when it cures.

For the next few months, we cut plywood pieces and glassed them in place. The hardest was fabricating the built-in water tanks that would be underneath the cabin sole. First we cut plywood mini-bulkheads separating the three tanks, then "baffles" to keep the water from sloshing around while underway – more tedious than difficult.

6/12/75
Cut last piece of bulkhead separating stateroom from head. Cut all athwart ship baffles. Decided on then marked forward tank position. Bought plastic PVC tubing for drains from forward areas (shower, chain locker) to bilge.

Helen cut all but two baffles while I cut last part of the bulkhead. I teased her about being too careful and almost got a tape measure up my ass.

We had this particular construction skill down, but next up was the daunting first real test of our ability to do something other than cut plywood and attach it to the hull with this toxic goo and fiber.

Building the "carline" would be a defining moment for us, and once finished, we knew we could do everything else somehow, some way. The carline is the large beam where the cabin sides and the side decks are joined together. Not only does it have to be strong, it has to follow a double curve by running parallel to the sides of the hull from bow to stern in addition to mirroring the banana shaped "sheer." When you look at the profile of most boats, the bow and stern are higher than the middle.

7/3/75

Freaked out again on positioning of carline. Clamped in fore and aft bulkheads. Misc. work.

Called Scottie three times to find out what the shit to do with the carline. After much thought, we decided to laminate it vertically rather than horizontally. All I could get from Scottie was that either I spend 3 or 4 hrs. working it out mathematically or eyeball it. Since I can't do the former, I suppose we will do the latter.

Still waiting on imports as Mario, the plant Custom's man, is always flustered and slow. We are in need of bolts badly.

It has been raining like crazy the past few days – sure doesn't help. Once we get the carline in, I feel all is downhill. This is really difficult and important!

Laminating strips of wood had the unexpected benefit of helping us contour all of our deck and cabin beams as well as the carline. When strips of wood are glued together into a curved position, once the glue has set and the clamps removed, it retains the shape. It doesn't spring back.

7/4/75

Got bearings back a bit. Worked out design of carline. Sawed 4" boards down to 3 3/8".

Worked out dimensions for carline which will require four laminates 3/4 of an inch thick x 3 and 3/8 inch wide x 20 feet long (approx.) and one other 3 inch piece cut at a 16 degree angle, which, when coupled with the deck camber and the other 4 laminates, will create a 10 degree angle. This 10-degree angle is the angle given for the cabin sides.

With the bulkheads permanently glassed in place, we had to calculate from Crealock's drawings where and at what angle the carline should pass through each one, cutting out the slots as precisely and carefully as we could. There were angles, but the teak planks were flexible enough to make the bends using our steel clamps. Starting modestly with two laminates, we painted the teak with catalyzed, red-colored Resorcinol glue. We then clamped the pieces together and added screws to keep the joints tight. Each day we added a lamination until the carline measured three inches by-three and three-eights inches. Because it would retain its shape, we were then able to lift the entire piece out of the slots and sand it with a belt sander. Having seen the amount of time factory workers spent hand-sanding hard-to-get-to places, we wanted to eliminate as much of that as possible.

The final step before permanent installation was to saw notches for the half beams that would span the space between the carline and the fiberglass hull to support the side decks. Very much the perfectionists with unrefined skills, we tried to make good joints. It took about three weeks from start to finish, but we did a pretty good job.

Perhaps the biggest stroke of luck was our personalities. One of the great mysteries in any relationship is how the person you marry matures – what kind of person they turn out to be. Love is blind in the beginning, so you just never know. As it so happened, in addition to becoming a fair carpenter, I was adept at design work and figuring out how to go about making things. Helen is a finisher, who saw each step through to completion. She too was learning and becoming good at working with wood. If we were pitchers on a baseball team, she would be the closer. Enjoying what we were doing tremendously, it was impossible for us not to occasionally gloat and recall the smirks we'd received from those skeptical of our plans.

We were having the time of our lives and discovering new techniques on a daily basis. Like a hummingbird, Helen was in perpetual motion, getting things done and done well. Waking early each morning to the clear blue Costa Rican sky, a little chill in the air, we would haul the tools out to their spots beside this fantastic, deep green, shiny, spectacular, monumental hull sitting in its cradle. The distinctive smell of teak filled the air where Helen and

I, alone, worked with a passion. It wasn't as though we could do things at a leisurely pace, either. There were bureaucratic deadlines and there was that damned thing called money. We were racing toward our goal, and it was going to be a dramatic photo finish to see who would win – the bank account or us.

About mid-morning, we would take a break and have hot tea in our porcelain tin cups using water that had been kept hot in our unbreakable, stainless steel Coleman thermos. After peeling a navel orange from one of our trees, we'd eat sections along with saltine crackers while sitting up on the hull overlooking the valley, the airport, and the picturesque town of Alajuela on the other side, some fifteen miles away – green half of the year; brown the other half – rainy season; dry season. After ten or fifteen minutes, we wouldn't stop again until the dark clouds and smell of rain told us it was time to gather the tools and lug them back inside, often just as the large raindrops began to fall.

This was a period of progress and blissful isolation. Normally, after the day's work was over, with the countryside fresh from afternoon showers, one or both of us would walk down the hill for groceries and five Pilsen beers (two for Helen and three for me). By taking last night's empties down in a cloth bag we nicknamed the "tote goat," we exchanged the deposit bottles for new full ones. Even if we wanted more to drink that night, the hill was too far to walk twice after a full day's work.

In the evenings I played my guitar, or we would listen to music as we wrote letters or kept up our journal. We were thrilled when one of our friends unexpectedly brought us a copy of an album he thought we would enjoy – Jimmy Buffett's A1A. Years earlier, back in the States, when I had been rebuffed by Helen, I did my version of running away and joining the circus. I became a roadie for ShowCo, a company that set up sound systems for rock concerts. That's when I first heard this unknown singer open for John Sebastian in Thibodaux, Louisiana. Sure enough, it was the same guy, and we felt as though he was singing right to us.

> Mother, mother ocean
> I have heard you call
> Wanted to sail upon your waters
> Since I was three feet tall
> You've seen it all
> You've seen it all
>
> - "A Pirate Looks at Forty" by Jimmy Buffett

It was encouraging to hear and enjoy music from someone who was, "Looking back at [his] background, trying to figure out how [he] ever got here," living his life "like a song." I started learning the chords to my favorites right away.

After dark we might smoke a little something if we had it, take our beers and go out to admire what we had done that day. Illuminated by a bare bulb in a droplight, this shining, masterful work of art never failed to give us a thrill.

It was absolutely incredible how such a seemingly small area could take so much time, energy and materials.

I would look at a project, such as putting the plywood decks over the support beams, and try to calculate how many days it was going to take. I always estimated what seemed like more than enough time, but never once did we finish on schedule.

Before we installed the plywood over the varnished deck beams and carline, we set the pre-cut pieces on a pair of sawhorses we'd made, prepared the surfaces and painted them with three coats of white. They were smooth as glass after Helen put on the final one. Not only was she good with a brush, doing it this way she was painting from above the surface rather than awkwardly painting overhead.

We were in a groove and making progress as fast as two people could, which begged a question that was often asked. "Why don't you hire someone and have them help with the work?" Labor was cheap and time was short.

Logically, I suppose we should have, but we were enjoying each other in such a splendid, unspoiled, esoteric, intimate way, the thought of having to put up with helpers or outside carpenters had no appeal, even though our pace required getting extension after extension and going through bureaucratic contortions to stay legal with our imported motor and passports.

1/7/75 [Helen]

Ben – San José to buy teak from Juan and go to hardware store.

I began by sanding the storage bin floor with new disc grinder. Painted over putty touch-ups under double berth. Glued and screwed teak braces to top. Glassed in double berth and closet bulkhead. Across from it, cut out drawer and door openings in head bulkhead. Puttied entire front of it and sanded. Sealed tops for bed storage.

Now waiting for Ben to return with Edwin Arguello for steak and shrimp dinner.

3/23/75 [Helen]

Our cozy house will be hard to leave. Glad the boat is the alternative. Tonight Ben and I are celebrating our love and happiness and slow, but nonetheless real, boat progress over a Missouri T-bone and a bottle of ROTHCHILD red burgundy. I'm really pissed we don't have wine glasses to drink out of. Maybe I will borrow from Cindy, if I can get down the hill today. So much to do. Yesterday, a special trip to San José for the purchase of glasses but no score.

3/29/75 [Helen]

The wine was sour because the cork had collected moisture after we waited two months to drink it. Steak was delicious with a sexual dessert.

7/27/75 [Helen]

Things going really well lately. Much work and much socializing in two days. So far we have ten half beams installed. Something to show off and also to get us more motivated – I've never felt better with a person in my whole life than with Ben. Yesterday we laughed heartily at being so on top of the situation. Situation, merely being life.

12

THE FINGER

IT WASN'T PIERCING. It was more guttural, more drenched with anguish than a scream. Flying down the stairway from the boat, I found Helen grimacing as she held her finger – pain, blood and fear. When she settled down from the initial shock, I looked at it and it didn't look good – red meat. The saber saw she was using had jumped and cut the tip of her finger, probably nicking the bone, making it doubly painful.

She held it possessively, blood streaming down her hand, dripping from her elbow, as we quickly walked to the house. It felt like I had been punched in the stomach when I looked at it. After hastily wrapping it in gauze from our medical supplies, without a car, I called a taxi: "La dirección es Ochocientos Vares Sur de la Bomba Chevron en Santa Ana, y rápido por favor. Es una emergencia." Upset with herself, she sat on the front porch holding the injured hand, while I rushed around putting up tools, including the table saw, which was the biggest and heaviest. Ralph would guard the inside of the house while we were gone.

Being careful is something we preached to each other daily with Clint Hanger, the San Francisco boatbuilder who lost part of one finger, in mind. Feeling like homesick twelve-year-olds at camp, I tried to comfort her as we waited for thirty minutes that seemed like an eternity. Arriving in a swirl of dust at the gate, our taxi driver took our plight to heart and stepped on it, making the trip a finger-jarring, one-car race to the emergency room at Hospital San Juan in downtown San José.

After waiting about 20 minutes, a nurse summoned her to a treatment room. I tried to follow, but was not allowed in. I'm sure they had seen spouses faint and injure themselves worse than the original patient. I cringed when I heard her scream from behind the closed doors as they injected the xylocain into the tip of her finger so the wound could be stitched. I hurt for her. All was quiet for the rest of the procedure, from which she emerged white as a ghost. Alone with the doctor for over 45 minutes, she walked out on shaky legs – dizzy, like a prizefighter who had taken a serious blow to the head.

We laugh about it now, and it has become a funny cultural story, but Helen didn't know what to think of what had just happened to her. I wouldn't find out about the details until a little later. At the hospital's accounting window I paid 25 colones, the equivalent of $2.14. We have the receipt taped to the inside of one of our journals.

She snuggled close with my arm around her as we rode in silence back to Santa Ana, took a left on the road to Salitrál and another left on the dirt road in front of the house where Ralph, as always, was glad to see us when we opened the front door. Helen's finger was starting to throb as she began telling me what had gone on.

The doctor, in a white starched physician's smock, seemed like a nice fellow as he examined the finger and decided that it did need stitches. She was able to understand that he was going to deaden the finger and that it would hurt a little, and yes, that was her yelling as the xylocain was injected. After waiting for the anesthetic to numb it, he had her put her hand on a tray underneath a bright light. Though it didn't hurt, she could feel the stitches as he put them in.

After sewing her up, the young doctor proudly showed her the repaired finger and asked how she liked the "puntadas." The stitched finger had a bit of a point on the end where the two sides of the cut had been joined together. Helen, not knowing that the word "puntadas" meant "stitches," thought the doctor was asking her if she liked the "point" on the tip of her finger.

She responded "No, no!" Shaking her head, she told him, "No, no, quiero rondo," as she made a curved gesture with her other hand – "rondo," round like the other one. Even though she was unsettled, she could tell he was disappointed by her reaction when he said something she didn't understand under his breath. With a look of resignation, he shrugged his shoulders and again put the finger under the bright light. Obligingly, he took a pair of surgical scissors, snipped off the sewn-up tip and began putting in a new set of stitches. That's why she looked so pale walking out of the emergency room, holding her bandaged finger sacredly in the palm of her other hand, shoulders pulled forward.

The next day I kept telling her that she was going to have to suck it up, be brave and it would be okay, but eventually we knew something had to be done to stop the throbbing that had bothered her all night. Afraid to look at it, I was not excited about undoing the bandage, but she couldn't take it any longer. As it came off, a wave of relief came over her once grimacing face. The finger had swollen, making the bandage too tight.

To be on the safe side, the next day Helen and I went to the "Clínica Bíblica" (Bible Clinic), one of the private "American" clinics staffed by English-speaking physicians, where Dr. Cabezas (Dr. Head) inspected the work done on Helen by the emergency room doctor. It looked fine so he told us to return in a week to make sure there was no infection and to have the sutures removed.

She was going to be all right, but the episode knocked the spunk out of us, which was a shame after the progress we had been making. The carline and half-beams supporting the deck were all bolted and screwed permanently in place. The underneath sides of the plywood deck had been painted to a fine glossy finish and they too had been fastened. The plywood cabin sides were screwed in, and we were in the final stages of finishing the water tanks when the accident happened.

It was discouraging. I stayed in the house with Helen the day after, trying to keep her mind off the pain by playing cards and cooking a good meal.

A day later:

10/5/75 [Helen]
Ben discovered by checking the level of "el bote" we were 1/2 inch off. Thus the cockpit beam he put in was off. No sense in continuing until fixed.

A combination of bad weather, discovery of the 1/2 inch, and me – he decided to take day off.

Joe and Mary brought us plates of food.

To top off our bad luck, Ralph's ears had become infected by some sort of bacteria or fungus, and he needed to see a vet. What's more, there was a shipment of marine parts that had arrived and migración was being difficult about releasing them. Rather than getting anything much accomplished on the boat, we found ourselves going back and forth to town.

10/10/75

Went in for Perko parts and were unsuccessful again. Edwin is to bring them out Mon. It seems we are missing two 3/4" thru-hulls. Helen went to have stitches removed but Doc wanted to wait until Mon.

Every trip into town was, at least, a half-day affair. First, we had to walk down the hill to Santa Ana and wait for a bus that would take us to the Parque Central. That usually took from an hour to an hour-and-a-half. From there we had to take a second bus to wherever we were going in town. Not only did this take a lot of time, we had to schedule our trips around siesta as many businesses closed for two hours in the afternoon. Coming home was the reverse with a walk up the hill.

10/13/75

Helen was to have her stitches out today and Ralph's ears were worse so she borrowed Bob's old Ford for the big outing. She did not have to have them removed as they were falling out with the scab. Ralph must have a shot each day for a week. Helen picked up the Perko order.

Then, hitting us while we were down:

Helen had trimmed one of the tank tops before her finger was cut. I finished them today using a disc sander rather than the saber saw.

Glass was a mess and as of now it has not cured. Perhaps the MEK is too old. The resin is only 1 mo. old and should be good.

Adding insult to injury, the plywood she was cutting when she hurt her finger had to be thrown away because the bad resin wouldn't cure, even after being painted over with a hot batch. We had to start all over again.

10/17/75
Still trying to get tanks together. Luís Ámador came by and exchanged the resin for some that was prepared with cobalt. We learned that the resin is usually shipped without cobalt, which is added later. Without it, it won't cure. I'm not mad anymore.

Helen's first real day back on job. She did painting, laminating, much misc. and housework.

On the positive side, thanks to the finger, we hired a maid that would drastically improve the quality of our lives and bolster our spirits.

Not that all of our headaches were behind us.

10/21/75
Had to go to town as belt sander has broken gears. This is a <u>typical</u> run and not an exception:

Took sander to three places, none of which could fix. Priced new ones, and they ranged from $200 up (double States prices for U.S. names; tax is about 100% to 150%).

Went to Customs to get Ralph's medicine. They would not give it to me because it should have gone to the other Aduana bodega as it was medicine. Must pick up tomorrow.

Found sander for $107 at Sears. Bought it, but they had no belts. Sears called another place, which said they had them. When I went, of course, they did not.

Finally found some rough belts.

Went to Superba for more gel coat and acetone. They are out. The only acetone is rumored to be at a pharmacy.

Caught a bus home that stopped at every gas station to put air in his tire.

I was lucky. Quitos, the driver of the Salitrál bus, was just going up hill to house.

When things don't go right, blame the natives.

Most Ticos do not have enough brains to do anything.

What I said was mean and untrue, but it had been a rough day, especially since I went everywhere on buses filled with people who really didn't give a shit about my sander belts. They had their own troubles. The bus driver with the leaking tire was probably not too happy with the way his day had gone, either.

If this relatively minor frustration upset me, who happened to be enjoying the hell out of being where we were, doing what we were doing and having fun with the people around us, it's easy to see how magnified that sentiment can be for others. Once, while retrieving some imports from Customs, I witnessed an extremely frustrated gringo who could speak no Spanish trying to deal with a Custom's agent who could speak no English. In the gringo's hand was a book titled, *Winning Through Intimidation*. I just smiled, sat back and watched the animated scene unfold.

13

BACK IN THE GROOVE

10/30/75
Installed part inner ¾" of cabin carline.

Re-stacked wood and now have enough room for two chairs on front porch. Took all large wood from back to beside house in shady area and now have back porch free of wood!

Cut inner ¾" of carline. Sanded and fit joints. Installed one piece the length on port side.

WHAT WE HAD DONE thus far on the boat looked good, and our configuration was catching the attention of others involved at the factory. From the beginning, I felt that placing the cockpit amidships in a boat 36 feet long was not the best use of precious room below deck. With the mid-ship cockpit design, the middle of the hull, where it is widest, is occupied by the engine instead of being used for living space. That our aft-cockpit version gave the cabin considerably more room was evident after we installed the floor beams and laid down the plywood floor.

This was one of those major steps for us as we could walk around on the inside of the hull for the first time. Now we could begin installing the cabin roof beams that we had been laminating on a plywood form we had made.

Once out of the clamps, we belt sanded and varnished them.

Progress can be deceiving in that it may take weeks to get ready for a single dramatic moment. The cabin roof beams had to be joined using a hand chisel to a double teak laminate that we called the cabin top carline. A double-wide beam next to the companionway took three tries, but we were stubborn about doing a good job – the forward hatch needed to be framed in, the corner posts fitted and the big beam underneath, where the mast would be stepped, fitted and installed.

12/22/75 [Helen]

Installed big beam in doorway. I helped Ben because of size. The beam weighs a ton and at this stage a scar would be like a death. Ben chiseled out the carline for it and the fit was tight.

I did sand all beams for final smoothness.

Ben cut down bulkheads. We definitely have a low cabin profile. It looks good.

Left for the plant at noon to pick up stanchions, fuel tank, mast step, whisker stay fitting, Plexiglas, bow pulpit. Jim brought us home in the van, and then we took them out to LA CASCADA for dinner.

12/24/75 [Helen]

I sanded with wet/dry paper the teak beams and carline preparing for varnish. By end of day my arm could have fallen off, and I wouldn't have felt it. Same day – Ben sanded through his skin. Terrible work but must be done for a top job.

Ben cut out doors for bed storage. Ben also installed beams that needed routing for electrical wire.

Quit around 4:00 and enjoyed the back porch.

Sanding by hand and with power tools was never-ending as long as we had *La Dulce*, but it was especially full-time during the construction. Done with wet or dry paper, we could do it for hours without stopping. At first the arm gets tired so we would switch the paper to the left hand until the same thing happened. Next we would put masking tape on our fingers so we wouldn't sand through the skin. After a short while the fatigue would go away, and we could go on for hours, thinking faraway thoughts.

6/6/75 [Helen]

Getting out of bed every morning is tough with sore, tired bodies. What's really hard is that Ben and I, both, have been working in our dreams: planting gardens, cutting wood, measuring, etc. That makes 24 hrs. 7 days a wk. on the go. Can't last but sure it will for quite a while.

The day's over and we, as usual, worked long and hard for 9 hrs.

12/2/75

Tried out the stanchions and they fit well except for a couple that can be bent the small amount needed. Then looked at the tank after we had unloaded it from the car. Something didn't look quite right. With fear in our hearts, we ran with it to the boat – it's heavy too – and hauled it into place. Sure enough, I had reversed the measurements. It didn't fit at all. After a real depressed feeling, to understate it, I turned it around and it fit perfectly. The only problem was the holes for the fuel lines were on the side rather than the top. After checking for a while, I discovered that at the plant they had reversed the measurements. The tank will fit as planned when the holes are changed. Jim came by around 1:00 pm and we took it back to the plant. It will be ready Fri. afternoon.

Cut holes for mast supports that frame in door to stateroom.

12/25/75 **Christmas**
All Bar-B-Q-ing chicken at Zaras' for dinner
BROKEN INTO
Ladrónes (thieves) had their eyes on us just waiting for us to make a mistake so they could steal everything they could get their hands on, and we gave them a window of opportunity. Normally, when we went out at night we had Rico or someone else watch the house, but this time, thinking we wouldn't be gone over two hours, we took a chance.

It wasn't until the next morning that we pieced together what had probably taken place.

Carefully, they had taken out the glass jalousies from one of the small windows overlooking our back porch and were ready to climb through. Ralph would have stayed lying down underneath the table while they did this. Then, just as they were about to come in, he would have gotten his Royal Irish ass off of the floor, walked over to the window, stretched with his front paws extended and yawned loudly.

"Dios mío, I'm not going in there with that dog."

About this time, he probably started wagging his tail at the thought of having guests to break the monotony.

"Me neither, amigo. Let's get out of here."

They probably assumed we had taken Ralph with us when he didn't bark, but barking a lot wasn't his style. True, this scenario is based on circumstantial evidence and conjecture, but I'll bet it's pretty close to what happened.

Nothing was taken.

1/8/76

Helen bought foam for the cushions and bed in the morning and glued teak trim in head door, sanded and taped up hatches to keep out sawdust.

Framed in seat with teak corner post. Cut out top. Glassed in head floor as well as seat in stateroom.

1/9/76

Helen made frames for ports. Took off tape from lavatory front that held teak trim and puttied voids. She also sanded down plywood sides to accommodate cabin roof. All this and gave me shit, too. Irritated when she read this, she called me sick. I'm not sick; Ralph is – of having his ears cleaned.

I had to go with Juan to Heredia for the last of the teak. I bought 115 board feet for the coaming, which was not great wood but should be adequate as it will be stacked on top of each other. In afternoon I put hatch in stateroom seat and glued three beams.

Ralph did go through a rough spell with his ears. Some type of terrible fungus or bacteria had invaded them both, and we had to clean them using 15 to 20 Q-Tips every morning and afternoon. Medicine from the States worked at first but the dark brown stuff started coming back after awhile.

A local vet gave us a vinegar solution that kept it at bay for several months until it too began losing the battle. It was a great relief when we again used heavy dosages of the anti-bacterial drops, and they cured the poor dog's itch. Before his recovery, one vet even suggested we might have to cut off his ears.

1/13/76 [Helen]

6 am – 8 am correspondence

Noon – Ben left for San José to check on motor installation, buy paint (sealer and epoxy), hardware store and food. Returned at five with our three-blade propeller $170 and the elbow where the water enters the exhaust line $50.

Again sanded joints and finished! Every piece of teak to be varnished is ready except the companionway, which Ben still needs to install. Sanded down bathroom piece and got depressed finding a new splinter – more putty. Sanded seat across from bed with wet paper. Puttied about 10 nicks in joints. Used disc sander in head to smoothen up hull sides. Painted white epoxy in bin across from closet hull. Swept out entire boat. Determined to get a vacuum!

Tired.

Strangely enough, Helen, Ralph and I were not the only animals living in our house. The other occupant, "Zorro," liked to start scampering around on top of the plywood ceiling in the crawl space beneath the tin roof just about the time we got into bed. A zorro, which we had never even heard of before, is a reclusive animal about the size of a raccoon. The entire time we spent there, we saw him only once underneath the house. Kind of washed-out like a late night bartender, he was a mean looking guy with white fur, black spots, pink mouth and sharp teeth. Curiously, we couldn't see an opening large enough for him to get into the space that he or she called home, but from the sounds it made, he was probably a bachelor. It may have been him who snuck out late at night and ate mangos, leaving the seeds on the top of the shed and on the ground but never inside the boat itself. We didn't mind him, and he didn't cause any trouble other than the sound of him raising hell up there. If he got out of hand, one of us would bang on the ceiling with a broom handle, which usually calmed him down.

1/14/76

I woke up at 4:00 am and could not sleep so I started on paperwork. I keep hoping it's the last. Ordered the main and staysail from Hood and sent a letter and check to Jim for $900 yesterday. Ordered fastenings to be sent to Tita to hand carry into the country.

Did some sanding while Helen sanded and puttied, the usual. María came over with a joint that we smoked at 2:30 and after beers I went to bed early. Helen sewed until 10:00 pm.

1/18/76

Sanded sealer while Helen cleaned up companionway joints. Also leveled up tops of cabin beams. One had to be done with planer. Cut grooves for electric wire.

Helen vacuumed the boat with vacuum borrowed from Chester Patterson.

I watched Super Bowl on a fuzzy screen, and Helen called Jane, Tom and Henry.

1/19/76 [Helen]

A bit of a restful day – good breakfast – late start and early ending (10-4 pm) Sanded beams again and carline. Discovered chisel to be a big help in cleaning-up and we both became attached to it.

Chester and Jean came by at 5:00 and Bar-B-Q'd steaks with us.

The cabin roof was about to go on and it had been a long time coming. As with the side decks, we were painting the surface before we made the installation so there would be a clean line between the cabin roof beams and the marfil-colored ceiling.

1/22/76

Helen put the third coat on two of the three plywood cabin top panels while I was screwing up one of them. The next day I threw a temper tantrum to end all. Drug my wet, paint-covered piece of ply that wouldn't dry over to corner of the yard and jumped up and down on it. Then we washed off the paint with turpentine.

We found the resin from Superba, cómo siempre, was again short on cobalt. When a bit of cobalt was added it cured in about 30 min. as it should rather than one day as it had been.

In the book I may write, I am reminding myself to add a chapter on what not to do when painting.

The solution to our painting problems was for me to let Helen do it. The piece I screwed up was the result of trying to apply the paint thicker so it wouldn't need as many coats. After Helen fixed it, the plywood for the cabin roof was cut to size and all of a sudden, in one day, we were able to screw the cabin top into place. *La Dulce* became enclosed. She began to actually feel and look like a boat.

1/29/76 [Helen]
We used no glue in between the first and second layer of the plywood cabin top. Instead we sandwiched a layer of resin saturated fiberglass mat. Used close to 600 stainless steel screws. Needless to say it was a long and exciting day.

Broke several screws screwing at an angle into hard ply.

Finished around 3:30 and sat inside the cabin now that it is enclosed, staring for good while. The cabin top looks big to us, especially compared to the factory boats, and adds a very new dimension.

By this time we had conclusively decided she was *La Dulce Mujer Pintada*, the Sweet Painted Lady,

I'm back on dry land once again
Opportunity awaits me like a rat in a drain
We're all hunting honey with money to burn
In a short time I'll show you the tricks that we've
   learned
Oh, sweet painted lady
Seems it's always been the same
Getting paid for being laid
I guess that's the name of the game

-"Sweet Painted Lady"
Words by Bernie Taupin, music by Elton John

In Puerta Vallarta on our drive to Costa Rica, I was learning the chords to the song when we saw a fishing boat named *Foxy Lady*, and one thing led to another in Spanish. Naming a boat is important because everyone wants to know what it means or what the significance is. Maurice Campbell had to explain the name, *CRUACHAN*, and his Scottish connection a million times in Costa Rica alone, which was not particularly easy.

The only other names we considered were *La Luz* (The Light), the name of our favorite cantina in San José, but that sounded hokey. From the movie *The Graduate* we thought about *Elaine,* or *Elena* in Spanish, which is what Costa Ricans called Helen, but in the end *La Dulce Mujer Pintada* won out because that's what we kept calling her as we worked.

Ultimately, we would shorten it to *La Dulce Mujer*, the Sweet Lady, because we got lazy when the time came to paint the lettering on the transom. Occasionally, someone would say, shouldn't that be *La Mujer Dulce*, and yes, it should have been after we dropped the *Pintada*, but we were so used to calling her *La Dulce* that we decided it didn't much matter if that's what we wanted to call her. As for naming our creation after a lady of the night: she was sweet, she was painted, she was expensive, and a bit gaudy. Further down the line, when we eventually bought a VHF radio, we began calling her *The Sweet Lady* to make it easier for those who didn't speak Spanish.

Our trips to the factory became less frequent, usually once a week if at all, but we still kept up with the gossip through Jim and Donna. Periodically, Jim's brother, Rick, an accountant, and Frank Day, the partner who had put up the most money, would come down to ask why production at the factory was taking so long. I felt for Jim during these visits because, not only does management have a hard time understanding production timetables, if you have been living in the States, you simply don't know the obstacles and the way things are done south of the border. Their well-intended and mostly simplistic solutions, more often than not, had Jim and me shaking our heads.

Rick would offer suggestions such as, "From an accounting point of view, I think if we work backwards we can clear this up." Frank was even more obtuse in his efforts to get the factory "back on track." With one of them thinking we should be "working backwards" and the other thinking that was exactly what was going on, we were bemused.

14

LA DULCE MUJER PINTADA

OUR MAIN SALOON was surprisingly large for a boat our size. The British have traditionally designed sailboats for rough weather, almost a constant off the coast of England. They don't like open space where a person might get knocked about. Our philosophy was different in that we figured most of the time living aboard our sailboat would be in port and that below decks should be as roomy as possible. To make it safe at sea, we put handrails in strategic places to hold on to when the going got rough … and it would.

The Volvo 36 horsepower three-cylinder diesel engine proved to be only moderately accessible and a pain in the ass to work on, but it was a dependable engine and, except for a couple of transmission problems, did a good job. A fuel tank filler with watertight cap went on the port deck along with a breather hose on the side of the hull.

Diesel engines require clean fuel since the injector sprays a fine mist into the cylinder as the piston rises, creating heat from compression that explodes it. To be on the safe side, we put two sets of fuel filters in between the fuel tank and the engine's fuel pump. The green Swedish engine had steel decompression levers. If for some reason there was not enough battery power to start her, I could lift the levers, and insert a hand crank. When it was turning as fast as I could get it to go, Helen would close one lever and that cylinder would usually start firing so the other levers could be lowered. If there was some juice in the batteries, the starter engine helped me and it wasn't very hard, but if we let them run down too low it took everything I had to get the large, heavy flywheel going fast enough. We made a locker for our tools above the fuel tank. In front of the locker we put a spectacular thick piece of cocobolo – a rich, dark reddish heartwood that had contrasting white sapwood on the sides.

In the cockpit we bolted the steering pedestal to a bronze plate underneath the cockpit sole that had adjustable bronze pulleys guiding the steel cables to the rudder quadrant. This is also where we put the battery box, electrical panel, cockpit drain thru-hulls, fuel filters and engine exhaust system. We had both electrical and manual pumps for the bilge, which was too deep as we could barely reach down and clean out the glop that would accumulate there – a problem we would eventually solve.

The cabin sole was teak with hatches and flush bronze handles that enabled us to access the three water tanks underneath. The aft tank was the largest, and the one forward was the smallest. Again, this was well before bottled water. We bathed in and drank the hose water that was available wherever we filled up, without a thought. Each tank had its own filler on the starboard deck. Once living aboard, we found that when it rained we could strategically place a dishtowel that would channel the water running down the side deck into the opening. We caught a lot of water that way.

On the port side we made a couch-sized "settee" with a teak bookshelf behind it that had a built-in stereo speaker covered with a colorful, hand-sewn "mola" from the San Blas Islands. We were listening to a lot of music, so a good sound system was essential. A 12-volt automobile stereo with two large, good-quality car speakers worked super in the confined area. In the main cabin we installed a Paul E. Luke soapstone and bronze fireplace that was vented with brass stovepipe insulated from the wood bulkhead by asbestos and hand-glazed Guatemalan tile. On top of the cabin, where it went through, was a brass "Charlie Noble" smoke-head that kept rain from coming in. The perfect fire, when we eventually got somewhere cool enough to have one, was a third of a synthetic log topped with mesquite chips for aroma.

On the starboard side we made an L shaped "dinette" with a bookshelf that was identical to the one on the port side. It held the other speaker. The table, constructed of three-inch wide teak boards glued and screwed to three-quarter inch ply, had a teak fiddle all around and was fastened to the floor with two substantial stainless steel pedestals given to us by the factory because they weren't adjustable – something the Tiburon 36' required. Above the table, attached to the ceiling beams, were our fishing rod holders. On the bulkhead we put a brass barometer, matching clock and kerosene lamp. Overhead was a Perko bulb light and a 12-V florescent lamp. Underneath the starboard settee was our wine bin – what a joke that was, as we never had enough money for regular sized bottles of decent wine. When we eventually made it to the States, I tore it out and put in a heavy-duty marine air conditioner that, at the dock, could cool the cabin quickly even with the companionway open.

Anchored out, we were always comfortable sleeping in our bed, or in the cockpit if it was especially warm, but tied up to a dock where the trade winds were often blocked, the AC made it livable. Ralph loved sleeping underneath the table with the cold air blowing directly on him.

Separating the stateroom from the main saloon was one of our most handsome pieces of wood sculpture, a one-inch thick, laboriously-made, louvered door. The grain of the wood was striking and it looked sensational open or closed. Forward of the main saloon, the stateroom had a double berth on the port side. Size-wise it was a comfortable double bed with a little taken off at the foot where the hull narrowed. The wider part (aft), where we put our heads and pillows, was in a small alcove where we wired two low-voltage lights on adjustable goosenecks to read by. The light was so focused that either of us could turn ours on without disturbing the other. The part of the fiberglass hull that our berth was up against was covered over with varnished teak. The forward hatch funneled in fresh air, and we had a fan when we needed it.

All of the plywood bulkheads were covered with varnished teak and every screw was covered with a bung, which is a round, wood plug that we aligned with the grain of the surrounding wood.

Across from the bed was a large cushioned seat next to a side bench wide enough to write letters on. Above, was a large drawer faced with a piece of teak that had extraordinary swirling grain and two smaller drawers – one for Helen and one for me, which she soon took over.

The stateroom had a closet big enough to hold my two guitar cases and lockers for folded clothes. Large storage bins were underneath the bed.

The head was forward of the stateroom, just aft of the sail locker, which was just aft of the enclosed chain locker in the very peak of the bow. When making the water tanks, we had made sure they held enough to shower every day. On the port side of the head was a round stainless steel lavatory and a chrome-plated bronze hand pump like the ones in the galley. The varnished counter top was made out of a special hardwood called "ron ron." It had a rich reddish-black grain that contrasted nicely with a teak door to the cabinet, secured with cast brass fasteners, that held our toiletries. Under the lavatory was a locker where we kept cleaning supplies. On the wall we put a mirror approximately 18" by 50".

Our head was a heavy duty Wilcox-Crittendon "Skipper" that had a four-inch diameter bronze piston driven by a three-foot handle with a black knob on the end. The only flaw was the pressboard white seat, which later cracked, pinching our asses every time we sat down. To solve this, we took it off, drew a pattern on a piece of cardboard and made a varnished seat and lid out of teak scraps that was much kinder to our rear ends.

To shower, Helen used two sinkfuls of water and I used one. She heated hers, but the routine and the objective was the same – to get that clean invigorating feeling that only soap and fresh water bring. For a while we had a handheld showerhead with a rubber end that fit on the spigot of the pump, but when it wore out and we were unable to find a replacement, we began filling up the sink and dipping a tin cup to pour the water over our heads and body parts. Long, luxurious showers these were not, but they worked.

Water from the shower went through a teak grating, down three-quarter-inch PVC tubing to the bilge, where it was pumped out by the 12-volt bilge pump.

Our portlights and the outside finishing rings were cast bronze made at the same foundry that poured the ballast – assembly required. Special bolts with wing nuts were what closed them tight against a rubber gasket.

Cockpit seats were designed so they would be long enough to sleep on. White cushions would eventually cover all but the bridge deck, next to the companionway. Like the deck this was made of teak with black caulking. A grating that encircled the base of the steering pedestal looked good and kept our feet dry.

What would make our cockpit distinctive was the laminated coaming that formed the seat back and pads for the Barlow two-speed headsail winches. Solid teak, it was about five inches thick at the top, expanding to eight inches where it met the deck. It was even wider where the winches were mounted. Though not planned, we decided to add a sturdy handrail athwart ship, as it was something we could hold on to in weather.

The galley, positioned on the starboard side, was the last piece of the design puzzle to fall into place. As our journal states, Lady Luck played her part in that we ordered a stove wider, but not as deep as the one we had initially wanted because it could be vented. The purpose of the oven vent was ostensibly to keep the cabin cool. This, we initially thought, would be a good thing, but what we hadn't taken into account was the fact that cooking food takes heat, which doesn't happen if it's going up a stovepipe without a flue. Additionally, it would have been complicated and cumbersome to install. We never baked very much anyhow, so we covered the vent with tin foil.

In sailboats the stove is usually gimbaled, allowing it to swing when the boat is heeled over keeping the top and burners level. You couldn't prepare hot meals very well underway otherwise. Ours was made by Paul E. Luke of East Boothbay, Maine, and it was a beauty – all stainless steel with a cast aluminum top and bronze burners. Propane, considered dangerous by some, we thought was the best way to go. Heavier than air, almost odorless, it can collect in the bilge if the proper safeguards aren't taken. "A spark and ... Boom!" were the dire warnings, but in all our time aboard we never knew anyone who had exploded. Originally, we built a box for the propane tanks on the side deck that drained overboard with access from the deck. We put a safety shut-off valve in the galley, but I turned it on and off with the valve on the tank itself as an added precaution. Later, after we added two feet to the transom, we moved the tanks to the newly created lazarette locker, making the original box an outdoor icebox. To insulate the stove cavity, we used asbestos and covered it with stainless steel finished with angle brass.

Next to the stove we put a trash bin and made a long, tall teak door that was secured with a nice brass latch.

To let light in and keep the galley cool, we put a rectangular portlight on the cabin side and a round one facing the cockpit, which also allowed the person in the galley to remain a part of any conversation outside. The companionway opening and the stairs to the stateroom were on the port side.

Our double, stainless steel sink was directly over the motor, which was boxed in with removable panels for access. If the engine had to be pulled (it would), we could take out the sink and lift it with a come-a-long high enough to maneuver it through the companionway.

The sink drained overboard through a one-and-one-half inch Perko bronze thru-hull with a heavy, bronze gate valve that could be shut off if something started leaking. On each side of the sink we installed a chrome-plated, bronze hand pump – one for fresh water and the other for saltwater to wash dishes. Rather than have an elaborate pressure water system with an electric pump and hot water heater, we elected to have only manual ones, the reason being, that electrical systems waste water, use precious battery power and were prone to break.

We made the countertop and icebox door, which could only be opened from the top by pulling up on a brass "O" latch, from unvarnished teak that measured seven-eighths of an inch thick by two-and-one-half inches wide. Too much cold escapes from a side door icebox opening. For as long as we had the boat, I toyed with installing mechanical refrigeration, but it never seemed quite worth it as we would have to run the engine an hour or two each day, and we didn't like the noise.

For eleven years we lugged ice that could last for six or seven days if we were careful. Clear block ice lasted the longest while a regular bag, like the size at convenience stores, would last for a day. Our icebox, with two shelves, was insulated with polyurethane foam that we mixed and poured one night, watching it miraculously expand.

The galley had four drawers fronted with teak and recessed brass drawer pulls. The varnished teak contrasted handsomely with the marfil-colored background. Space for our spices was aft of the galley counter where we built a secret compartment, which was too much fun for adolescent minds. Most canned food would be kept in storage bins under the settees.

Under the stove we made a locker for pots and pans. Our first locker door, the one for our wine bin, had louvers, but they were time consuming to construct and dangerous to cut because my fingers had to be close to the table saw blade. The others we made with vertical strips of teak, about two-and-a-half inches wide, leaving about a quarter of an inch in between for ventilation. They looked just as good and were much easier to make.

The companionway was secured with a solid teak door adorned with bronze latches and hinges. The varnished teak main hatch slid back and forth on stainless tracks.

2/7/76 [Helen]
Cleaned up boat.

Sort of tired from day of sanding. Looked at boat from Roberta's yard. Quite a shock as we had never seen it broadside due to the trees on our side. Weren't really thrilled with what we saw. Ports were too high.

Cut the port openings one inch to lower and will have to fill in on the top.

Sanded by hand and with a belt sander to round-over the curve where the cabin sides met the cabin top. It looks pretty good.

Chester over to see progress after hernia operation, and we had a few.

2/12/76 [Helen]

Big bad day! Applied second layer to top – one layer 3/4 oz. mat, one woven and 3/4 oz. mat. Used seven gallons of resin. Batches too hot but did adhere properly. Three-hundred screws 1 ½" #10. Mucho caulking!

To our surprise, it wasn't strong enough over main cabin. Really pooped, solid labor from 9 – 3 pm.

Despite the reinforced double beam over the galley, we found the cabin top too springy forcing us to put a four-inch-square teak post built hollow like a wood mast underneath it for support. This, like the cockpit handrail, was one of those unplanned things that turned out well, doubling as something to hold on to when we were at sea.

Helen did the lion's share of the non-stop, ongoing painting and varnishing with the exception of the cabin top. Enamel paint would have been fine and could have been brushed on, but at the time, we decided epoxy would weather better. After trying to brush the epoxy on:

2/22/76

Terrible paint job. The epoxy did not go on well leaving gloppy brush strokes. We really created a big mess and were very disappointed over spoiling our beautifully prepared surface.

Patterson's for usual visit – this time spaghetti – Chester has had the same problem with epoxy and recommends spraying it on. Now the problem is finding a compressor – he has a gun.

2/26/76 [Helen]

A bit sluggish but sanded epoxy preparing for spray job – maybe Friday.

Sanded till blood appeared on fingertips and decided it was impossible to paint on Fri. because the surface, due to wet and dry sanding, seemed too moist.

3/3/76 [Helen]

Painted. Guido Anderson arrived about 8:30. He's an old man who has a mute little boy as his assistant. Compressor blew a few breakers. The outcome wasn't any better. The sides had lace curtains and the top was too thick and rocky.

Very upsetting day.

Guido later visited all duded up with wife and two kids. Exhausted, we were in our robes. Oh well!

3/5/76 [Helen]

Ben sanded and puttied top for third time. Love/hate relationship.

I went to Ensambladora Automotritz for copy of contract between John, Jim and Ben. Then to B. of A. for copy of bond we have for motor. Lastly, to R. Smyth for copy of the request for an extension. Scored all three copies and took them to the lawyer. He said we needed the bank extension prolonged and also proof of the past extension. I'm so sick of extension this and that.

Early evening because painter arrives at 7 am.

This time we finally sprayed on a coat that was acceptable.

The teak deck was dramatic with a herringbone pattern at the bow. After the teak had been laid one strip at a time, we put masking tape over the wood leaving only the grooves for black caulking. What a mess. It took me a full hour to clean up after a long day of forcing the thick black stuff in between the planks. As pretty as they were, they lasted only four years before they began leaking and had to be pulled and completely re-done.

The forward opening hatch was teak with three panels of green tinted Plexiglas to allow light inside. Two brass supports held it open.

What was especially satisfying was that our boat was unique and becoming quite a piece of handcraft. We were doing a good job, and we were having a ball.

15

EL JEFE NUEVO

THOUGH WE HADN'T been spending much time at the factory, we had heard from various sources that the biggest threat to efficiency and production was becoming our buddy, Scottie. It was truly a shame. His behavior had become erratic to the point that he was regularly showing up for work late, sometimes after drinking. As a result, Scottie, the only real shipwright in Costa Rica, was told that he was no longer part of the team and that he should clean out his locker. It was sad on a personal and professional level. A stressful job, especially in a foreign country with a different language, can wear a person down, and I think that's a big part of what happened.

Who could possibly take his place? Frankly, Helen and I were surprised when we heard that TransAm Marine was going to make *me* an offer to work for them. The speculative dilemma – how could I possibly take on a job at the factory and finish our boat? It was the rainy season, making it impossible for me to do anything after a day at FibroTécnica. That would leave only Saturday afternoons and Sundays free. The only reason we were even considering it was money, and we talked long and hard about it for days before my scheduled appointment with Rick and Frank to discuss the possibility. Jim and Donna had gone back to the States to spearhead sales.

5/11/76 [Helen]

Ben was supposed to meet Frank at 9:30 at the factory, and they didn't show up so he left. The afternoon for Ben was great just being back and working on our boat. Drastic change in discussion about working: to fart these guys off. It's better for us to go to the water in five months instead of eight. Too much work for Ben besides – he would have 64 days to work on our boat (every weekend in eight mos.) and no time off. These guys are aggravating when it comes to showing up on time. If they can't even do something so simple, no wonder their business is hurting.

What ticked me off the most was that I had to walk down the hill at 7:30, take the Santa Ana bus to Parque Central and then catch the Lourdes bus to the factory to make it there for our 9:30 appointment. They had a car and still arrived two hours late. I saw them pull up as I was calling Helen from a pay phone outside the gates of FibroTécnica and told her I was on my way home – to hell with them.

After being stood up, I called Frank the next morning and told him that I didn't know what they had in mind but, whatever it was, it wasn't going to work out.

In a bit of a panic because they were scheduled to leave Costa Rica in a few days, they drove out to our place with a last minute proposition.

5/13/76

We talked all day and came up with a deal: 4 months – 5 maybe, the use of a Land Rover, access to materials *from the factory at their cost, $600 a month and more if deserved, 12:30 – 4:30 would be my hours. They knew they needed someone at the factory to look out for their interests as well as do what I could to improve production that had become disorganized.*

This was very cool. In the international version of *Time Magazine*, there was an often-run ad showing a macho male sitting on the top of a red Land Rover holding a glass of José Cuervo Tequila. Now we had one just like it. Helen took a photograph of me posing on ours.

The day after I accepted their offer, I learned of another problem that obviously factored into my employment (and perhaps Scottie's lethargy). Hauled out on the east coast of Costa Rica at Puerto Limón, the wooden boat, *Calma*, that had been made from the plug, was starting to come apart. Because FibroTécnica had been skeptical of the decision from the beginning, they had made Jim and the boys sign a paper relieving them of any responsibility for the all-wood version of the Tiburon 36'. The cost of any repair would fall squarely on Jim, Rick and Frank's shoulders. I was their only hope to salvage that mess.

5/14/76
We drove with Rick to Limón to Mike's boat. It rained and the boat leaked everywhere. I went over problems with Mike.

After going through the Panamá Canal, Mike had sailed to Limón because the boat was leaking like crazy. Since there was no dock where repairs could be made,

Mike had her lifted out of the water with a crane. Though we didn't know it at the time, *Calma* had sailed on her one and only voyage, never to float again.

The way the agreement with me was set up, Jim, Rick and Frank were paying my salary, but the factory was in on the deal too, since they were selling us parts at their cost and loaning us the red Rover for our personal use. Though technically Dañiel and Don Johnny were in charge of the factory and its seventy Costa Rican employees, I was working on the floor. What I said carried a lot of weight with both them and the workers.

Since I was a stop-gap employee who was only marginally qualified, my first piece of sage advice to Dañiel and Don Johnny was, "You need to get someone down here who speaks Spanish and knows what they're doing as far as sailboat production goes."

My first bright idea to make production more efficient was: tennis shoes. There was a very distinct pecking order at the factory. Carpenters did not clean up after themselves, their ayudantes did. That was part of the problem and it was something I knew I couldn't change. The other part of the problem was the hard-soled shoes they were wearing. Often held together with masking tape, they attracted even more crud than regular soles. After weeks of work on a boat, it looked as if an army had marched through it. Every scratch on the finished gel coat had to be buffed out, as did every glue stain.

My initial suggestion was to require each worker to come to work in tennis shoes. As Dañiel explained, that would be impossible. They couldn't afford them based on their salaries. Also, since tennis shoes were an import item, the duty made them even more expensive than in the States. The pay scale varied from three colones (36 cents) to eight colones (about $1.00) an hour. For each worker to spend $20 on a pair of tennis shoes for work wasn't financially feasible. So I suggested that the factory buy them for the workers and use their tax exempt and mass purchasing power to keep the cost down. I was told that that too was impossible because the workers would use them to play soccer during their off hours, and the shoes wouldn't last.

They did love fútbol. Lunchtime was thirty minutes long and the guys would down the food they'd brought from home in about five minutes and then, between the two large metal buildings, play soccer with a ball made of used masking tape.

Finally, I suggested that we buy the shoes but insist they be left in their lockers at the plant. I know Dañiel didn't think much of this idea either, but he relented and the factory bought everyone a set of shoes. Taking three months to arrive and clear Customs, it was a mini-Christmas when they did. With shoeboxes all over the place, the men were joking and laughing as they each tried to find a pair that fit.

In theory I suppose the tennis shoe experiment was a good idea, but it didn't take long for the rubber soles to crud up with fiberglass resin and random junk from the factory floor just as the others had. Several months later, everyone was back to the hard-soled shoes held together with masking tape – no shortage of that.

I did better with factory equipment. Rockwell was a good brand of industrial quality tools, including pneumatic ones that worked from compressed air. A representative agreed to fly down from the States to help us re-stock those that were in short supply, especially drills. You could never have enough of them. In order to screw something properly, multiple sized holes had to be drilled. Without having to change bits, two drills make a job go twice as fast. The woodworking shop also got some major tool upgrades, including a new fourteen-inch planer. In the United States everything was available and in Costa Rica very little was. Virtually everything had to be imported and go through Customs.

Getting marine parts was another importation quagmire. At my request, Lewis Marine Supply, a company Helen and I had been buying from since we became *Ben and Helen Harrison, Boatbuilding and Repairs*, sent a representative down from California to help Dañiel and me work out a comprehensive list of parts that each boat would require. That way, in theory, when ordering we could just say how many boats we were ordering for – three boats = three sets of hardware.

These were the big problems that involved management. But what I really liked about my job, most of the time I was helping solve smaller day-to-day construction problems in Spanish with the workers.

I was learning a lot including the reason why Helen's and my Spanish conversations about building our boat had left so many with puzzled looks on their faces. Since a sailboat in Spanish is a "velero," it seemed logical to me that the verb "to sail" would be "velar." When Don Johnny overheard me use the word, amused, he told me that in Costa Rica "velar" means to mourn, as one would mourn the dead. Instead of telling people we were building the boat so we could sail and live aboard, we had been telling them that we were building the boat so we could mourn the dead.

The biggest screw-up that occurred on my watch, and it was a pretty good one, was the mystery of the sinking mast. Stepping the mast and installing the rigging were two things that were being done in the States. For some strange reason, on one of the boats the rigging would be tightened and tuned, only to be loose the following day. When the same thing happened again, Jim called me to try to find out what was going on.

In the darkest corner of the factory, one worker was in charge of bedding the ballast after it had been lowered into the hull. He was supposed to fill the voids with sand and resin, then glass over the top with woven roven. What I didn't know was that my guy, on his own, had decided to save the factory money. Rather than waste all that resin, he filled the voids with polyurethane foam, the soft stuff used for insulation, before cosmetically fiberglassing over the top. With the mast stepped on the ballast, every time it was tightened, it sank further down into the soft foam.

Inside each boat there was a molded fiberglass liner that made getting to the affected area a real problem without major work to the boat's interior ... unless we came up with a simpler solution, which we did. By cutting out the drain pan in the head there was just enough room under the liner to cut out the fiberglass layers, dig out the foam and pour resin underneath the mast step. It wasn't easy but it beat tearing up the cabin floor.

It was true that my workload had increased with my new job, but the strain didn't come from work hours alone. A lot came from the work-related social hours we were obliged to spend. Instead of having friends over once or maybe twice a week, they were dropping by or inviting us out, four and five nights a week. We'd been in Costa Rica for almost two years and had become high-profile gringos on a daring mission, which was about to become even more exciting the closer *La Dulce Mujer Pintada* got to the water.

As evidence of our elevated status, we were invited for dinner at the Santa Ana postman's house. Naturally, we had to reciprocate and thought that red-sauce, ground beef spaghetti would be a good dish to serve. It didn't dawn on us beforehand that the postman and his wife had never eaten pasta, but it was obvious by the hesitation and looks on their faces that they had no clue how to get the noodles and sauce slipping and sliding around on their plates into their mouths. Even after watching us twirl the noodles with our fork, it's tricky until you get the hang of it. They were stoic, bless their hearts, and insisted that they had enjoyed the meal though they didn't eat very much.

The factory closed at 4:30 in the afternoon, but by the time I got out of there it was often dark and raining as I drove home in the Land Rover. With our newfound mobility and paycheck, I could now stop and shop more often at Más X Menos Supertienda or the fancy carnicería across the street. The meat in Central America was tough and lean. Ground beef for meatloaf, spaghetti or hamburgers was fine, but the only really tender steak was the tenderloin, which was pricey. The best deal was a fish called "dorado" (gold). I had never heard of it before but it tasted great and cost only 45 cents a pound. Of course, I would soon learn that dorado is the same as dolphin (not Flipper) in Florida or mahi mahi in Hawaii.

Canned tuna was cheap as well and, between us, I'm sure the number of tuna fish sandwiches eaten was in the thousands. We were working so hard, we could eat as much as we wanted whenever we wanted. For variety, the cafetería at the plant served a hot lunch of beef or chicken that always included fried plátanos and gallopinto, a mixture of reddish/black beans and rice, for 75 cents. In Costa Rica, no matter what the main course was, it almost always came with a side of rice and beans.

6/22/76 [Helen]

Art and Tita Sunday for B-B-Q short ribs. Ben "my slave" all day while I read Circumnavigators, *which is now my favorite book. It has given me much drive to circumnavigate with Ben. When Ben first mentioned it, I didn't feel the urge but now that I have read the accounts of those who did, it sounds so exciting and adventuresome. Yesterday we talked of building another boat for $20,000 building fee in some exotic part of the world receiving four $5,000 installments while building. Before, this idea left me cold – but I've changed. It's a delight to construct a vessel, and I'm learning so much about tools, design and math.*

More peach trumpets are blooming by our gate. My garden looks great. Okra ready in three weeks maybe. Tomatoes have shown through. All onions finally eaten. Good fluffy lettuce.

Worked in darkroom and developed a terrific 11' x 14" teak milling scene.

6/28/76 [Helen]

Put in our best Sunday. Glassed in starboard bench. Cut the doors in the seat backs as well as finished storage bins under starboard bench.

At one point we worked twenty-eight days straight. At the end of a long stretch like that, everything began to take longer. We eventually learned that we could accomplish the same amount of work, and better maintain our sanity, by working five-and-a-half or six days a week.

Back at FibroTécnica the big news was the arrival of Dennis Garrett. Don Johnny and Dañiel had brought in someone who knew about production fiberglass sailboat construction and who could speak Spanish fluently. We hit it off from the beginning.

16

BACK TO THE FACTORY

ON OCTOBER 30th, 1976, two years and one month after we arrived in Costa Rica, it was time for us and our boat to leave our wonderful place in Santa Ana. When we moved in, we told the Krumpkys, our landlords, that the longest we could possibly stay was one year. We had been there for over a year and a half, and they were anxious for us to leave to make room for family.

The government deadline to launch *La Dulce* was January 12, 1977, giving us two months and twelve days to work on dry land before transporting her to Puntarenas and putting her in the water. Because we had formed such a close relationship with Dañiel, Don Johnny and Dennis, they were kind enough to allow us to bring the boat back to FibroTécnica to finish as much as we possibly could in that period of time – a huge favor. Though exposed, the boat would be next to a large covered work area that had some major tools that would speed things up.

We would be positioned next to *Calma,* which I had had trucked in from Limón where nothing was getting done. Going quickly from bad to worse, at least at the factory she had a chance.

Two days before the truck was to come to Santa Ana, I took down the makeshift shed that had more or less covered our work for such a long time. It came down with ease once I took the nails out of the corrugated tin panels.

10/28/76 [Helen]

Tore down shed. The last wing we lifted and shoved off. Scary. Roberto hung around and bugged Ben.

Put cockpit drains in with screws and caulk-tex. Repaired main hatch so it slid better. Installed door. Put 'thru jolis' (thru-hulls) in cockpit floor. Packed. Installed hose under pit.

I left for Chester's with a $100 to buy food, 50 meters rope, more hose and beer.

Iris Chacón on TV at nine.

As frantic as we were, we still didn't want to miss the Iris Chacón Show. She was a healthy painted lady who dressed so provocatively that she looked undressed in the few clothes she actually wore. We'd been gone for over two years, and the only TV we watched on our black and white portable Sony with a seven-inch screen, other than an occasional movie in Spanish or in English with Spanish subtitles, was a children's show with adult humor, "El Chapolín Colorado" (The Red Grasshopper), and Iris Chacón, who sang and wiggled everything, and I mean everything, as she belted out and danced salsa numbers in front of a high-powered Latin band.

While we worked, we sometimes listened to the radio on our Zenith Transoceanic. The only two songs in English played regularly were "The Disco Duck" and "Give me an 'F' give me a 'U' give me a 'C' give me a 'K'" – the introduction to Country Joe and the Fish's anti-Vietnam

War anthem, the "Fish Cheer." Bad words, like those on the "I Feel Like I'm Fixin' to Die Rag," don't sound bad to those who haven't grown up with the language.

When we eventually began integrating ourselves back into U.S. society, there would be songs, movies, expressions and events that everyone knew, which we had never heard of. It was a Rip Van Winkle phenomenon, waking up after being asleep for years to find the world a different place than when he began his siesta. We'd only been gone for five years, but the year before we left San Francisco was spent paying attention to almost nothing but our sailboat plans. Add to that the time it took us to catch up to North American culture after arriving in Key West, which is pretty out there anyhow, and we'd lost the Seventies – an entire decade.

Though it was the last time we would attempt to watch Iris in our little plywood house, falling asleep before the end of the show, this wasn't a period of reflection. It was a time of exhaustion, momentum and the anticipation of another big step toward the launch of *La Dulce Mujer Pintada*. Foremost on our minds was the dangerous task of getting her loaded onto the truck and driven safely back to the factory for our final push to the water. Over a year ago, when she was unloaded at our house in Santa Ana, I wrote in the journal: *I don't know if we will ever get her out now, but I'll wait a while to worry about that.*

We were now dealing with over 20,000 pounds (ten tons) that needed to be jacked up at least 36" above where she was resting.

After manhandling the same heavy timbers we had used for unloading, I began, with help from our friend,

Tomás, to jack the boat up so the truck could back the lowboy trailer underneath. The most we could go up was about an inch at a time, rotating corners. More tedious than physical, going carefully up at this pace was draining, as any mishap could easily crush me or Tomás or both of us. Even if we survived, there would be a lot of damage to the boat.

Very little that we had done up until this point had been truly life threatening. This was. I didn't like it, and I didn't want Helen anywhere nearby. The worst-case scenario would have been for one of the four pyramids of stacked wood holding the cradle to collapse from an imbalance. Maybe we would have been able to scramble out from underneath and somehow right the boat again without too much damage, but the more likely outcome would have been serious injury or worse. We had to go slowly, be very, very careful and, most of all, have patience.

There was a collective nervous sigh of relief at the end of the day when we had her up enough, we hoped. It had been dry and that would help the truck's traction climbing the slight incline up to the road, once she was loaded.

10/30/76
Up at five.
Truck didn't show up until 1:00 pm. Due at 8:00 am. Really loused-up our timing.
Heavy rain.

The logistical problem we encountered loading the cradle onto the flatbed trailer was again the downward slope of the land toward the aft part of the boat, forcing us to jack up the rear to eye level – dangerously high – twice as high as the front.

When the truck arrived, we found it still wasn't up quite enough to clear the flatbed, yet I was afraid to go any higher. The only other option was to dig down, as we had when unloading it.

This was by far the biggest event to take place in Santa Ana since who knows when. Neighbors, factory workers, Tomás and I were all taking our turns with the shovels digging trenches for the tires. Men, women, children and Ralph were all there to watch, help and share the moment. The excitement level was high *before* we broke a water line that sent everyone scattering and laughing until we got it turned off at the meter by the road. Later, Chester and Jean would show up with five pizzas and a case of beer, which hit the spot after we had dug deep enough to slowly back the trailer under the cradle and lower the boat onto it. Chester had had our aluminum mast and booms extruded in El Salvador. They were then transported to TracTaco, his factory on the outskirts of San José, where he painted them and fitted the hardware. They were waiting for us at the factory.

Though getting the boat on the trailer was a triumphant first step, in the end, despite all of the action, tension, laughter and drama, the day ended on a sour note. Because the truck had arrived late, we didn't get it loaded and secured with chain until a heavy rain soaked the ground, making it muddy and slick. Even so, Oscar unsuccessfully tried to drive the big diesel Mac tractor-trailer up the incline. The only perceptible movement was spinning tires that dug into the wet dirt at the entrance.

10/31/76
The driver showed up at 7:00 am. Today it didn't much matter because of the mud.
He got stuck immediately.

A local farmer drove his tractor to the site to try to help by pulling the truck. We all agreed this should work but again, there was no movement. The tractor bucked and strained until one of the steering bars snapped. With difficulty, he was able to drive it the short distance back to his place where it would have to be welded. I offered to pay, but he refused.

Chester came by with two panel trucks that Helen and some helpers filled with our tools, boat parts and gear. This would be our last night in Santa Ana. Once the boat was at the factory, we would be living in the Apartamentos Laisa where Jim Ryley and TransAm had rented a place that they were generous enough to let us stay in – another big favor.

That night we discussed strategy with Chester, Tomás and Dennis – more pizza and beer.

So far, the truck was still stuck, we had broken a tractor and it began to rain again late in the afternoon. Needing to find a bigger machine, Helen and I woke up at 5:00 am and drove to a construction site about a mile down the road where I remembered seeing a John Deere "digger."

"Señor, tenemos un velero Ochocientos Varas Sur de la Bomba Chevron y no podemos sacarlo con un camíon solamente porqué hay mucha lluvia. La tierra es resbaladizo. Podemos pagarse sí puede ayudarnos." (We have a sailboat stuck up the road because the ground is slippery. We are willing to pay if you would help us get it out.)

He agreed, so shortly after 11:00 am, during his lunch break, he followed me up the hill and around the corner. When he came upon the scene, his jaw went visibly slack – this was obviously a bigger job than he had envisioned. Fortunately, there is a reckless abandon and machismo among workers in Costa Rica when they encounter a challenge. Without hesitation, he joined us in trying to decide the best way to go about it.

First, he tried pulling. No go, not enough traction. Next, the driver of the digger squeezed his machine through an opening after a few fence posts were chainsawed down in a flurry of wood chips – the same ones that had been replaced after unloading. By lowering the stabilizing supports, he would be able to push with the hydraulic arm without slipping backwards. Everyone in place, we tried again and again. We were moving her slightly, but we didn't have quite enough oomph to get her over the incline and onto the road.

The operator was going to have to get back to work soon, so we improvised one last-ditch effort. With some heavy line that we would later use for anchoring, I tied our Land Rover to the truck. Everyone laughed at the rope, saying there was no way it would hold, but this was strong stuff. In four-wheel drive, with people standing on the bumpers for weight, we gave it another try.

Unbelievable!
Land Rover pulling Mac, which was pushed by John Deere.

Bucking, sliding, huffing and puffing, engines straining, rope stretching, boat shivering, slowly she began to move for the first time. We didn't stop until we had pulled her up onto the road. There was much backslapping, hugging, cheering and clapping. It had taken three days, but we had done it.

The John Deere driver refused more money than we agreed upon even though it had taken much longer and was a lot more difficult than he possibly could have imagined. The boat looked like a mountain perched high upon the trailer. I wouldn't doubt for a minute that even today some of those who were there decades ago still think about the boat that was built just off of the road to Salitrál – 800 Vares Sur de la Bomba Chevron.

After seeing the John Deere off and untying the Land Rover, *La Dulce Mujer Pintada* was on her way back to FibroTécnica, and we were indirectly on our way to celebrate at La Luz. Sensing something was different, Ralph looked back from the Land Rover at the yard he would never see again. As we began to drive off, tears welled up in Helen's and my eyes as we looked at each other and said good-bye to the little plywood house where we had loved each other very much and built a boat, just the two of us.

After a stormy beginning, we were married on August 30, 1972.

On top of the world in Buena Vista Park with a panoramic view of San Francisco.

Marine architect W.I.B. "Bill" Crealock at his office in Carlsbad, California.

Nicknamed the "Golden Grommet," the Pontiac Executive we drove in to Costa Rica with 98,000 miles on the odometer at the beginning suffered a breakdown. Not a car passed as I replaced a radiator hose. A thunderstorm provided the water to refill the cooling system.

The sawmill just outside San José where our teak was cut into planks.

Helen, Ralph and teak in front of our plywood house in Santa Ana.

La Luz—the best bar in the world near the boat factory in Lourdes, San José, Costa Rica.

The factory workers laying up our hull. The half of the hull in the foreground has the balsa core that will be sanded and covered with fiberglass. In the background is the plug for the mid-ship cockpit Tiburon 36'.

The boys and I in front of our hull.

Scottie, Jim and I next to our hull just after it was taken out of the mold.

The ballast being poured. It was made of molten railroad track and weighed 7800 pounds.

The hull, being passed by a bus, on its way to our rented house, Ochocientos Vares Sur de la Bomba Chevron, in Santa Ana.

Turning heads.

Unloading the hull after it had been brought to the house from the factory. Scottie, the shipwright, is on the right.

Santa Ana, where we built the boat, is the onion capital of Costa Rica.

Royal Irish Ralph on the back porch stacked with teak.

More ox carts loaded with coffee beans and produce passed in front of the Santa Ana house than did automobiles.

Two gringos and one Tico next to one of the thousands of Land Rovers in Costa Rica.

Helen took this picture of the inside of the hull as we were constructing the shed. In the distance is the valley and the city of Alajuela.

Making a template so we could transcribe the curve of the hull onto 3/4 inch plywood.

Helen glassing in a bulkhead.

The finger healing after she ran the sabre saw down it.

The baffles that would keep the water in the water tanks from sloshing around under sail.

The carline and half-beams that had been one of our difficult early challenges.

We were not overwhelmed, just sitting down on the job after a big day. The water tanks had been installed, bulkheads glassed in and cabin sole cut to size.

Helen cutting out where a porthole would go with a sabre saw.

I'm smoothing out cockpit beams prior to starting on the coaming.

Measuring the cockpit coaming and winch pad.

Building the laminated teak coaming.

Building our dinghy, *Dulcita.*

Helen belt sanding the teak deck.

Cleaning up after caulking the deck using turpentine from the bottle we regularly refilled at the hardware store.

Ralph and I and an Imperial beer.

The hull as seen from the mango tree in our neighbor's yard.

Family portrait taken in our yard in Santa Ana.

We were up there.

Tomás and I jacking up the hull so the lowboy flatbed could back up underneath the cradle and the boat could be taken to the factory before the final drive to the sea.

Finally, we were able to load the boat onto the trailer.

Trying to get the boat out of the yard after most of the construction had been done. It was a big deal.

Production of the Tiburon 36' was well under way when *La Dulce Mujer* returned to the factory. These three would soon be on their way to Puerto Limón where they would be loaded onto a freighter sailing to Miami.

Profile of *La Dulce* just after she arrived back at the factory prior to launch.

The ten-ton boat with mismatched "fajas" (straps) being lifted off of the trailer at the launch. That's me in the foreground.

PART TWO

Helen and I at the factory entrance moments after our boat had passed us on its way to Puntarenas to be launched.

1

THE BIG SPLASH

THE PHOTOGRAPH OF US standing in front of the factory on the day our boat was trucked to the water says a lot. Thin and fit, wearing our work clothes, we've got an "aw shucks" look about us combined with grins that jump out of the picture. We weren't Don Quixote and Dulcinea, and we sure weren't "loving pure and chaste from afar", nor were we "marching to hell for a heavenly cause," but what we had done was akin to dreaming an impossible dream and reaching for an unreachable star.

Moments prior to the photo, Oscar, our driver, and Rafael, his helper, had driven past us in the truck loaded with our sailboat as it left the gates of the factory headed down the mountain on its way to Puntarenas. We were about to get into our Land Rover for one of the last times and catch up with them somewhere between San José and the bridge. If the boat fit underneath, we wanted to launch at high tide the next morning. From the back seat, Ralph kept a keen eye on the road.

An hour and a half later, we rounded the turn and came upon the truck parked just this side of the metal structure that had an overhead clearance of fourteen feet, nine inches. Oscar had managed to beat us with only a small head start. Maybe it was better we didn't watch him round curves, passing trucks filled with produce.

Climbing up the timbers of the cradle and over the gunwales, I needed to see from eye level if there was going to be enough room. Very slowly, we started, with Helen relaying hand signals. There were several things we could do if the boat didn't clear, but according to my calculations, we had about two inches. The simplest solution would be to let some air out of the tires; the worst would be having to remove the main hatch. I sat in the cockpit, as Oscar slowly pulled onto the highway. By eyeballing, I really couldn't tell if we were going to fit underneath until we came within a couple of feet in front of the riveted steel beam that was the lowest part of the superstructure. As we eased along, it looked as though we were going to make it and sure enough we did, by slightly more than two inches. Hallelujah!

For the remainder of the trip, we followed the truck to a small campesino pulpería on the outskirts of Puntarenas, where we would stay until morning. After eating from his bowl, Ralph came in and sat on the floor between us at the little restaurante/bar while we had some fish, rice and beans. Having more sense than I, Helen climbed up into the boat and went to sleep. Pumped as I was, I needed to spend some time with the boys in the bar before loading Ralph into the car and going to bed. This would be our first night on the six-inch foam mattress we had cut to size with a hacksaw blade. Under a sheet with a 12-volt fan blowing directly on us, it was comfortable and not too hot.

We were up early the next morning and there was a lot to do before the tides were right. If we launched before or at high tide, we wouldn't have to fight the current. But anytime after that, the water would be pushing the boat against the pier, making it difficult to pull away without banging against the barnacle-encrusted pilings.

No boat can enter into or leave a country without documents, but this was obviously a different situation than most, and I'd lost a lot of sleep on this one. We knew from the beginning that it wouldn't be practical or economical to register the boat in Costa Rica. So, early on, we had written to California and Texas to see if either would register it. Thanks to my mother's Lone Star State address, Texas did, and the application asked for only the essentials. It was approved and our boat was listed as: "Model: Custom 38'." The only problem was that the paper itself didn't look very official. It was a five-by-seven card with the barest of information super-imposed over the state seal of Texas. What we were legalistically attempting to do was launch our boat and then ask Customs to treat it as though it had sailed to Costa Rica from a foreign port (Texas). This was a big one because if they refused, we could be hit up for thousands of dollars in taxes. On the other hand, if they accepted it, as we hoped they would, we could immediately take our papers to the Customs House to get our sails and a lot of other critical imports from their bodega without paying duty on them. Edwin Arguello from the factory had helped make the arrangements. Now he was on the bus from San José to make sure all went well and to take our Land Rover back to the factory.

It was a short drive from where we had parked overnight to the commercial pier used for loading and unloading freighters. First on our to-do list was go by the Dock Master's office and pay for the use of the crane. We wouldn't confront Customs until after the launch, when the boat was officially in the water. Finding the crane operator and doing the paperwork took longer than expected, but what really threw our timing off was a train that went down the tracks and stopped for over an hour on the oil-stained, brownish-black pier, blocking the entrance. There are piers for small boats like ours, and there are big piers for ships. This was a big one with a big crane at least fifty feet above the water.

At first they weren't going to allow Helen to go where the big splash was about to take place due to an accident that had recently happened with another small boat they had tried lifting into the water. The Dock Master matter-of-factly told us how the owner had wanted to film the launch and that just when he happened to be underneath, it fell and "crushed him flatter than a cucaracha." On and on, I told him how she'd done half the work, and that it wouldn't be fair, etc. After we wore him down and promised that she would stay out of the way, he agreed with a reluctant shrug of his shoulders, "She's *your* wife."

Once our driver had carefully backed the trailer down the four hundred foot pier in his "Big Mac" big rig, the crane operator and his assistant began pulling out the straps from a storage shed at its end. The "fajas" (straps), that went under the hull and connected to the crane's cables, were a mismatch. One was shorter than the other. "Okay," we decided, "fuck it. Let's rig it and see how it looks. It might work with the shorter one on the bow."

Though the boat would be tilting downward at the bow during its ascent from the cradle and descent to the water, it looked as though there wouldn't be any problems if they were tied together so that the forward one didn't slip off the bow. This, like the drive down from San José, was an all-or-nothing situation. Nothing could replace all that we had done.

High tide was 8:00 am and we were going in around 11:30 am, so there was going to be a serious current problem caused by tides that average from eight to eleven feet. Several days later, recounting what had taken place, Dennis' comment was, "Sometimes you just have to go for it, don't you?"

I suppose the most remarkable aspect of the launch was the un-remarkableness of it. There were no bands, streamers or well-wishers at an event that was witnessed by maybe ten Ticos who didn't even know us. Helen and I filmed it on our Super-8 movie camera.

1/12/77
The launch went smoothly, and the crane operator carefully lifted her off of the cradle. As she first moved, Helen cracked a bottle of Korbel Champagne – the same that was served at our wedding reception, which relieved us of the burden of launching an improperly christened boat. A critical step. Slowly, he edged her over the water about 50' below. When she was in the water, the straps were left on because the tide was going out and would have pushed her against the pier.

With the boat in the water, still in the straps that held it away from the pier, Helen, Rafael (the helper, not our dog) and I climbed down the ladder on the side of a creosote piling and jumped onto the deck. The first thing Helen and I did was go below to make sure there were no leaks while we still had the ability to pull her out if there were. Further complicating our tide predicament was the fact that the mast was tied down on the side of the boat that was next to the pier. Worried about maneuvering her away from the pilings without banging her up, we weren't quite sure what to do but, whatever, it was up to us and us alone.

The first time I started the engine, it died. Hands shaking nervously, I bled the fuel line – warm diesel fuel squirting on my hand, going into the bilge – and restarted it. Jesus Christ it was hot with the sun bearing down on us. Then, luckily, good will and nautical generosity came to the rescue in the form of a tug operator, who graciously offered to pull us away from the dock. I don't know how we would have done it otherwise. With lines cleated off fore and aft, Rafael dove into the water and cut the rope holding the two straps together. As the tug pulled us away, the straps were released. Safely away from the pier, we uncleated his lines, yelled thanks, and motored away under our own power.

Everything was working! We were smiling. The wind against our sweaty shirts felt cool. Then, before we rounded the point, some five minutes later, an awful smelling smoke started pouring out of the companionway. With Helen at the helm, I jumped down below to see where it was coming from. It was the exhaust. When I put the galvanized pipe together, I had used a product called Permatex on the joints. The man at the hardware store where I'd bought it told me to be sure to put this brown gooey cream on the threads, and I had. This would have been a good idea if the pipe was going to be used for water, and a bad idea for a hot exhaust. Though it burned off pretty quickly, it left a lingering odor below deck that would last several days.

Awkwardly getting used to the way she steered and how the controls worked, we pulled up to the icehouse and let Rafael off at low tide. He had to climb the ladder up to the dock. Our dog, Ralph, had gone with Edwin to the Yacht Club.

This is when Morris came into the picture. He and his lady lived aboard *Falcon*, a black-hulled, 45-foot cutter that was anchored near the entrance of the estuary. An experienced sailor, he knew the area and figured correctly that we needed help.

Morris explained that we could not get in to step the mast but agreed to pilot us to the Yacht Club.

High tide in the Puntarenas estuary is not unpleasant as it is filled with the clean water from the gulf. At low tide, the water is a dirty brown and there is a rotten stench in the air. Docks that were only two feet above the water at high tide are anywhere from eleven to thirteen feet from the water's surface at low tide. The pilings, covered with barnacles and an assortment of underwater sea life, don't smell good when exposed to the heat. The shoreline becomes a soft brown mud with trash, broken bottles, sunken boats, abandoned motors, all exposed. A third of the time the estuary is pretty; a third of the time it's ugly; a third of the time it's in between. As we rounded the sandy point in our smoking boat, it was at its worst.

There were no channel markers in the "estero" and the Yacht Club, where we wanted to go, was at the other end.

So we motored over and cautiously tied up alongside *Falcon*. We didn't know Morris that well, but, as we would learn, boaters help each other out. He knew the estuary, which is tricky. Trailing his dingy with an outboard, he piloted us to the Yacht Club.

"Yacht Club" sounds pretty snazzy, and a lot of Costa Rican bigwigs were members, but it lacked the opulence commonly associated with the word "yacht." It was nothing more than a large open-air deck with a metal roof covering tables, a bar and a grill. They had moorings and a launch that would pick you up and take you ashore, sometimes more quickly than others, depending on the importance of who was blowing his horn. The reason we were willing to pay five dollars a day for our first few nights was that we had yet to rig our anchors, and we didn't have oars to row our dingy.

Within a matter of hours, this creation of ours was now something we had to protect – a major new responsibility. Morris understood and helped us pick up the buoy. It's hard to be a skilled boat person until you've actually done some boating.

The Hotel Viking, within walking distance of the Yacht Club, had a small outdoor restaurant on the gulf side where we had a tired dinner before returning for our first night on the water. With the forward hatch open, we could see the stars as we immediately fell asleep.

1/13/77
High tide was around 8:00 am so we left early for "Cocal" where we would step the mast. This frightened me as much as the launch. We kept our fingers crossed that

the rigging, which was measured and cut the day before we left the plant, would be the right length. After struggling and some minor scratches on the mast, we got the lower forwards, uppers and backstay on. We were unable to attach the forestay or headstay as the plate was not on for the former and Vega had forgotten to drill a hole larger on the pulpit. To secure the mast forward, we temporarily used a halyard.

As the result of mis-measuring, I was one foot short on the port lower. The others fit.

Returned to Yacht Club where I helped some gringos when I should have been working on our boat. We walked to a nearby store to buy some canned tuna as the stove is not hooked up yet.

I then went to Felipe J. Alvarado, a Custom's broker, to check on getting the sails, etc., out. He said we couldn't do it because we were a Tico boat, the problem we had anticipated with the Texas registration. Customs ok'd it, and we are set to get them out tomorrow morning.

Without knowing us, Customs, unaware that we had built the boat in Costa Rica, checked our passports and casually accepted the stateside registration document. We were told we could pick up the boxes the next day.

1/14/77
I left for Customs to pick up the sails, chain, etc. Helen worked below organizing the mountains of things that were everywhere. I got the shipment without any problems and bought a bottle of rum and one of guaro.

We unpacked all afternoon with the little fan running and then took a nap.

I went out to buy some more tuna after blowing our horn about 50 times for launch. The sooner we get our dinghy and independence the better.

I called Dennis and asked him to swage another aft lower for us.

1/17/77
Terrible day. I first went to Puntarenas for papers – none of which were ready – returned.

Helen then headed for San José with some things we were going to leave at the apartment. She left once and had to return because I hadn't remembered to give her the rigging length. She finally left about 11:00 am. I was depressed the whole day wondering what in the world I was doing on this scary water and why we didn't just sell the boat? Morris brought over a pair of hand carved mahogany oars, so I put on the oarlocks and rowed in for the first time when Helen finally returned with the cushions we had forgotten and three huge bags filled with stuff. A remarkable load for the bus, which delivered her to the icehouse. It was 9:00 pm when she arrived. Barely stayed awake for beefsteak.

Completely new to this, I was worn out, undone by fatigue and the strong winds that had come out of nowhere the night before.

[Helen]
My arms were about to fall off after gathering up everything we needed in S. José. Got taken for 13 colones

214

when I had ridden the bus for ten minutes and realized I needed to get off. Apt #4 first then to see Meisner at B. of A. to cash a $70 check. By 3:00 at FibroTécnica working away with Dennis. He did all the swaging. I bodega shopped and rooted around in the office. By 5:00 we were off to La Luz, celebrating the finding of his residency papers and my day coming to an end. Took remaining bocas back to Ben on boat who was bummed out. Too much work – I agree – physically and mentally we were both exhausted. He picked me up in our "new car" – the dinghy.

2

TO PANAMA FOR
A STAMP

THE CHANGE IN OUR CIRCUMSTANCE and climate had been abrupt. Going from seventy-degree mountain weather to ninety-degree tropical weather was brutal. Our skin was white and the clothes we wore were drastically different from what we were used to. Instead of long pants and work clothes, I began wearing shorts and a T-shirt to keep the sun off of my back. Helen was reduced to shorts, a bikini top and a T-shirt for protection outdoors.

The boat that had once overlooked Alajuela, steady as a rock, began rocking with the waves. We could hear the water slapping against the hull at night in anchorages where disaster seemed always to be lurking.

Our visas were expired and our time in Costa Rica was officially over when we left Puntarenas with our exit "zarpe" (visa) on the third day after the launch. Since the government wasn't overly concerned with foreign recreational vessels, we felt we could hide out in legal limbo at Joe Hill's for two, maybe three weeks to get ready to make our bureaucratic journey to Panamá. If we wanted to come back, and we did, we first had to sail to another country, get our passports stamped, and stay for forty-eight hours before returning with a clean slate and the right to stay for six months with an option to extend for another six. It was a paperwork trip that was forcing us into an unfamiliar ocean before we had time to work out the kinks and finish the work that still needed to be done on *La Dulce*.

The sails had not yet been unfolded or raised when we received our exit papers in Puntarenas.

1/19/77

Left at low tide for Joe Hill's and ran aground by Nicoya Ferry. Got out about an hour later and motored over. It was a bit rough. Dinghy and generator bouncing.

At Joe Hill's we took a mooring after dragging anchor a few times.

The bottom around Joe Hill's was hard and the current's swirl makes it difficult to set an anchor. The moorings, 55-gallon drums filled with concrete sunken into the sand, were more secure. From a steel eye in the cement, a chain and some line were attached to the buoy that Helen managed to pull onboard with our handmade teak boathook. It's a tricky maneuver. The helmsman can't see the buoy that the person lying on his stomach on the bow is trying to pick up. At that very moment, our engine decided to quit going into gear. A pin had fallen out of the shift mechanism into the bilge. Had Helen missed the plastic ball, we would have been in a pickle.

The captain of the sailing yacht, *At Ease*, another new arrival, was a little pissed at us for snaring the last mooring before he did. *At Ease* was a very expensive, well-maintained, 60-foot sailing vessel that was being delivered to the Caribbean from California for another event on the racing circuit. The bleached blond captain and crew, wearing Top Sider shoes, monogrammed shirts and khaki shorts, were deeply tanned professionals. With no other moorings available, like clockwork, the three of them expertly set anchors, launched their 14-foot inflatable dinghy powered by a 25 horsepower Evinrude and came ashore.

For ground tackle, we carried a twelve-pound Danforth as well as a thirty-five-pound and a forty-five-pound CQR or "plow" anchor. The secret to anchoring, we would learn, is chain. Once we bought two hundred feet of five-sixteenth inch BBB that fit our manual windless, a chrome plated bronze Plath, most of our anchoring problems were solved. Chain is harder to pull up but, due to its weight, the angle the anchor digs into the sea bottom makes it hold better, plus it acts as a shock absorber for gusts of wind.

While in Costa Rica, we had only twenty-five feet of chain shackled to the anchor, using line for the rest. Even using the forty-five-pound anchor our holding power was adequate, not great. A weight conscious racing sailboat like *At Ease* carried only the minimum.

On dry land, sitting around at the Hacienda, drinking beer, we listened to the captain and crew speak yacht talk. With a slight sunburn on our pale bodies, Helen and I were paying close attention, as there was an awful lot we didn't know. They were cocky, but it was obvious they had spent years sailing. A valuable lesson was about to be learned from them – Neptune, God of the Sea, doesn't like anybody very much. He feels humans are outside intruders so He teases and tortures them unmercifully.

While we were seated at the big table, the sun setting and the kerosene lamps being lit, the wind kicked up a little. The tide, having just turned, was now on its way out. Startled, one of the crew members suddenly realized that their boat had drug anchor and was aground. Racing to their dinghy, they flew into action. At first they tried to motor off into deeper water. When that failed, they attached a halyard to their dinghy and pulled the boat sideways in an effort to reduce the draft by heeling her over. When that too failed, they put anchors off to port and starboard, attaching lines to the top of the mast by tying them to halyards normally used to raise the sails. This way, the boat would remain upright, standing on her keel, as the water receded.

It was starting to get rough when we loaded Ralph into the dinghy and rowed back to our boat. By dead low, the wind was blowing so hard that I started our engine in case we needed to put it in gear to take pressure off the mooring. Through the howling wind and rain, we could see their silhouettes in foul-weather jackets, holding flashlights as they walked around the hull that was standing high and dry. Then, at the worst possible time, a gust of wind came up causing the port anchor to let lose. *At Ease* had stood for a couple of hours but the winds were too strong and blew her over hard. Luckily, no one was underneath when she fell. Having landed that violently on her side, there must have been damage, but the hull and deck appeared to be intact when they left for Panamá early the next morning – after she had righted herself and floated off of the bottom with the incoming tide.

When Helen, Ralph and I arrived at Joe Hill's in *La Dulce Mujer Pintada*, it was not officially Joe Hill's anymore even though that's what most people still called it. The story we had been told, late one night Joe's wife suspiciously drowned. After answering official questions for a few weeks, he and another woman mysteriously disappeared. It had been re-named the Hacienda Nicoyana by Mike and Sally, a young couple who had taken over. Mike, who resembled a redheaded version of legendary mountain man Paul Bunyan, and Sally, his attractive blonde wife, were rugged hard-working people who we would have the good fortune of getting to know well.

The gathering place was a two-story wooden building with living quarters upstairs where Mike and Sally lived. Underneath a tin roof at ground level, there was a large table surrounded by leather Costa Rican rocking chairs (the same kind we had traded our car for), sitting on an uneven stone and cement floor. The kitchen was off to the side. The Hacienda's library contained hundreds of worn paperback books that could be checked out by writing your name and the title on a notepad. This is where I discovered John D. McDonald's Travis McGee series. Every title has the word for a color in it, and I read every one that was there. Travis McGee, knight in tarnished armor living aboard his houseboat, *The Busted Flush*, docked in Ft. Lauderdale, unconventionally took on the unscrupulous to help the defenseless, which always required the aid of at least one beautiful woman.

Everything at the Hacienda was on the honor system. When a person wanted a beer (five colones or about 60 cents), he got it out of the large ice bin and put the cap in his assigned gourd that hung on the wall – a box of matches, one match goes in the gourd – some chips, the top of the wrapper. At the end of the stay or every Thursday, if you were there long term, they counted your objects and you paid for them. There was no electricity, just kerosene lamps. There was an outdoor shower on the beach and an outhouse out back.

On Mondays and Thursdays, the *Sábalo*, a launch owned by the Hacienda, made the ten-mile trip to Puntarenas. Anyone who wanted could catch a ride for ten colones. It made two stops along the estuary: the Mercado Central and the Casa de Hielo (Icehouse) as the latter is how food stayed fresh and the beer cold.

During rainy season, a short way up the hill, a small river with a waterfall emptied into a secluded pool for bathing and skinny-dipping. Surrounded by palm trees and tropical foliage, the water was close by at high tide, retreating fifty to sixty feet at low tide. At night, under the moonlight with the tide out, the beach moved – it was alive.

Thousands of small hermit crabs clicked and slowly wandered about until they sensed outside movement. In unison, they would stop, go back into their adopted shell and pretend that no one was home. Most evenings at the Hacienda were quiet and lovely. From our cockpit or through the open hatch over our bed, we could see so many stars they seemed to saturate the heavens.

Anchoring the dinghy after rowing to shore took some getting used to. If the tide was high, one of us would let the other out at water's edge, then wade out as far as possible without getting our clothes wet and throw the six pound anchor out into deeper water. The objective was to avoid carrying it any farther than necessary because ours was overbuilt and heavy. If the tide was out, we carried her up a ways on the beach before setting the anchor so we could retrieve it later without swimming. When *La Dulce* was anchored out or on a mooring, we tied the dinghy against two cylindrical white rubber fenders on the port side where we had installed a fold-down, bronze step to help us get on board. Ralph could jump down into the dinghy from the deck. When he was getting back on board he stood on the middle seat, reached up with his front paws, put them on the cap rail, then with a boost from the rear, he was back on board.

Towing a hard dinghy is not a good idea – too much can go wrong. So before making any passages, we fastened the main halyard to a line that was fastened to both ends of the dinghy. With Helen at the winch and me guiding it, we lifted her up on the cabin top where we tied her down on teak davits.

The Hacienda was a good stopping off point for boats in transit from California to the Panamá Canal and vice versa, as there aren't many well-protected anchorages along the West Coast. People sailing through generally needed to stop for a while, get provisions, fill up with fuel, water and recuperate. The anchorage was constantly changing.

1/20/77 [Helen]
Had a good beefsteak dinner. Cabin has a warm tone at nighttime. Still just using two cabin lights.

1/21/77
Put on staysail track, winch and cleats. Bolted down bow chocks and prepared for sail tomorrow. We should be ready.

Morris arrived last night after a blow at Tortuga Island.

An anomaly on a brand spanking new boat in Costa Rica, which we had built ourselves and launched only six days earlier, we were quite a show – pale as tourists on an almost completed sailboat. The brass and bronze, that we favored over chrome, still glistened and shined with gold colored newness – everything did – and everything was untested. Before we could actually sail, now that the necessary hardware was in place, the sails had to be unfolded, put on their track and rigged for hoisting. Somehow we would have gotten *La Dulce* ready to sail by ourselves, but it was very kind of the more knowledgeable people around us to lend a hand.

1/22/77
Morris and Ken came over to help us get the sails ready. The jib was no problem as cables came with the sails. No problem with the main, either. The staysail was weird. Upon Morris' urgings, we decided to rig it without using the boom.

About 11:00 we dropped the mooring and motored over to the Falcon *for Debbie and Sean. We then put up her sails and were sailing in light air. Later, with a breeze of about 12 knots, she heeled over nicely.*

Was it exciting? Did our cheeks hurt from smiling? You bet. We kept our fingers crossed that all would hold together under the considerable strain of the wind against the sails.

When we returned, Helen called her mother and father from Jesusita, and we had a party on the Falcon. *Ralph and I made a grand exit by falling out of the dinghy when Morris handed him to me.*

Though we lacked the ease that comes from routine, the dinghy was working out with only one minor glitch. The reason we looked so awkward rowing it at first was the lack of a "skeg," which is a small keel on the bottom that helps it go in a straight line. It took us a while to get the hang of it. The person rowing had his back to Ralph who always stood in the front like George Washington crossing the Delaware, while the people passenger(s) sat on the back seat.

To come up alongside, you row directly toward the side of the boat. Then, with just the right amount of momentum, one oar is pulled onboard while the other turns the dinghy sideways and into the fenders. Once alongside, standing in the dinghy, we'd tie off both bow and stern lines. As awkward as we were, this was no easy feat, especially if the current was racing.

Our poor dog didn't know what the hell was going on. Obviously, he was bewildered and perturbed that we would leave the cool mountains of Santa Ana and bring him to the water. What did we think he was, a duck? He wasn't a bad swimmer, but he needed a destination where he knew he could get out. For those on board *Falcon*, looking down upon Ralph and me thrashing around trying to get into our dinghy, it must have been theatrical. The water in the Gulfo de Nicoya is filled with bioluminescent plankton. When it's dark and the water becomes agitated, they light up brightly like thousands of fireflies.

We had so much to learn.

1/23/77
Helen and I took her out alone and had a great sail. The boat handled super in a variety of light air. Lost our first fish bite as we were too busy tacking. Really moving up the cut to Joe Hill's on our return, we were complimented on her looks when we went ashore.

1/25/77
Helen rowed over to a nearby beach with Ralph while I worked on electricity.

We then ran into Linda and Winfred. I helped them move their boat, which was tough as the motor needs repair and the anchor is hard to pull up. They came over for dinner bringing some beef and fresh fish – fish stew and tomato sauce. Had first J in a long time.

Tomorrow the fathometer and knotometer go in.

Linda and Winfred had lost the use of their engine because it "ran away" from them. When the governor malfunctioned, it started running faster and faster, until it would have exploded, had Winfred not had the presence to shut off the fuel.

Before leaving Costa Rica, we felt it was absolutely necessary to install the fathometer so we could see how deep the water was and a knotometer so we could tell how fast we were going. Both would turn out to be virtually useless, but we didn't know that. We were just going by the books. The fathometer and knotometer have to be mounted below the waterline, so we were going to careen her – let her lie on her side as the tide goes out, giving us the opportunity to drill holes in the hull before the tide rose again.

1/26/77 [Helen]
The fathometer and knotometer still aren't in.

The Costa Rican patrulla boat showed up at Joe Hill's and anchored in between our boat and Linda Ruggs'. They were looking for a tug but managed to make us so nervous we drank a rum at noon. Then the heat of the day was upon us. Looking forward to decent bread, I followed the recipe to a tee but, once again, it was hard and flat.

Spent evening singing at the grand table for beers. Captain John showed up on a trimaran. When he discovered his dinghy was gone, he completely lost it before he finally settled down. Tide had carried it out. He shot flares, accused everyone of being a thief and prayed to his God – pretty wild place here.

When the patrol boat arrived, we happened to be below deck. Since our visas were outdated, we cautiously closed all of the hatches, making it look as though no one was on board until they left. Whew!

1/28/77

Most important was going over charts with Winfred who is familiar with the southern part of Costa Rica.

Also decided to take Linda and Winfred up on their offer. They gave us $100 cash in exchange for a $100 check, knowing we would need it to clear Customs in Panamá. It was really good of them. With only $20 in our pockets, I know they think we are absolutely naïve and a bit lunchy to wander around so out of it. The culprit is really the haste with which we have to leave.

I need to get all generator work done tomorrow and the next day. The factory loaned it to us, and we need to return it.

The pace was frantic. Sunday was the day we were going to put in the fathometer and knotometer.

1/30/7 7

The big day. We eased over to a sandy place we had chosen about 1 hr. before high tide. With an anchor aft, we tied her to a tree for'd positioning her about 1 ft. off bottom. Then I worked on wiring port and starboard running lights.

La Dulce *started leaning over about 1:00 pm with the help of a halyard attached to the Danforth anchor about 200 ft. to port.*

We drilled the hole in her a couple of hours later, while the boat was really at a slant. Got fathometer in without trouble and then went to knotometer. She went in but not smoothly. After we were finished, we went up for a beer.

I returned early to check and found water on the cabin sole. It had come in through a scupper that leaked. Scared me. As we straightened up, we could see that it had gotten books, including our journals, wet as well as all of the port bench lockers.

About then I checked installations and found fathometer to be fine. The knotometer was leaking both at the base and through the hole. It had been ordered so long ago we lost the fitting. Had I not checked we would have sunk. We patched it with the last of our Boatlife calking and drove a peg of wood into the hole.

The boat was a total mess.

2/1/77
I worked on connecting as much as I could, and quite a bit came together. Aft running light, fathometer, knotometer, compass, searchlight, all were connected – the wires were run through clips.

2/3/77
Washed everything down and packed things away for the trip tomorrow. Around 10 am went across to Don Johnny's island where we dropped off the generator and filled our tanks with water.

Phil and Helen of Moontide *came by to look at fathometer. They found it to be working and explained how to read it. We were afraid it was not working properly.*

Our last night, we spent playing the guitar.

Ralph has discovered fishing and will go for hours. He seems to be having a great time on shore so we'll see about sailing.

We left about 10:00 am and had a great sail over to Herradura. We were really close when Helen started having stomach pains. She became pale and her stomach hurt badly. I asked her if she thought we should return to J. Hill's. Casper, the Doctor who had a boat moored there, was to arrive today. She hesitated, and I decided we should – she agreed. So, we came about and headed back to where we had begun.

Everyone at the Hacienda was surprised to unexpectedly see us again. Fortunately, by the time we got there Helen was feeling much better. "Never leave port on a Friday," is one of many sailing superstitions. We never would again.

On Sunday we once again sailed off and made it to the bay at Herradura, the first leg of our trip to Panamá. The only calamity on our second attempt to cross the Gulfo de Nicoya was the loss of our fishing rod and reel after it was jerked out of the cockpit by what should have been dinner.

Such were our first days of "the cruising life."

3

WHALES AND
BLUE WATER

2/6/77

Winds were light, had to motor part of the way across the Gulfo de Nicoya. A fish hit the fishing lure and pulled the rod out of the boat, and we could not find it after circling several times. It really upset us both more than I can say. As broke as we are it was a tremendous and STUPID loss. I get credit.

Arrived at Herradura about 5:00 pm and motored to anchorage. A little frightening for not many reasons, but being as green as the water, it is all a bit spooky. Anchored with 35 CQR for'd and Danforth 12 H aft. – holding well. Took Ralph to beach, and I walked to a small store to buy bread – only building and we are only boat.

IN THE YEAR 2014, we would have been able to tie up alongside expensive pleasure craft and sport fishing boats at the Herradura Yacht Club's large floating dock. But in 1977, the lone building on the beach was a faded blue and pink wood grocery/cantina with two metal porcelain tables advertising Cerveza Imperial and six brown folding metal chairs set in the sand underneath a rusted tin roof only slightly taller than I was. Field-workers' houses must have been farther back in the bush.

2/7/77
Found $10 in bathing suit so we decided to go to shore and buy a beer. Met a guy named Carlos who bought a couple for us, and we showed him the boat. It was blowing fairly hard so La Dulce *was rocking but the anchors were holding well.*

There is an art to anchoring, and we weren't even close to getting the hang of it. The phrase "holding well," that often appeared in our journals, would more aptly be described as nervous "hopeful wishing." Had there been other boats in the anchorage, we would have felt a lot more comfortable – someone to talk to about things, maybe even sail with but, at the time, there simply weren't many boats or people in that part of the world.

Leaving Herradura early, the next stopping point that had been marked on our charts was Manuel Antonio, but when we arrived at dusk, the protected area looked too small and dangerous with a lot of swell. Scared to anchor and scared to be out at sea all night (something we had never done before by ourselves), we reluctantly decided to sail on for the next anchorage. As the glow of sunset faded, knowing full well that darkness is when invisible sea monsters come out to torment and cause trouble, we really had no other choice.

Before the moon came out, it was pitch black. An overcast sky hid the stars and made it hard to see any horizon or point of reference. We would have to sail a compass course while keeping an eye out for freighters who weren't necessarily looking out for us. They might not even feel the impact if they ran over a boat like ours.

Technically, a sailing vessel has the right of way, but realistically some ships are so large and going so fast, they take long distances to change course and miles to come to a complete stop. When green and red bow lights are visible at the same time, it means they are headed right at you, and a perpendicular course needs to be taken immediately. As frightening as natural phenomenon seem at night, freighters are really the number one danger.

I took the first watch while Helen made some rice and beans down below where the cabin lights reassuringly reflected off the varnished teak. Without much experience at steering by compass, I was the first to become confused as to which way to turn the wheel to make a correction. When the sails started flopping and our speed dropped to the point where we lost the ability to get back on course, I had to make an awkward 360 degree circle with a somewhat controlled jibe to get back to our heading. Naturally, Helen anxiously called out to ask me what was happening.

"Nothing dear, I just accidentally steered us in the wrong direction."

Under full sail, we were heeled over enough that the gimbaled stove was angled as she held on and cooked. Where you want to go and where the wind wants you to go aren't always the same, but on this night we were in sync, moving nicely on a beam reach in the swell of the mighty Pacific Ocean, just the two of us, just like the merchants and pirates of yore.

It was challenging, exciting, thrilling, and exhausting with plenty of terrifying things to worry about consciously and subconsciously – we were not very good sailors. Novices at anchoring and neophytes at navigation, there were some important basic seafaring fundamentals that we didn't know how to do, like reef the mainsail, i.e. make it smaller, which would have helped that first night when an ass-kicking squall came up quickly.

After my two-hour shift, Helen took over while I got some sleep. Without a self-steering vane or autopilot, one of us had to be at the helm all of the time. It was going to be a long night. Taking over after her watch, I noticed some low clouds rapidly passing between me and the moon, but didn't think much of it until the wind started picking up causing us to heel over until the lee rail was under. Then a blast of wind knocked us over on our side dumping the air out of the main. Heart racing, I wasn't sure what to do but hang on. Helen scrambled up from below, where books and things were flying across the cabin, just in time to get hit in the face with a heavy sheet of rain. All I could do was come up into the wind, causing the sails to start flapping violently, slowing us and curtailing our ability to steer until the sails became unintentionally back-winded blowing the boat dangerously over on her other side until the air spilled out, and we again righted. We had no control over *The Sweet Painted Lady* until we started the engine so Helen could motor into wind, and I could crawl up the side deck to drop sail.

Holding on to the mast with one arm, in driving rain with spray coming over the sides, I had to take the halyard off of the cleat and let the mainsail drop. Not even bothering to try to tie it down, it flew off to the side and was dragging in the ocean. After uncleating the halyards for the headsails, I had to go on all fours up the deck to pull the staysail and jib down. On my stomach, with the warm ocean water pouring over me and the cold rain so heavy I could barely see the cockpit, it was a struggle just to hang on. I could briefly see better when a bright bolt of lightning accompanied by an almost simultaneous crack of thunder lit up everything.

Meanwhile, with the wind blowing somewhere in the neighborhood of twenty-five to thirty knots, the jib sheet by the cockpit was jumping around so ridiculously that it tied itself into a knot on the lifeline, meaning we had no control over that sail and couldn't get it down.

Having done all I could, I crawled back to the cockpit where a very frightened, shivering Helen let me take over so she could go below for our foul weather jackets. Wet and cold with hands and knees shaking, there was nothing else we could do but stay away from the whipping sheet tangled in the lifeline. Ralph was holding on with all four paws down in the cabin.

As things unraveled, it was abundantly clear that we easily could have been hurt, or worse, knocked overboard and died, even wearing our safety harnesses. Finding someone who has fallen into the water at night is almost impossible. If something bad were to happen, there was no way of calling for help. Even if we had had a VHF radio with a range of about 15 miles, the odds were slim to none that anyone would hear the transmission or be able to find us if they did. Helen had put together an extensive medical kit, just in case, because any injury would be something we would have to deal with as best we could until we got back to civilization – like the ordeal Maurice Campbell had to go through after he lost his big toe.

Then, as suddenly as it had come up, the rain stopped, the moon reappeared, and the wind settled down. Just like that, it was over. Our eyes met as we sat together in the cockpit, motoring through the chop that was left behind. After catching our breath and regaining some composure, we began sorting things out and getting the sails back up.

Had we known what we were doing, when I noticed the low fast moving clouds against the moon, I would have called for Helen to bring up the foul weather gear and take the helm. Noticing the early signs gives you time to drop the foresails, tie off and reef the main. If the winds were really strong we could have let the sail out a bit and steered more downwind until it passed. Eventually we would learn that what had scared the shit out of us was no big deal – a squall – something that happens all the time, but on this occasion we were shaken to the point that it was hard to sleep for the rest of the night. Without saying anything, we sat in the cockpit looking out at the silver-gray ocean illuminated by the pale light from a half moon.

Though daybreak is a wonderful thing, I have never particularly liked sunrise at sea. The clouds still look dark and ominous. The decks are often wet with dew. It takes a fresh water shower to take away the salty, greasy feeling that accumulates overnight. Only after a couple of hours does the sun climb high enough to dry the decks and make the clouds look white again and the world beautiful once more – blue sky, clear blue water, an occasional flying fish skimming across the surface.

2/10/77

As sun came up we could see Isla del Caño dead ahead. Although super simple our navigation was right on.

Again the anchorage looked beautiful but over our heads. We just did not feel confident about it so we headed on. Ralph has thus far refused to go to the bathroom so we are worried. The morning was great – we saw dolphins all around the boat several times.

Ralph, after much coaxing and a water pill finally peed to the relief of us all.

Biologists have concluded that dolphins have more time to play than any other mammal and that they are intelligent enough to enjoy it, which is what they appeared to be doing as they swam alongside our boat to observe the onboard mammals looking at them from above. It was magic lying down on the bowsprit out over the water, as they came within a few feet of our hull, swimming at exactly the same speed as they periodically breathed through their blowholes. Poetic athleticism and graceful power, their form was filtered through rays of sunlight penetrating the ocean's lazy swells. Ralph didn't bark as he excitedly circled the decks, watching them break the surface when they came up for air. He had a curious tail-wagging expression as he looked at them and then back at us as if to ask, "What the hell are those things?"

They were unbelievably entertaining when they showed off by occasionally jumping completely out of the water. On this our maiden voyage, we were mesmerizingly comforted by these strange, large, gray animals streaking alongside our dark green hull under jib, staysail and main, smiling at us with eyes that seemed wise. The only sounds other than our voices and Ralph's feet on the deck were the wind and the water as we made our way south toward Panamá.

It was the whales later on that spooked us even more than the squall.

As scary as night can be, there was a warm comfort from the cabin lights below deck. By locking the wheel, the helmsman (or helmswoman) could go down briefly to put water on the stove for coffee, tea or to get a snack. Even so, the Titanic factor was always on our minds. We weren't going to be cut open by an iceberg, but you never know what's out there or what's going to happen. Trouble seems to wait for night.

As the sun got higher and higher in the sky, it would become sweaty-hot without a Bimini top to shade the cockpit. Adding to the discomfort, our only two outdoor cushions were the hard type that could be used for flotation. Hugging the coast with a breeze barely strong enough to sail in, we were surprised to see another sailboat coming up from behind. It was a Dufour racing sailboat, the only other sailboat we would see on the trip to Panamá and back. With a 120% genoa, they passed us like we were standing still. *La Dulce,* a cruising boat, was never going to be that fast, but it was clear that we needed to get a larger headsail for light air – one more thing to buy – somehow. Starting the engine would have increased our speed, but it also would have used fuel and heated up the cabin, which was the only place halfway comfortable for Ralph, who panted with irritating regularity. In between our duties at the helm, we took sweaty naps, trying to catch up on sleep.

Arrived at the mouth of the Gulfo Dulce at dusk and motored past Golfito where we hove to until morning.

Worried about entering the harbor at night, a boat is "hove to" when the sails are back winded and crossed with the rudder – sailing, but not really going anywhere. Though we didn't have to steer, we did have to stand watch for a second night in a row.

2/10/77
Motored to "Lit and Lil's" – about one hour – and it was fantastic. It looked like some paradise in the South Pacific.
We anchored rather well and went in for a beer, which they didn't have so we had tea. About half way through the anchor drug and we touched bottom. Nothing serious but we worked our asses off for an hour and a half, trying to get back into position and get the anchor to hold. Had to put on the 45 lb. CQR in place of the 35 lb. but got her taken care of.

The Gulfo Dulce is a big, deep bay with a shoreline that drops off quickly. The only way to secure a boat is to put an anchor out from the bow and then tie a stern line to a tree on shore so the boat won't swing around and drift away.

Had a bit of guaro with Lil. Returned to boat for huevos rancheros and back to Lit and Lil's with the guitar, which bought us dinner. Drank our guaro, played for an hour or so and had a great meal of chicken and dumplings. Jeff, Cindy, Lit, Lil and a blond guy (Mick?). Had a good evening.

Guitar nights weren't always good, but most were. In these remote areas without electricity, there wasn't much entertainment other than socializing, checkers, chess or books that were passed around. In the evening people enjoyed listening to amateur music underneath a kerosene light that illuminated palm trees on the beach through open doors and windows. There was no television reception and very little available on Spanish speaking radio.

Lit was a skinny man in his 50's. Darkly tanned, he never wore a shirt. A lot of us didn't – shoes either – they just got wet. Lil, also in her 50's with gray hair, was stockier. On hot evenings after having a few, she would take off her shirt exposing a sturdy, no nonsense, no see through, size "D" bra above a white stomach with little red spots that young eyes can see even from a distance. She only stripped down with certain people she confided, implying that what she had done was somehow risqué.

2/13/77
I cleaned the engine's water filter and put in some stanchion bolts where they had leaked in the previous

days rain. Then rowed ashore for a shower and to get more stores. We got some good things – fresh beans, okra, tea bags.

I played, and we returned for a tuna casserole and retired after trying to read. Certain bulbs are scarce. Our reading light bulbs are in the compass.

We decided to leave at noon tomorrow for Panamá rather than tonight.

As the crow flies, Puerta Armuelles isn't far from Golfito, but traveling by water we had to round Península Burica, an overnight voyage, to get there. Forewarned that the anchorage was an "open roadstead," curious wording for an unprotected harbor, we knew there would be no breakwater or enclosed bay. It turned out to be nothing more than a huge industrial steel pier that stretched out into the ocean far enough that white refrigerated ships could come alongside. Mobile cranes lifted pallets of bananas off rail cars and lowered them into the hold. There was no place for us to tie up.

We were the lone boat anchored in the harbor where day and night it was loud from ship's generators and the diesel motors that powered the heavy equipment working around the clock. We were constantly worried about dragging anchor and washing up on the beach, so we didn't sleep much. Had this happened, it could have been the end of our Costa Rican Adventure. It would have been difficult if not impossible to get *La Dulce* off the beach through the thundering surf.

In every port of entry, protocol dictates that a yellow quarantine "Q" flag should be hoisted, signaling the Port

Captain that the boat has come from another country and is requesting permission to enter. Sometimes a boarding crew would come out, but usually after waiting a while, we would go to their office with our papers. We lowered the dinghy. I rowed to a steel platform that was at sea level. There I tied our tiny rowboat to the vibrating metal and climbed the stairs to the top of the pier carrying our oars so they wouldn't get stolen or knocked into the water by the swell. We had been told that dogs weren't allowed onshore, so I felt awful looking back at poor Ralph following me with sad, sad eyes. He had no concept of bureaucratic rules. For him, "There's a beach over there!! And you're going over to the pier that that leads to the beach!! I need to go the bathroom dammit, and you left me behind. Why?"

2/16/77
The head of migración told me it would be $45 and that I would have to go to Cuidad David over 50 miles away. I told him I only had $40, which was true, so he called his boss and did us a "favor." He stamped our passports as leaving on the 18th and charged only $35 for which we got no receipt.

When I returned from this, I rowed back to the boat and was about to eat dinner when seven officials came tromping on board and stuck their fingers into everything.

Ralph has been a problem but finally took a shit on the Astroturf, cabin top and side deck. He's having a hard time not being able to go to shore.

If Ralph could have talked, we surely would have received an Irish Setter earful about some of our recent decisions regarding where and how we were living. Once cleared, we replaced the "Q" flag with the flag of Panamá that Helen had sewn on our Bernina sewing machine.

2/17/77
Went to port captain and obtained the "zarpe" for 25 cents – the only legal charge and headed out as soon as we could.

Motored to Punta Burica and had a beautiful afternoon sail with another amazing dolphin show. We are heading directly for Puntarenas.

2/18/77
Motored, sailed, and hove to during the night. As sun rose we found our fuel to be low. She had been at 1/4 tank when we left which I thought gave us ten gallons. Decided we should return to Golfito. Maddening.

With only five dollars to our name, we needed to find Glen who would cash a $15 check so we could buy some food and fuel at 50 cents a gallon. It wasn't long after daybreak that we made the course change and got the bejesus scared out of us. Having religiously read all of the articles in *Cruising World, Sail* and *Yachting* magazines for years, one of the recurring stories is about boats that had been sunk or attacked by whales and how the crew had survived for months in their tiny inflatable life raft, without food or water, before being miraculously saved by a Japanese fishing boat that happened to be off course.

There were several theories on these occurrences. One was that the boat, from a whale's eye below, looks like another whale and the attack was really an attempt to mate, which is a truly scary thought – being sexually assaulted by a horny humpback.

The other leading theory was that inadvertently, the whale surfaced where the boat happened to be.

We had just changed course for Golfito when we were spotted by fifty or so black whales with white markings that decided, in unison, to swim right at us. It was obvious that they were on their way to eat Helen, Ralph and me or fuck our boat. The only suggestion on how to fend off whales was offered in an article written by a cruising couple who claimed that by banging the inside of their hull with pots and pans, an aggressive whale had decided to leave them alone – if, in fact, the whale was planning an attack in the first place.

Skittish, there was no doubt in our minds that we were in danger. Helen took Ralph below deck and closed all of the ports so when they lifted us up and flipped us like a flapjack, we would not take on too much water until we righted ourselves. We both put on our safety harnesses and, yes, Helen did take out several pots and pans just in case.

We would later learn that these were pilot whales and that we should have been marveling as they surrounded *La Dulce,* swimming beside our boat as the dolphins had on the earlier leg of our paperwork journey. But, at the time, my heart was racing as the sea was almost black with them. This went on for about ten minutes before the super-pod, again in unison, decided to move on.

Fortunately, when we belatedly realized how ridiculous our reaction had been, Helen came up with Ralph who walked around the decks looking at them and wagging his tail.

Sailed for Lit and Lil's but changed course as it was rough and raining there. Barely made it into Golfito with our fuel and sailed right up to the harbor opening in the rain. Had a few beers and a great night's sleep.

Anxious to get back to the Hacienda and Puntarenas, we bought 20 gallons of fuel and sailed to Lit and Lil's for one night.

2/21/77

Just as we were about to leave, we drug anchor and the boat came close to shore. I started to pull us out by the anchor and pulled us onto a coral head. The tide dropped so fast we were aground. It did come back up, and we sailed most of the way to Captain Tom's.

Tom, a gruff one-legged Vietnam Vet with a gold front tooth, had a scruffy house on a beach inside Golfito. A popular stopping place for boats in transit, it just didn't sit well with us after having spent time at the much more scenic, Joe Hill's. That afternoon I changed the oil in the motor and transmission and cleaned all of the filters, including the oil filter, as I couldn't find replacements – a nasty undertaking that had me sitting on the cramped galley floor, sweat pouring off in the stifling heat and stagnant air that smelled of stagnant water and hot motor oil. To get the old oil out, I had a hand pump that spit the thick black liquid into a bucket.

I played that night and was totally upstaged by a female guitar player. She was good.

Leaving the next morning, we sailed most of the day. When the wind died as darkness came upon us, we motored all night, passing Isla del Caño and the lights of Quepos:

2/25/77

We could just see the Gulfo de Nicoya when the sun came up. Motored until 11:00 when we finally got some wind. Ran to the pass and then broad reached to Joe Hill's. Helen took the helm, and we screamed in.

Mona, Casper and Glen were there – had a red snapper Helen caught in the afternoon. We howled at the moon until all hours. They seemed glad to see us, and we were glad to be back.

At least we were beginning to look the part of sailors. Our public parts were a dark tan and our private parts only slightly less brown as we had been away from shore without much reason to wear anything other than to protect sensitive areas.

La Dulce Mujer was looking much less new as the brass and bronze were acquiring a natural salt-water patina, and the hull's green topsides had some nicks and scrapes. Our dinghy had become much more used, especially with Ralph jumping in and out of it as we rowed him to beach after beach. He was glad to be back at a familiar place where he could fish and cool off in the water. This would be the beginning of his affinity for seafood. Ralph could actually catch puffer fish, which he would bury in the sand for, I suppose, a rainy day.

4

AIN'T IT GOOD

TO BE BACK

AFTER MAKING THE TRIP mostly unscathed, we were back in familiar territory and safer than we had been since being forced by Customs to venture out. Our meager but welcome income was the two-hundred dollars a month that I was being paid to write an Owner's Manual for the Tiburon 36' (on our Remington manual typewriter).

Looking at us one might conclude that we were well off, and we were to a degree as a fairly handsome, young couple on a fancy new 36-foot boat with a haughty Irish Setter, yet we had no money and no credit cards. Banking, as we know it now, was as far off as were computers, ATM's and GPS's. SatNav, as it was called then, was feasible only for commercial ships and mega yachts that could afford it and had room for the large ball that had to be mounted on top of the bridge.

2/27/77
Started on owner's manual and it went fairly smoothly. Helen rowed over to Jesusita to make a phone

call with Mona but decided against it because they have added a five-colone charge even for collect long distance.

Wrote letters in the afternoon, and went in for music. Three guitars and a banjo for a wild one.

The next day, a Monday, we sailed to Puntarenas to clear Customs and hoist the Costa Rican flag.

2/28/77 [Helen]

The port captain remembered our launching and immediately we were Costa Rican friends. It was over in a breeze, and we sailed to the icehouse for 100 lbs. and also to the market for food. Choppy as hell for Ben rowing the dinghy (about a 25 knot wind from the N). We even sailed out of the estuary – main only – until the middle of the bay where the wind died. Returned with two liters of red rum.

There was a moderately priced rum named Flor de Caña that we bought occasionally, but usually we could only afford the cheap stuff that was poured from five-gallon metal drums into used unlabeled clear bottles, plugged with a drugstore cork. In Costa Rica, no bottle of any kind was ever thrown away.

Back on our mooring at the Hacienda, it was time for me to make a trip to San José via the *Sábalo*. Now that Dennis was in charge at the factory, I needed to remain involved, get specifications and make drawings for the Owner's Manual.

I also needed to cash a check at the Bank of America. When we left the States all of our money was put in the B. of A. in San Francisco because they had a branch in San

José, Costa Rica. We had been assured that it would be easy to cash checks, but it turned out to be damn near impossible with a three-week waiting period, until we met Bob a gringo officer who made our lives much easier.

3/1/77 [Helen]
The Sábalo left with Ben and more people than it should have been carrying for Puntarenas. Joe Hill's is loaded with sailboats. This last week it has been fluctuating between 12 and 19. I hung around the hacienda and traded my dinghy with Sally to let the bottom dry out before its new paint job.

I read Dove while a norther blew 35 knots. Singing onshore didn't develop. Because of the wind, everyone stayed on their boat.

3/3/77 [Helen]
Painted first coat on dinghy. Unexpected change in color. Paint doesn't store well on a boat. The heat and motion disturbs a can if it's been opened already. Casper gave me one quart of white. Did a mountain of laundry. Finished Dove and cooked noodles and tomato sauce for myself. It's no fun cooking alone. The spirit is missing. Can't wait to cook for Ben tomorrow. Really can't wait to have food on board again. Our hanging basket is empty.

The normal cruising yacht in Costa Rica began its voyage in the States carrying hundreds of cans of food including canned bacon, canned hams and everything they could possibly stuff into storage bins, to the point that they were generally floating well below their waterlines. In most cases these people had been preparing and planning their trip for years.

Our stores consisted of maybe five or six cans of tomato sauce, a dozen pouches of Maggi instant soup, rice, beans and some noodles. Produce that didn't need ice was kept in a mini-hammock that hung in the galley. Coming back from San José on the *Sábalo* after cashing the check, my "tote goat" was filled with bags of fresh onions, peppers, tortillas, Monte Verde cheese (made by Quakers in the mountains), La Selecta bread, ground beef and a 100-pound block of ice.

3/4/77 [Helen]

We hibernated listening to Buffett's "Changes in Latitudes, Changes in Attitudes." Cooked enchiladas and had a great time. Ben said the city was rough and what a delight it was to be home. Everything is looking up at the plant. We leafed through our calendars and reminisced about the bad along with the good.

3/5/77 [Helen]

After Dañiel came by in his new race boat, Ben wrote from 9:00 to 12:00 am. I went to shore and screwed in the teak strips on the bottom of the dinghy using the brace and bit and the last of our 3M-5200 caulking – the job turned out well. Swam. Visited Pacifica from California who had been dismasted by a shrimper boat in Nicaragua. Looks as if Ben and FibroTécnica will be doing some work for them.

This last trip of Ben's to the factory has substantiated his credibility among owners of boats in need of help at Joe Hill's.

All of the breakdowns I've been witnessing speak strongly of a lot of poorly constructed boats and too much use of mechanical devices by people who don't know how to fix things.

Spent a romantic night on the cabin roof.

With our only income being $200 a month, we were always dead-ass broke. Fortuitously, unexpected opportunities presented themselves. The boats coming through Joe Hill's and Puntarenas sometimes needed repairs, and there was no one else in the area other than Helen and me who knew as much about sailboats. For years we had been immersed in every aspect of marine construction. If anyone knew where to find parts or make do with what was available, it was us. All of our tools, including the table saw, were stored below.

At first we thought about chartering our boat as a way to earn money, but it didn't take long for us to figure out that we didn't want other people on board, expecting us to wait on them and cook their meals. It came to pass that *Ben and Helen Harrison, Boatbuilding and Repairs,* was not as far off of the mark as it had been when we left California. Odd jobs here and there made a big difference to us financially, and we got to hear the boating gossip.

Everyplace is a *Peyton Place,* but one might think that in the confines of small sailboats, there wouldn't be much hanky-panky going on. They would be *so* wrong. In one instance, while Helen was visiting with the wife of the

253

couple aboard *Pacifica*, the husband walked into the main cabin naked in the middle of the afternoon to say, "Hello."

3/16/77
Ate dinner on the Freya *with Bart, Diana, Peter, Pati, Mona and us. Peter cooked a gourmet chicken wok-style and we later got tickled remembering how important cooking was to us in San Francisco. Still is, but in a Costa Rican way. We recorded the conversations and Ben's singing. Afterwards, Diana and Bart came over for tea with us ... and more! Group sex is* not *our bag.*

Then there was the trimaran with an attractive couple and their young son. We had met them just after we launched and had a wonderful sail on their fast multi-hull. From another boat passing through, we learned that in Golfito during a shore party the husband had snuck away with another woman. When the wife realized what was going on, she found someone of her own to sneak away with. Everyone, of course, was stupid drunk, but that sordid night of alcohol-fueled debauchery ended their relationship.

As it turned out, cabin fever between the legs was rampant. Joe Hill, himself, had run off with another woman after his wife mysteriously drowned. But the randiest of them all was a handsome man sailing alone on his beautiful wooden schooner. He was continuously propositioning any remotely available female, married or single. With testicles that hung out of his short shorts when he sat down, his basic approach was, "Don't you want to have some fun?" Some did. He was persuasive, persistent and focused. Those of us there on a semi-permanent basis generally behaved ourselves. It was those passing through that caused the majority of the trouble. The loins of many of these travelers may have been burning for "forbidden fruit," but our stomachs were constantly growling for real food.

3/17/77
Had beans and cornbread and a fight because Helen failed to leave me some beans. Ralph got them. We aren't poor but we sure can't afford any good food.

3/18/77
I wrote all day on the manual after cleaning topsides. Helen cleaned all day and it was a hot one. Below deck I sat with a towel on the cushion with another to keep wiping the sweat off.

We had two eggs over rice with tomato sauce.

3/19/77
Cleaned the boat really well because Don Johnny is expected. Dañiel sped in with a female model who was being photographed in one of their powerboats.

Cornbread and beans. But beer at the house.

We were continuously cleaning the boat because wonderful Ralph was a slob. Wet and sandy when he came back from shore, he was always shedding red hair. Using salt water that we hauled up on deck in a bucket with a rope, Joy dish detergent was, at the time, the only product that worked well with brine.

3/20/77 [Helen]

Chester and Jean came out to rent a cottage for Semana Santa. They bought us lunch, which was the first time we'd eaten at Joe Hill's in the three months we've been around. Watching our colones!

Cornbread (the only bread we were able to make) and beans were a staple as was rice flavored with Maggi soup. If we had even a small fish to mix in with it, fried rice and onions was another entrée. But better food would soon be coming our way because the factory, in partnership with the stateside investors, had decided to manufacture an aft-cockpit 38 foot version of the Tiburon 36'. It would be called the Cabo Rico 38', and I was going to be a part of a new production team helping design and build a new boat that had been inspired by Helen's and my hard-headed insistence on a different cockpit location and below deck configuration. The reality was that ours was the prototype for the new sailboat.

Setting things in motion, stateside investor Frank Day and his girlfriend, Susan, arrived at the Hacienda on April 2, 1977, aboard Tiburon hull #19 that had been launched in Puntarenas as a demo for prospective buyers. After rafting up for the evening and a full moon party, the next day:

4/3/77 [Helen]

We left Joe Hill's after huevos rancheros and much talk about the 38-footer. Sailed thru the smaller pass to the Tortugas where we again rafted, shelled and watched red, orange, purple and black crabs tottle thru the sand.

Then, with Frank and Susan on board our boat, we set sail for Bahía Ballena (Whale Bay) for an overnighter.

Frank sailed the whole way and really got Dulce *moving. We ate ceviche and drank Bloody Marys before arriving.*

Bahía Ballena was what the Wild West had once been. The only building onshore was a one-room saloon with three horses tied up to the wood hitching post worn smooth by leather reins. There were no cars, only horses swishing their tails and twitching their skin to ward off flies. The place smelled like horses and manure. Skinny flea-bitten dogs were sleeping in the cool dirt under the shade of the porch when we "yachties," looking as though we were from another planet, walked in. Actually, Helen and I blended in fairly well, but Frank and Susan were wearing fashionable sailing attire. On the dirt floor were three passed out real cowboys that could have come from a Larry McMurtry novel – hats, boots and spurs. Had they suddenly come to life while we were there, they probably would have thought they were hallucinating or being invaded by aliens.

After marginally cold beers, we had another beautiful sail back to the Hacienda where we cooked and talked well into the night.

4/5/77
Worked hard with Frank all morning on the new boat and got quite a bit accomplished. The girls went into Jesusita while Frank and I went over the owner's manual. With the girls gone, we also talked about money,

which I always hate. I asked for $1,000 per month. He was hoping for less.

Had fried fish dinner. Frank had accidentally dropped our oarlock off the pier, so I was not in a good mood. We looked for it at low tide but could not find it without a flashlight.

4/6/77
Found the oarlock. Then Frank and I settled on $800 per month with a bonus if things work out well. Not bad considering.

I would ride the *Sábalo* then bus up to San José on Mondays, stay at their apartment while I worked at the factory, and then return to the Hacienda via bus and *Sábalo* on Thursdays. The grind was about to begin, but not before Helen and I gorged ourselves. The owners of Jesusita, the small seven-room hotel located on the beach of a nearby island, needed a vacation themselves so we agreed to watch their place and keep the generator running while they were away for the weekend. Our pay was a good bottle of Bacardi Rum and all we could eat from their freezer. On our first moonlit night, after having outdoor sex on a table beneath the veranda, we ate at least three pounds of shrimp with a loaf of fresh bread.

4/14/77
For breakfast we had steak, bacon, eggs and potatoes until we couldn't eat anymore.

All day I sat in a leather rocking chair and read James Clavell's *Shogun*, a gripping novel about the Far East that begins with a riveting sailing ship-in-a-storm sequence.

Fried two chickens for dinner.

And continued reading about "joss" (luck) and "pillowing" (what we had done on the table without a pillow the evening before).

At the factory, my responsibility was to supervise two carpenters who would make the deck and interior mock-ups from which we could make the molds. But before we could do that, we needed to extend the hull by two feet at the transom – make the 36-foot hulls into 38-foot hulls. This is where Dennis did something that was not only brilliant, it would eventually benefit *La Dulce* by allowing us to add that same two feet on to our stern.

He designed and the factory workers made a two-foot long "half-mold" that would fit on two existing Tiburon hulls that had been laid up without a transom. By lengthening two hulls before permanently extending the main mold, we could begin making the full deck mold and interior molds. Though there were still some Tiburon 36' boats in production, the future was clearly the Cabo Rico 38'. Over two hundred would eventually be built.

Dennis and I worked long and hard on the interior layout trying to come up with acceptable plans. The powers that were wanted to cram as much below as they possibly could while I advocated a simpler version. They won, but with Bill Crealock's input, we did a pretty good job of achieving what they wanted and still have enough room to move around the cabin. *La Dulce Mujer* slept four with one head – theirs – eight with two heads. In hindsight I think they were right. Most cruises on a boat of this type would be of the weekend or two-week variety with friends and children along for the fun.

Going back and forth to San José without Helen was tough, but the work was exciting. The hardest part was dealing with stateside visitors coming and going at the Apartamentos Laisa where I stayed. Usually, they were bosses and/or their friends on a "working vacation," ready to party. It was almost impossible not to go out with them since they didn't speak Spanish or know their way around. Every week it seemed, I was a boat specialist by day and social director at night who still had to get up early for work in the morning. Almost every night in San José we ended up at La Luz – still the best bar in town.

5

DIRTY MAGAZINES AND NASTY WOMEN

COSTA RICA HAD WHORES GALORE – still does. There wasn't much that couldn't be arranged involving sex. Many successful Costa Rican businessmen had a mistress. Sex was everywhere, yet there was a puritanical streak within their social fabric. Dirty magazines were almost impossible to find as it was against the law to sell them. A man could buy a woman and see everything there was to see in the flesh, but he couldn't buy a *Playboy* magazine because they had pictures of naked women. This cultural phenomenon enabled us to become purveyors of smut so we could eat better – a continuing challenge even with my new salary because we kept pouring money into our boat. We had learned that girlie magazines were a hot commodity with commercial fishermen. Not only did we encourage everyone who visited us to bring them, it gave us an excuse to go through them ourselves.

7/20/77 [Helen]
Left around noon along with Nomad. *No good sailing wind so we motored to the shrimper in front of Chap's*

house and made a fantastic trade of three smut magazines for a bucket full of jumbo and medium shrimp. Sautéed some in garlic butter and boiled the others for hot sauce.

The nasty women arrived with Frank Day, my main boss, on Wednesday, August 23, 1977, from the United States of America.

Picked up Frank and two ladies – Betsy and Pat, a yacht broker from Ft. Lauderdale. Went by apartment and then to La Luz, Arturo's and Orleans. I got into it a little with Pat.

Our boat still needed a ton of work before we could realistically sail off into the sunset, so while I was away working in San José, Helen doggedly, in her inimitable way, kept making the progress we needed in order to make our boat seaworthy, comfortable and good looking. When we were together at the Hacienda we played, but we also worked our tails off. From an immigration perspective, we had been living in Costa Rica for a long time – since October 28, 1974, over three years, and the day was coming when migración was going to make us say, "Adiós."

My work at the factory, if you could call designing and supervising the construction of sailboats "work," was as enjoyable as it gets, and I was collecting a paycheck. The downer came when Frank arrived with two snooty females from Ft. Lauderdale instead of his girlfriend, Susan. It was a social disaster.

Helen and I both went to San José to meet them as we were mistakenly expecting the same congeniality we had enjoyed on Frank's last visit when he hired me. Helen, who hadn't been up to the big city for a while, thought the factory looked better than ever. Dennis and I were eager to show off the considerable progress we felt we had made.

Production was much more organized as there was a flow that kept minor snafus from disrupting any of the many steps toward a finished product. Two Cabo Rico 38's that were almost ready to be shipped sat impressively in their cradles in the middle of the factory. From the floor, they looked mammoth as the shiny hull reflected the fluorescent lighting. Climbing the stairs to the catwalk outside Dennis' office, we were able to look down at the cabin top, complete with teak decks. Like schoolchildren smiling because we felt we had done a superior job on our class project, we anxiously awaited praise from the visitors. We were caught completely off guard when, rather than being impressed, they were grumpy. All they did was criticize, bitch and moan.

8/24/77
Shit hit the fan. These people are the most arrogant, stupid assholes I have ever come in contact with. They were rude to Don Johnny and so unbelievably bad mannered. They acted as though they were mingling with lepers, and that they were the mighty gringos all-knowing, all-powerful, and rich (even though they don't pick up many tabs).

I was really depressed as was Helen.

Frank didn't know about the agreement that had been communicated to us on the sheer stripe. Additionally, they were all pissed off because they had invested in advertising even though I had written them that the date they wanted delivery could not be met.

Frank was a thick man who had played college football, probably an offensive tackle or guard. In Denver he owned a ritzy car dealership specializing in exotic automobiles. We had been told that it was so upscale there were ferns, like the California fern bars, hanging in the windows. Wearing steel rimmed glasses, he had a boyish look and, when he wanted, a charming personality. Pat, the yacht broker with blond hair and blue eyes, arrived in a pink pantsuit that had a Doris Day look. Betsy, several years younger than Pat, was a cute girl with a good figure. Perhaps they were lovers, perhaps not, but it became obvious that she was simply along for the ride.

At the factory we had been working as hard as we possibly could and had informed them, in writing, in advance, when they could realistically expect delivery of the first two boats. Getting a new boat into production isn't an easy thing to do. Often, at this stage taking a little more time to do things right saves time and money in the long run. Still, even though we were proceeding at what I considered a rapid pace, as far as they were concerned, we were behind schedule. That was problem number one since they had ignored our timetable and gone ahead with advertising that would be running too soon to be as effective as it would have been had it been better coordinated.

Our second problem: we at the factory had been told by Jim, *not* to apply color to the sheer stripe that went along the top of the hull. Our instructions were to sand and prep it for paint so the buyer could choose the color he wanted after the boat arrived in Florida. Frank went ballistic. He was extremely upset that a color hadn't been applied when the hull was being laid up, as we had been doing with the Tiburon 36'.

This small skirmish was but a prelude to a bad, bad weekend together afloat on our own *La Dulce Mujer Pintada*. Already, acrimony was in the air.

8/25/77

Woke up at 5:30 in the morning and we all caught the bus to Puntarenas. About half way there, Frank started on some line of crap.

The line of crap was a conversation Helen and I overheard between Pat and Frank sitting in the bus seats directly behind us. Their back and forth was generally about how stupid Costa Ricans are and how difficult it is to get anything done as a result of their incompetence. The more we heard, the more we became enraged over what they were saying about our workers, and the way they were saying it. In a low voice I told Helen that I probably wasn't going to be working for them anymore.

The more Frank kept telling Pat how lazy the Costa Ricans were, the madder I became.

8/25/77

I turned around in my bus seat and said, "Frank you are the most arrogant asshole I have ever met, and I don't know if I want to continue working for you."

That set them back a notch. I should have been fired on the spot for insubordination but I wasn't. He tried to box me in with, "So you are a Tico now and not a gringo."

I explained that I had not transformed into a Costa Rican, but what he was saying was total bullshit. I knew firsthand that the workers were doing a remarkable job, all things considered. Working with fiberglass is not easy, comfortable, or healthy.

I figured the gig was up then and there, but surprisingly, they didn't tell me to go fuck myself – the reason being, that they badly wanted a free weekend cruise on our boat, on our dime. Pat and Betsy, who obviously felt they should be catered to, were never around when it came time to pay for anything. Frank always had short arms for pockets as deep as his were rumored to be. Not only were we providing the boat with ourselves as crew, we ended up buying most of the groceries. Perhaps we would have splurged more if what was available was better, but realistically, we were buying the best ingredients available at the central market in Puntarenas. If they had wanted, they could have bought more upscale food in San José and brought it with them on the bus.

Then, while they waited in the shade onshore, Helen and I loaded the groceries aboard our dinghy and rowed out against a strong current to the boat. After taking Ralph to shore, we rowed to the icehouse and bought a block that weighed about 110 pounds. For lowering it into the dinghy, there was a pair of tongs on a winch bolted to the icehouse dock. As the block descended, Helen (who was in the dinghy) stayed out from underneath until it was at eye-level and then guided it into the bow. After rowing back out and tying off alongside *La Dulce*, I chiseled the block into four pieces with our ice pick so they could more easily be lifted up on deck and put into the icebox.

Then I rowed to the dock and picked up their gear, taking it to the boat before returning for them. Four was the most we could carry in the dinghy and with Frank being heavyset, that was two trips pulling hard on the oars against the current. Helen and I had become pros at getting in and out of the dinghy. The hard part was getting people who were unaccustomed to life on the water from the smaller boat onto the larger one. It usually required some pushing, often making it an indelicate procedure. We just hoped the stanchions were strong enough to withstand the weight of Frank's 250-pound body. If they had failed, he would have fallen backwards into the dinghy, which would have been a disaster considering how fast the tide was running.

Once we were all aboard, we started the motor and loaded the dinghy, Helen winching it up with the main halyard while I guided it to its wood davits on the cabin top. After we secured it, Helen motored slowly forward so I could more easily pull up the line, chain and anchor. Underway, as we cleared sandy point and headed for the Hacienda, *they* complained about the heat.

The sail, about two hours, was pleasant enough, but there was tension. Pat didn't care for dogs and was not into sharing the cockpit with a loveable panting Irish

Setter sitting next to her. Ralph knew this too, but he had a dog sense of humor and kind of leaned into her. Clearly, our guests didn't like us and the feeling was mutual, but we did manage to get there without further incident. After we picked up the mooring, Helen and I untied and lowered our dinghy into the water, doing a reverse of the drill we had done in Puntarenas. Moving them and their belongings down from our deck and into our little rowboat was still awkward but not quite as intimate as it was on the way up thanks to gravity.

There were several cabins up in the hills at the Hacienda. This was where they were staying after having dinner ashore. Helen and I weren't invited to join them, but that was okay. Like Ralph, Mother Nature also had a sense of humor.

Cozy and dry below deck, Helen and I closed the companionway and ports when heavy rains and wind came blowing through so hard that Mike and Sally were unable to prepare dinner or light the kerosene lamps in the semi-outdoor kitchen. The winds were so strong, they blew rain through the open-air cabins making everything, including the sheets in "Lemon Drop," wet. From the companionway, while drinking their more expensive rum, we could vaguely see flashlights moving around up in the hills. The rain continued with lightning and loud thunder. Gently rocking in the well-protected harbor, securely tied to the mooring, we were almost chilly when we snuggled in bed after a dinner of hot pasta and fresh vegetables.

The next morning at breakfast, under a clear sky, they didn't look too good or well rested. The circles under Pat's eyes made her appear older than she had the day before.

8/27/77

It's hard to write exactly what makes these people so rude. I can't help but believe it is some sort of insecurity. Frank has been better than the rest but the chemistry between us is like magnets of opposing polarities.

Took them to the Tortugas. Lost a fin.

Had a little spat over having meatloaf. It wasn't good enough for Pat. Betsy asked if there wasn't something else that could be made with hamburger that would be "edible." I said I was really in the mood for it and assured all it would be edible.

We all slept on the boat because they had checked out of cabins.

I was ready to strangle the whole lot of them over the meatloaf dustup. Popping up through the companionway like a jack-in-the-box with enough steam built up to blow a gasket, I probably scared them as I explained how much they were going to like the meatloaf. We had been in Costa Rica for so long, we had forgotten that in Ft. Lauderdale the only place that served meatloaf was Luby's Cafeterias.

8/29/77 [Helen]

Left for Puntarenas at 6:30. Saw two turtles mating. Ben made good omelets and received no thanks. It was high tide so we were able to tie up and unload them at the fuel docks.

Bought some more food and sailed back to spend our 5th wedding anniversary at the Hacienda instead of Puntarenas.

Beers at Hacienda.

The mating turtles were leatherbacks, the size of a compact car. This was not a frantic or hurried fornication, and we made sure not to bother them enough to spoil their long, passionate love session. The male reproductive organ is housed in the base of its tail so he mounts her from the rear holding her tightly with his flippers. As Helen and I marveled, our guests appeared uninterested.

In retrospect, most of the blame for the fiasco rested squarely on Frank's shoulders. He was the hotshot boat manufacturer who had invited the fancy yacht broker and her companion from Ft. Lauderdale on a promotional trip. He probably paid their airfare. Both women had on expensive designer clothes when they arrived and most likely thought they were coming to an exotic paradise where they would be treated like royalty eating steak and lobster.

My go-fuck-yourselves confrontation on the bus, the food problem, the wet sheet problem and lack of electricity problem, all contributed to a vacation they probably laugh about to this day as one of the great misadventures of their lives. They looked downright exhausted and disheveled when we said goodbye.

6

FEAR AND GUARO

THE DEBACLE WITH FRANK and his lady friends was yet another sign that it was time to leave. Our visas, which we had extended a second time since our return from Panamá for a stamp, were about to expire. Although I probably could have stayed on at the factory working for Don Johnny, Dañiel and Dennis for a while longer, it was time for new horizons.

Living aboard *La Dulce* and visiting foreign ports was to be our climax, the grand orgasm of our tenacious efforts, but despite all of our preparation, we knew we would soon be exposed to God only knows what. Our original plan was to return to San Francisco where the fireplace would warm our floating home, but we soon learned from other sailors what a hard trip that can be and how the Papagayo and El Niño winds can unexpectedly howl down from the Sierra Madres on the West Coast. We heard how beautiful the Caribbean is – Roatán, Honduras, Key West and the islands of the Antilles. After quite a bit of thought, we decided to change course.

Getting ready to depart this beloved and relatively safe harbor was now more urgent than it had seemed only a few days earlier, and it was affecting us mentally. Though the drumbeat of danger was always close to the surface, like soldiers about to be sent to the front, there were some wonderfully gay times and memorable evenings – boats, bosoms, guitars, palm trees and clear water.

Working hard to get *La Dulce* ready, we bolted down the remaining sail track and put up a used Bimini top, one of our more fortunate acquisitions from *Calma,* that we bleached and cleaned before installing. It was as though we had added a Florida room to our house. Ralph approved. In between the sun, fun, fear, guaro and beer, we were learning a lot and often the hard way. One big lesson we learned was, *always, always* check the oil before starting the engine. If the dipstick comes out with something that looks thick and grayish, salt water has siphoned from the exhaust manifold into the oil pan and cylinders and the motor will be severely damaged if you try to run it. We learned that on September 2, 1977. Not only was it slow to start that afternoon, huge billows of white smoke came out of the exhaust. Something was definitely wrong, we knew that, but we had no idea how bad it was and were obviously not as concerned as we should have been.

Left Puntarenas with two cylinders working and spent the night at San Lucas Prison Island. We were greeted by a prison guard and asked to anchor closer to the camp.

I was trying not to run the engine, which forced us into the lagoon of the prison island where a guard insisted we give him the key to our ignition.

9/3/77

Awoke at 6:00 to leave with the running currents but delayed a bit by the hefty guard who was still asleep. Rather ridiculous situation. Had to motor around point but then made good time until we passed Isla Azúcar and Isla Elena.

That men and women are different there is no doubt, but it is more than physical.

"Do you hear that, dear?" says the woman.

"No, I didn't hear anything," says the man.

"Listen, there it goes again," she says.

"What are you talking about?" he'll say until it becomes apparent that something is wrong or needs to be done. The wise man listens to what a woman has to say because it is a warning sign of something about to happen. The female is *never* wrong in her premonitions. Women intuitively are constantly vigilant in their protective genetic awareness. At the same time, men tend to go into a denial phase until the problem becomes obvious. Had Helen been in charge of checking the motor oil, we wouldn't have been pulling the engine. She knew something was seriously wrong before I was willing to admit it. The old myth about having a woman on board being bad luck is total bull. Not only can you admire them in daylight and snuggle with them at night; they will help the smart man avoid problems.

The more I fussed around with the engine, the more apparent it became that something serious had happened and it wasn't anything I could fix nor could it be repaired in place. The best thing to do would be to pull it and take it up to the factory in San José.

Figuring we were screwed anyhow, we decided that while the motor was being repaired, we might as well haul the boat out of the water and bring the "half-mold" down so we could add two feet to our transom – a ton of miserable fiberglass work, but we had wanted to do this from the beginning. I arranged for a truck to bring the mold down and take the motor back on the return trip. Cambrae, the chief mechanic, agreed to fix it after hours for 3,000 colones – $350. Of course, we would have to order parts – how many and at what cost we didn't know.

Leaving the Hacienda, we hoped that we would have wind so we wouldn't need to use the motor and risk further damage on the way back to Puntarenas. At least by this time we had learned to reef the mainsail – a concept as old as sailing ships. When there is the right amount of wind or less you fly as much canvas as you can get up. When it starts blowing, you've got to reduce the amount of sail or bad things happen. The secret is knowing when. The axiom is that it's time to put in a reef when you first start to think it might be a good idea. There is more leeway during daylight, but at night, it needs to be done before getting into a windblown pickle with waves coming over the bow while holding on for dear life as we had done on our maiden voyage.

On the way back to the estuary, we had to put in a reef and later shake it out as we rounded the point of Puntarenas where the waters were more protected. Pacific Marina, where we would be hauling out, was just outside of downtown Puntarenas on a sandy road that followed the coastline. Bill and Crissy, the gringos who ran the place, lived in an apartment upstairs. He was a thin man who wore nothing other than a pair of cut-offs with a pack of cigarettes in the front pocket. Crissy, his skinny wife, was battling menopausal hot flashes at the same time she was trying to quit smoking. She could become animated.

Bill, who was always pulling on an unfiltered cigarette, was of no help whatsoever in Crissy's efforts to stop because an x-ray of his lungs showed them to be in miraculously good shape while hers had problems. It turned out to be a bird, rather than Bill, that did the most to get her through those tempting moments. An old friend had left them his parrot after he died of lung cancer. Every morning the bird imitated the cough that it had heard for years, sounding exactly like a person coughing up terrible things. Hearing that bird gave Crissy strength and us the giggles as we could distinctly hear every tortured nuance of his horrendous morning tobacco cacophony.

9/21/77

At around 6:30 I rowed over to Pacific Marina to be sure all was ready. Returned and Lalo came over with skiff to tow us over to the dock. At about 8:30 we were pulled around to the car and, after a few dives by Don Pancho, we were hauled up.

We had the boys – Raul and Beto – scrape the bottom while we removed the rudder, backstay and exhaust thru hull to make ready for the mold. Also roughed up the transom so the fiberglass would adhere.

The "car" was what they called their heavy-duty "cradle" with steel wheels on railroad tracks. By rolling it down an incline into the water, the boat could be floated onto it. Then, with a diesel-powered winch pulling on the cable, the boat could be pulled up on dry land. It was virtually fool proof, but only one boat could be out of the water at a time, and that was going to be us for several brutal weeks. Ralph was the only one who didn't mind the haul-out as he slept on the cool sand in the shade underneath the boat or gallivanted up and down the sandy road sniffing and pissing. At high tide, he'd go for a swim if he felt like it.

Next door to Pacific Marina was Clara's, a small store where we could sit at one of the three tables, drink beer and buy food items like canned tuna, that we often ate right out of the can with lime juice. After cleaning up from an exhausting day, it was heaven.

Though Clara's played a role in our temporary existence, two other bars were favorites. One, of course, was the always-wonderful La Luz in San José. The other was El Fela in Puntarenas. The boca they served with each beer was a deep fried fish about eight inches long. Delicious with lime, especially in the heat of the afternoon, they were so crisp you could eat all but the head and spine. A Pilsen beer was five colones so we dined there often, sitting outside in the shade on padded 1950s kitchen chairs around a worn Formica-topped table.

9/8/77

Cambrae down – bent rod so we pulled motor. It is really heavy and caused much strain. Pulled her out with halyard, which scared me to death as the motor weighs over 600 pounds. I am really sick over it.

After glassing on the two-foot extension in the stifling heat of Puntarenas and putting the repaired Volvo diesel back on its mounts, we couldn't wait to return to the Hacienda Nicoyana. As redheaded Mike said, mostly in jest, as we sat in the leather rocking chairs around the community table looking out at our freshly painted green hull, "You can hardly tell where it's stuck on." *La Dulce* finally looked the way we had originally envisioned when we were discussing our plans with Bill Crealock in Carlsbad, California, just days before we drove across the Mexican border. Finally, she was complete and her lines aesthetically balanced.

On the first Sunday of each month at the Hacienda, there was a potluck dinner we always looked forward to. Often Mike would fry some mahi-mahi or roosterfish to go along with the other dishes brought to the table. Occasionally, a fancy yacht would pass through, sharing food that we normally could only dream about, like corn fed beef. One especially fancy motor yacht had a walk-in freezer. Once we were all gathered under the tin roof, the drinking and eating began. The party often continued well into the night with after dinner music.

I was in particular demand because most at the Hacienda Nicoyana were hearing "A Pirate Looks at Forty," "Come Monday," "Tin Cup for a Chalice," "My Head Hurts, My Feet Stink and I Don't Love Jesus," "Trying to Reason with Hurricane Season" and "Banana Republics" for the first time. We, at the Hacienda, just happened to be living the life Jimmy Buffett was singing about, and it was very heady and emotional to hear words that described us put to melody. Throw in a mixture of country standards, some Cat Stevens, John Prine, Crosby, Stills and Nash, and Helen and I were drinking free. Often others would join in the foolishness, and we became an impromptu band under the faint hiss of two kerosene lamps.

Nights were so lovely with the tall coconut trees leaning out toward the water. On the beach after dark, hundreds of small hermit crabs would bustle around making a slight clicking sound until they saw or sensed motion. There wasn't any of civilization's background noise – no cars, no planes, not the hum of a refrigerator or canned laughter coming from a television – only the sound of wild parrots, flying two-by-two, squawking as they came to roost at sunset or a fish breaking the surface. Cooking was done with propane, and ice from Puntarenas kept the beer cold.

Except for the Hacienda's Coleman lanterns, the only lights reflecting off of the water in the semicircular bay protected from the weather by a jagged hilly island, were from boats. Everything was so vividly quiet. Rowing in the moonlight, the oars would disturb the water as they pulled us through the darkness, making tiny fluorescent plankton light up in magical display that also lit up the bodies of anyone who thought a moonlight swim might be fun while millions of stars looked on.

These were good times that often led to lovemaking after Helen and I finally got into our comfortable bed underneath an open hatch that funneled the breeze over our naked bodies. The sound of water caressing the hull, living our lives like a song, there was no one there but us and ten or twelve others whose home could sink at any given moment.

One almost did, but together we saved it on an action-packed afternoon. She was a wood planked double-ender owned by an elderly couple that had tried to clean and paint the bottom using the tides. It had not gone well. As the tide came up, water began pouring over the gunwales into the cabin, a major disaster in the making. Mike got his gasoline pump working and we contributed a spare 12-volt bilge pump that helped, but as the saying goes ... there is no better bilge pump than a frightened person with a bucket. We bailed until we thought our arms would fall off and then kept on going until the boat righted itself enough to stop the water from coming in. Totally exhausted, our arms like rubber, beers were on them.

They had a hell of a mess on their hands, but they hadn't lost everything.

7

COSTA RICA FAREWELL

NATURALLY, WE WERE SAD about leaving Costa Rica, but we didn't have much time to get too choked up since we were frantically preparing for our departure and earning some last minute money. At the Hacienda Nicoyana/Joe Hill's, yes, it was emotional, and we felt the same about leaving our friends at FibroTécnica, but it was time. One night about a month before we left, an expatriate at Arturo's said, "You are the only gringos I know who came here and actually did what they said they were going to do." As I looked at the reflection of Helen and me in the mirror behind the bar, he had a point, but we were part of a success story that involved a lot more people than just us. Not only were dozens of the Tiburon 36' produced, the factory eventually made over 200 Cabo Rico 38's, beginning with those first two that I had been a part of. Costa Rica, and our many and diverse compadres, had been good to us.

10/25/77
Helen sanded for'd hatch while I worked on the cap rail. I quit around 2:00 pm to write "Attachment A," the specs for the new Cabo Rico 38' that will become part of

the standard contract for sale and purchase. It was my last task, and it was good to get it finished.

10/26/77
I went to the factory in an official capacity for the final time to deliver it.

3/9/78
Connected Helen's galley light and installed the stern light without bulb. I hope we can find another. I then worked on fitting the head door. Helen worked on the galley until we had a pretty big fight. I came to the conclusion that she is a workaholic, and I am an alcoholic.

We made up, went to shore, came back to the boat, and made love.

3/16/78
I finished the anchor roller installation, and we made general preparations to leave. Malcolm showed up and we (Mike, too) sang until late – our last session. Could have played for hours more. Sort of sad.

Once again we sailed to Herradura and then Golfito, which would be our last Costa Rican port. The water there is similar to the Puntarenas Estero, but the town we could see from the anchorage was a blueprint of colonialism and United Fruit. Maybe it was me, but the identical rows of run-down, wood-framed employee-housing units built on stilts alongside the company store was depressing in the March heat.

It was an uneventful passage except that the fuel line to the engine had an air leak that kept causing the engine to quit. Unable to find it, a mechanic came out and embarrassed me by locating it in a matter of minutes, fixing it with the turn of a wrench. That problem solved, while getting ready for the second part of our adventure, I almost screwed up big time when I left our camera in a taxi.

3/23/78

I cleaned the deck after reading for a while. Got the port side done. Helen cleaned the inside, especially the rods and reels. She was about finished when she discovered the camera was missing. We looked everywhere before tracing it back to the carga taxi that carried the ice on Monday. I had left it in the cab. Jesus, was I depressed.

Our only lead to finding it was that the driver had said he was from the town of Palmar.

3/25/78

I caught the bus to Palmar and arrived about 9:30 am to start looking. No luck for an hour, so I went to a bar and asked. The lady there seemed to know the taxi driver and said I should ask about him at the furniture store. A boy led me there and, after several funny sequences, I finally got the camera back. I paid all the folks off: forty colones for the camera, five colones to the kid, and ten colones to his mother.

I later found out that they had tried to sell it but no one could figure out how to work it. In getting it back I explained that it was all my fault, etc. <u>I was really lucky!</u>

Rode back to Golfito with Red who I met at a bar at the crossroads, and he stopped at every bar on the way. Finally stopped at Emma's where we had beers. It was fun drinking with the madam of a whorehouse. On the way out all her girls were saying, "Foto guapo."

"Guapo" means handsome, but I'll bet they say that to all of the guys along with "¡Qué grande!" Of, course I took their picture as they posed smiling.

Needless to say, Helen was glad to see me – with the camera.

Though the fuel line was fixed, the alternator wasn't charging properly, the propane regulator for our stove crapped out and immigration caught us with an outdated zarpe. At first Customs wanted me to go back to San José for a "proroga," but I managed to talk him into a new zarpe, which would give us a couple of days to solve our problems. The closest place to buy a propane regulator was Villa Nelly.

3/29/78

Hopped on a bus at 10:00 and got there just before noon. Had to wait until they opened at 1:00 and then had to wait until 2:30 for the return bus. Finally, after about an hour waiting for a water taxi, I arrived.

At least the stove works. We had a good stew for dinner.

The alternator checked out meaning there was a bad connection somewhere that I had to find as I sweated profusely. I cleaned every contact in the system for the second time and it finally worked.

The last thing we did before leaving was stencil and paint the words "*LA DULCE MUJER*" on the transom. Her official name was now officially shortened from *La Dulce Mujer Pintada*, The Sweet Painted Lady, to *The Sweet Lady* because we were tired.

We left Costa Rica for Panamá around 10:00 o'clock in the morning on an outgoing tide under full sail for Isla Montuosa, which had been marked on our charts as a place we could anchor overnight.

Happy about coming upon the small isolated island, we were disappointed when we got closer as there really wasn't a good place to anchor. Only the lee of the island offered any protection and even there the swells were two to three feet causing us to roll continuously. On the southwest side, jutting out of the water like Mayan stelae were jagged tall rocks over which thundering surf sent plumes of spray high into the air. Facing this fury and the sound of crashing waves was a house with smoke coming out of the chimney. Who in the world could be living there?

I'm sure there wasn't any reason for me to feel as though we had stumbled onto an Alfred Hitchcock movie set. I'm sure there was no reason to be scared, but we were out in the middle of nowhere all by ourselves. We hadn't seen any evidence of human life since leaving Golfito the day before – no boats, ships, islands, nothing. There was no dock or boat pulled up on the beach that we could see on this speck of ground south of Isla de Ladrones, the Island of Thieves, and Isla del Coco, a shark infested island that is said to be the inspiration for Robert Louis Stevenson's *Treasure Island*.

The truth is we were lucky to have even found Montuosa navigating by dead reckoning. Despite all of my studying on how to navigate by sextant using the sun and moon, I couldn't get a line of position to come within a hundred miles of where we were. Later, during our stay in Roatán, I would learn how to use the sun and the stars, but we had a long way to go over open water before we got there.

Naturally, Ralph wanted to go ashore. I did not want to go ashore, but how do you explain that to a dog that is standing there wagging his tail and looking into your eyes. Maybe whoever was in that house with smoke coming from the chimney and no visible way of going to and from civilization was afraid of dogs. Maybe they would slit our throats, steal everything we had and sink the boat. Who would know? Not far from us was the island of Coiba, our next stop, where there was a real prison filled with Panamanian prisoners. Maybe these were escapees.

Launching the dinghy in the swell wasn't easy as *La Dulce* was moving up and down so much our fenders couldn't keep the little boat from banging our topsides. After casting off, as we got closer to the beach, the thundering surf threw us forward until we hit the sand and jumped out to pull *Dulcita* up from water's edge. I suspect very few feet have touched Montuosa – eight of ours did as the sun was setting. We saw not a soul that evening or the next morning. Whoever it was they kept to themselves.

On Coiba, a day's sail away, there was a fishing camp on the banks of a small, protected bay. "Panamá" means an abundance of fish. On our way from Montuosa we had two mahi-mahis on the line and brought in a nice wahoo. We even had a big marlin hit the lure and break water before the line parted.

We rested for a couple of days at Coiba, writing, fishing and walking on the beach as Ralph romped in the surf. On the third day, we set sail at sunrise for Punta Mala and the Gulfo de Panamá on our way to the Panamá Canal.

4/27/78

Sailed out from Mala into an east wind of over 25 knots. We tacked once and saw we were making no progress so we went out to escape the current. Rough and nasty night on a beat. Lost radar reflector and saw quite a few ships.

The radar reflector was a ball-shaped aluminum contraption that we tied high in the rigging. Its purpose was to make sure our boat would be visible to other ships on their radar. When it blew off and hit the water, it slowly sank into the same whitecaps that were coming over our bow, hitting us in the face as though someone was standing in front of us throwing buckets full of saltwater.

4/28/78

Tacked and headed for the Perlas Islands. Could only point up some 70-80 degrees but had a pretty day with a mild sea and breeze.

Tacked at dusk to go farther north. Sighted the light at Punta Bone and the many ships in a traffic pattern funneling toward the Canal de Panamá. Wind increased at dusk so we sort of loafed and beat with double reef and staysail.

Still vividly etched in my memory is the sight of twenty, maybe thirty freighters converging on the channel leading to the canal. They were getting in line in much the same way airplanes line up for takeoff.

Then the weather got worse.

4/29/78

Helen woke me up to ask what land was off our port because it didn't make any sense to her. I was shocked to see Punta Mala again. We had been carried back some 50 miles in eight hours unbelievable as it may seem.

We started again across the Gulf but this time, full-speed ahead. The day was nice and we talked and made love. A freighter passed our stern just afterwards so close we could hear its engines.

As usual the wind picked up at dusk and blew harder than ever. I reefed the main, changed genoa for jib, then put another reef in the main, before dropping the jib. We raced through the night under double reefed main and staysail.

A rough night with a lot of spray.

Personally, I have never witnessed two people doing it, but I'm fairly sure some sailors on the freighter that crossed our stern got an eyeful. With binoculars they would be looking down on our cockpit from the bridge. Coming up on us fast, we were just finishing when we heard their diesel engines. There wasn't time to rush down for clothes as they passed quickly and realistically there probably wasn't much they hadn't seen already – two tan naked bodies with red faces covering themselves as best they could with their hands.

The biggest threat to our well being, other than freighters, was not the waves crashing over the bow or the wind blowing at gale force, it was fatigue – especially for sailors without a good self-steering vane or autopilot. Two years later, after arriving in Key West, an "Aries" self-steering vane would be our first major purchase. But off the coast of Punta Mala, we had to take shifts, sleeping in turns or the sea would wear us down, potentially causing mistakes like the one I made the next day.

4/30/78

Helen took over and let me sleep from 12:00 to 3:00 am, so I took over to wait for dawn and let her sleep. As the sun came up, I could see the mountains of Colombia.

We caught a jack and a dorado of which we ate part and fed the rest to Ralph.

Coming up on the Perlas that evening, exhausted, I screwed up and misidentified an island. I mistakenly motored at full speed toward the wrong one. Luck and luck alone is why we didn't hit a rock or run aground before realizing my miscalculation. We had to use our spotlight to snuggle in close to land and the protection of a small inlet. With a feeling of sublime relief, we dropped anchor for the first time since Coiba.

A vintage pilot book we had been given described the waters off of Punta Mala as the most "vexatious" of passages for the sailing vessel. Amen.

5/1/78

Woke up sore and exhausted but alive and well. Took Ralph ashore, and we collected some shells and a small fern. Helen gave me a haircut and I cut my beard.

Motored over to Mafafa and were greeted by canoes. Went in town for ice and a cold beer – none – bought a bottle of gin, one of two that had been on the shelf for a long time ($5). Bought some fruit and eggs.

Motored over to another anchorage where we cooked dorado tempura and drank warm gin before going to bed still exhausted from the trip.

Technically, we should have cleared Customs before setting foot on Panamanian soil, but the Perlas Islands were so out of the way there weren't any government officials and no one cared. Mafafa was a tiny, extremely primitive village of straw huts, dirt streets and no automobiles. Alone in the anchorage, except for dugout canoes pulled up on the beach, we found one old Coca-Cola cooler that was run for a couple of hours each day. It contained only a few off-brand sodas. I don't know that I have ever felt more like a spectacle than I did there, walking around town with a big red Irish Setter among natives wearing only the basics, living in grass shacks in a town without ice.

We moved to another nearby anchorage because we were self-conscious. The warm gin was hard going down.

5/2/78

I woke up because I had to let out more scope and stand watch during the night.

We didn't leave until noon because it was raining, which gave me a chance to catch up on the journal. We did a lot of talking about the boatyard that we may someday set up.

We think we will go to Roatán and write the book on our experiences, then to Florida. There, we will fix up the boat and then, if feasible, begin our boatyard. The location is critical so we will have to search thoroughly. One of the U.S. islands would be good if we could find a spot.

Sailed at noon back to 1st anchorage and caught a mackerel on the way. We've never seen so many fish.

5/3/78
Woke up to another rainy day but decided to go regardless. Helen rowed Ralph in and began the day by capsizing the dinghy. After bailing it out and returning to the boat, we sailed out in a light shower into strong winds and motored until we had rounded the point against the current. Then we flew. We averaged 6 1/2 knots for 2 hours and must have been doing 7 1/2 knots – for sure 7.2 knots – for 2 hrs. Left at 8:30 and arrived 22 miles later at noon.

The anchorage at Pedro Gonzales is well protected and beautiful. We arrived at fiesta time and at least five canoes with large outboards came up and were scratching the topsides. There were another fifteen on the beach. Everyone was drinking and two came over to ask if they could <u>give</u> us (not sell us) some "ROJO" marijuana, which I felt compelled to refuse. Drugs are not something *you take through the canal. I hated to say, "No," as it was red as red could be.*

Spaghetti without meat, and read.

5/4/78

Had trouble deciding whether to go. After an hour we left with the wind to our backs. Had a good sail. Caught a mackerel, red snapper and a long needlefish.

We arrived at Contadora and are amazed at how fancy it is. Clark and Yvette, whom we met in Golfito, are here. We cleaned our fish and put them in Clark's refrigerator. Then we all went in for a beer at $1 each.

There is a small store on the island where we bought some long missed items – Cheez Wiz and crackers.

We returned to the boat for a while to rest and then came back for a going away party for Bill and Pam of Sunchaser. I played for a rowdy group that danced.

Contadora Island, fifty miles from Panamá City, was a big resort on a lush, hilly island that catered to the affluent. Heads of State often retreated there to contemplate the problems of the world. What we couldn't figure out when we went ashore was all of these weird-looking gringos wandering around – pale, long hair, chunky bodies, sloppy T-shirts "Norlin Island" written on the back. Everyone was speaking English. What was more confusing were all of the "NORLIN ISLAND" banners hanging from prominent balconies of the Hotel Contadora.

We soon found out that the resort was hosting a Gibson guitar convention aimed at music storeowners who had been flown in for the event. Norlin Enterprises, it turns out, was a South American conglomerate that had purchased Gibson and Epiphone guitars. When we wandered into one air conditioned convention room filled with guitars and musical products, no one seemed to know whether we were part of the convention or not, although we looked a lot healthier. I was handed a free cold Heineken, and by chance began to hear the amazing tales of Mudge Miller, head salesman. After he convinced me that Gibson was the greatest guitar ever made, I confessed that we were from one of the boats anchored nearby and that I didn't own a music store. Without missing a beat, he proceeded to tell us about his boating experiences. Whether anything he said was true or not, I have no way of knowing, but he sure had us laughing. Seems that he and his wife had received a windfall and purchased a yacht, which they felt would improve their lives and the image others had of them. Unfortunately, the reverse happened within the first week. Seeing "Head Cleaner" in the "head," he used it on his head when he showered – the hair eventually grew back.

So much of a story is in the telling and Mudge knew how to draw it out for maximum effect. Realizing that yachting wasn't for him or his wife, they sold the boat and soon after, as fate would have it, happened upon on a Rolls Royce. He couldn't pass it up in large part because they were going to drive to a family reunion out in West Texas.

Once there, inconspicuously sitting in the town's gossip café, he overheard two old farmers talking about the relative success of Mudge's family members. As for his brother Bill, they thought, by the looks of his brand new station wagon, he must be doing pretty well. Sheila, his sister, must be doing well, too, they agreed, what with her new Cadillac. Mudge could not wait to hear about himself and the Rolls Royce when one said to the other, "I don't know about Mudge though, driving around in that old Packard no matter how slick it is."

What we didn't know at the time was that Norlin Island was part of a corporate enterprise that was in the process of screwing up two legendary North American guitars that had been played by many, many great musicians. My first quality guitar, after learning on a Sears and Roebuck "Stella," was a Gibson ES-175, which I bought in 1958 and still have. Norlin's strategy to increase profit was to capitalize on the brand name, but reduce production costs. First, the company moved Gibson manufacturing from Kalamazoo, Michigan, to Nashville, Tennessee. Labor was cheaper there – and less skilled. Tragically, the production of Epiphone, another fine instrument, was moved from the States to Japan and turned into a low-end product.

5/5/78
It was a fun morning. We returned to the boat to read and nap. Helen went to sleep early. I finished Looking For Mr. Goodbar *and sat outside with Ralph for an hour.*

Sitting in the cockpit of the wonderful boat that we had built, as day turned to night and the many lights from the resort began reflecting off the water, a feeling of euphoria, that would repeat itself for years to come, brought tears to my eyes as Ralph, with my arm over his shoulder, sniffed the ocean breeze.

Contadora was quite a contrast compared to Mafafa, the little native village with one Coca-Cola cooler.

Tomorrow we would be heading for the canal and Panamá City.

5/7/78

We slept in and left Contadora an hour later than planned. Motored and sailed keeping up with Sirius *who is surprisingly fast. We got some good pictures of each other's boats under sail. They got me catching a fish and Clark caught a big dorado.*

8

THE PATH BETWEEN
THE SEAS

DAVID McCULLOUGH WROTE in the Preface to his monumental book, *The Path Between the Seas*:

> The creation of the Panamá Canal was far more than a vast, unprecedented feat of engineering.... Apart from wars, it represented the largest, most costly single effort ever before mounted anywhere on earth. It held the world's attention over a span of forty years. It affected the lives of tens of thousands of people at every level of society and of virtually every race and nationality. Great reputations were made and destroyed. For numbers of men and women, it was the adventure of a lifetime.
>
> Because of it one nation, France, was rocked to its foundations. Another, Colombia, lost its most prized possession, the Isthmus of Panamá. Nicaragua, on the verge of becoming a world crossroads, was left to wait for some future chance. The Republic of Panamá was born. [2]

For the French, whose earlier efforts to build the canal failed, the strategic importance of a passageway between the two great oceans was obvious. Having previously dredged the much longer Suez Canal linking the Mediterranean to the Red Sea and Indian Ocean, it seemed a logical and, more importantly, a profitable thing to do. It was less than 50 miles that they had to traverse. In 1855 a railroad had been completed across the Isthmus and financially it was a bonanza. Dividends for the Panamá Railroad Company, the world's first transcontinental railroad, were 15% on the average and went as high as 44%. A one-way ticket was $25 in gold. Fortunes had been made and even greater fortunes lay in store for anyone or any nation who could build the path between the Atlantic and Pacific Oceans.

Foremost among the reasons for their failure was a lack of engineering capabilities and a failure to appreciate the severity of the tropical diseases. True, the railroad was highly profitable. But what was blithely overlooked was the fact that the rail, 47 and 1/2 miles long, had taken five, not two years, to complete at a cost of eight million dollars, six times the original estimate. Thousands had died in the making and almost all the deaths were from cholera, dysentery, fever, smallpox, malaria and yellow fever for which there were no cures. The French and the rest of the civilized world believed that these diseases were caused by "noxious effluvium" – poisonous marsh gasses, hence the name malaria meaning "bad air."

---

[2] David McCullough, <u>The Path Between the Seas</u> (Simon & Schuster, 1977).

Piously, when the U.S. took over the project, the high death rate of the French was attributed to their decadence. Survival depended on one's moral fortitude. "Debauchery, sins of the flesh, moral or physical cowardice, were sure paths to ruin." Great credence was given to the testimony of those who saw mountains of wine and champagne bottles and who described the French years as a "genuine bacchanalian orgy." As it turned out, the U.S. would be no better as the circumstances did not lend themselves to virtue, nor did the sicknesses, in reality, distinguish between sinner and saint. One historian claimed that, "in all the world there is not, perhaps, now concentrated in any single spot so much swindling and villainy, so much foul disease, such hideous dung-heap of moral and physical abomination as in the scene of this far-framed undertaking of nineteenth-century engineering." "Everything which imagination can conceive that is ghastly and loathsome seems to gather into that locality. Gambling of every kind and every other form of wickedness were common day and night." The three most thriving collateral industries were gambling houses, brothels and coffin manufacturers. [3]

The lack of medical knowledge was the greatest enemy of progress, by far. During the construction of the canal, hospital bedposts were set in canisters of water to foil ants. These canisters were the perfect breeding place for mosquitoes, and being located in close proximity to the infirmed, they spread yellow fever, malaria and dengue

---

[3] David McCullough, The Path Between the Seas (Simon & Schuster, 1977), pp 145-147.

fever at an even more rapid rate inside than outside the confines of the health care facilities. The sad truth was that as early as 1881 a few men of medicine had figured out that the mosquito was the culprit, yet the medical establishment laughed at them. It was common knowledge that "bad air" and lapses in virtue were the true culprits.

About a year after we arrived in Key West, Helen and I both came down with malaria that we may have contracted in Panamá as it can remain dormant for years. First, I had the worst fever I have ever experienced. In 80-degree weather, I was shivering in bed, covered with blankets. I shook uncontrollably for hours and couldn't go to work singing at Two Friends, a bar on Front Street. The next day, a little beat up, I figured I was well enough and performed that night. The day after, the fever hit me again. With malaria, every 48 hours little crescent-shaped organisms in your blood go ballistic for about six hours causing the fever.

I thought I was going to die in the doctor's waiting room. He wanted to do tests. When I mentioned that people on the dock thought I had malaria, he couldn't believe it. This went on for a week – high fever, couldn't work; no fever, could work. My boss thought I was nuts coming in every other day until the doctor finally gave me the quinine pills, and I was immediately well. When Helen started getting the same symptoms, we knew right away, and she was prescribed pills that same day.

Before we could go to the Balboa Yacht Club at the canal entrance in the American Zone, we were required to anchor not far from thirty-three freighters also waiting. There, we were boarded and "admeasured" by canal authorities who measured the depth of our bilge, and the length and width of our waterline to determine, from a complicated formula, our tonnage so they could calculate what we would be charged for the passage. Unable to proceed to the Balboa Yacht Club until Monday because Customs was closed, with our stores depleted, we had to settle for what food and drink we had onboard, which wasn't much. Just before dark Bob and Brenda, whom we had met in Costa Rica and worked within the Zone, picked up our spirits considerably when they came by in a sailboat and dropped off cold beers. We had contacted them from Contadora, so they knew when we would be arriving and where we would be anchored.

While we marveled at what we were about to witness and experience, Ralph was perplexed. There was a strictly enforced rule forbidding pets from going to shore, and there wasn't anything we could do about it during daylight. He could see the shore and wanted us to put the damn dinghy in the water and row him over there. He was even more upset after we made our way to a mooring buoy, cleared Customs, blew our horn for a launch and left to go ashore without him. He was one happy dog when I snuck him in after dark in our dinghy.

Helen's parents, who were dying to go through the canal with us, landed in Panamá the very day we arrived at the Balboa Yacht Club. The canal was very much in the news those days, and they badly wanted to experience it first hand while it still belonged to the United States. The imminent transfer of ownership to Panamá was not sitting well with many Americans, including Helen Sr. and Henry Andrae, devout Republicans. After all, hadn't we built it and run it like clockwork since 1914? We got to explore this subject and others more than I ever imagined as H & H decided to save money by staying with us on our boat rather than rent a hotel room.

PANAMA CANAL TREATY OF 1977 (summary)
President Jimmy Carter and Panamanian Chief of Government, Omer Torrijos, signed the Panamá Canal Treaty and Neutrality Treaty on September 7, 1977. The agreement relinquishes American control over the canal by the year 2000 and guarantees its neutrality. On May 4, 1904, Panamá granted the United States the right to build and operate the canal and control the five miles of land on either side of the water passage in exchange for annual payments.

My ideological problem was that if Henry and Helen were against the transfer, then I had to be for it even though I wasn't sure. When we were with "Zonies" Bob and Brenda, I was against it. In his early 20's, he worked on one of the big tugs used to maneuver large ships. She taught in the Zone's English speaking school. Both had been born and raised there as had generations before them.

The rationale behind the 1977 transfer was to help stabilize a region that was becoming increasingly unfriendly to "patriarchal" U.S. The Panamanians were tired of being a "Banana Republic," where the real power was held by foreigners. In their eyes, we had overstayed our welcome.

Helen and I, without the benefit of daily newspapers, magazines and world opinion, had little sense of where Central America as a whole was headed politically. Based on what took place not long after we left, we were like the very nearsighted cartoon character, Mr. Magoo, who through blind luck, oblivious to the dangers around him, confidently marches on. We were aware of shadowy "covert operatives," but had not a clue how close real political and militaristic upheaval was following behind us as we slowly worked our way toward Honduras and the Bay Islands. It wouldn't be long before the entire region would be affected by the Nicaraguan Sandinista-Contra Cold War battles that pitted American financed rebels against socialistic movements.

Fortunately, the people in Central America didn't take out their general aggravation with North America on us personally. Though we were living onboard a fancy varnished yacht with what must be an expensive dog, we spoke Spanish and our attire had years earlier become Central Americanized.

On Monday, May 8th, I went to the Port Captain's office and paid $85 to transit the canal and was penciled in for early Wednesday.

5/9/78 Tuesday

Helen Sr. and Henry went downtown and bought over $200 in groceries while I fueled and filled water tanks. I went to Customs and got the crew list squared away.

About 4:00 I found my impeller was bad when I belatedly checked the motor. Helen and I rushed to the

*Volvo place, which had one. Easy repair but lucky I
caught it beforehand.*

The rubber impeller is what spins and pulls the sea
water through the manifold keeping the engine cool.
Overheating in the canal would have been a nightmare,
especially without a spare.

Clark and Yvette on *Sirius,* in addition to having
enough canned goods to last them a lifetime, had well-
organized boxes of tools and spare parts, including fuses,
impellers and diesel engine injectors. They had a wind
vane to steer them and electronics to help them navigate.
Years had gone into the planning of their trip from Texas
through the canal to Costa Rica and then back again. We,
on the other hand, were so low on money, we were unable
to buy many spare parts, and all that we had in the
cupboard was our usual – rice, tomato sauce, spaghetti
and Maggi soup. Relying on the food we bought along the
way, *La Dulce Mujer* always sat high on her water lines.

For most private boats, going through the canal is an
all day affair and a grand twice in a lifetime experience.
Since it takes a minimum of six people to make the transit
– a canal "advisor," the captain and four people to handle
lines – our friends would help us and then, a day later, we
would take the train back to Panamá City and help them
make their transit. Unwritten etiquette dictates that the
host boat bring along plenty of food and drink. Thanks to
Helen Sr. and Henry, experts in that field, we were ready.

5/10/78

We went through the canal! Yesterday our schedule was confirmed and at 7:00 am, Alfred, the advisor, boarded. Clark, Yvette, Matilda, Bob and Brenda arrived earlier. We left relatively soon after for the 1st lock with controlled fear.

I was at the helm.

We motored for about an hour up the channel while two freighters passed us. The lines were coiled – two for'd, two aft. A large loop was made on the ends that would go to the line handlers on shore.

The locks at Miraflores were our first.

We eased into the 1st lock behind a Mobil tanker and the handlers heaved monkey fists to us. They hauled up the lines and put the loops over the bits. Clark and Bob worked the foredeck. Yvette and Helen the aft. The water boiled into the lock but not as bad as expected. The real thriller was when the freighter in front of us started its propeller.

In addition to the advisor that instructed us throughout the trip, there was a line handler on each side of the lock who would throw us a "monkey fist," a baseball sized ball at the end of light line. We would tie the monkey fist to our more substantial line so the handlers on shore could pull it up to industrial sized cleats on either side of the lock. When the water came rushing into the lock, and we began rising, we had to take up the slack to keep us centered. The size of the locks, and the forces that were put into play are truly extraordinary – thousands of gallons rush in from both sides. Looking up at the mammoth black hull of the cargo ship positioned in front of us with lifeboats as big as *La Dulce*, we were but a speck. The tanker wasn't full, so it was sitting high enough in the water that we could see the top of its gigantic bronze propeller that was wider than we were. Ships look big in the ocean but they are enormous when viewed from about forty feet astern.

After the lock had filled and the doors opened, the ship's prop began thrashing, blasting tons of bubbling white water backwards at us as it slowly moved forward to the next lock. The prop wash was much worse than the water filling the lock. We stayed tied to the lock as we danced around in the turmoil until it settled down. The linesmen on the sides of the lock then threw us our lines, and we motored up behind the Mobil tanker for the second trip up.

The second lock went the same as the first, but in the third lock we were rafted up to Fantasia. *The prop wash was bad but no lines parted.*

This was not the way we wanted to go through the Pedro Miguel Locks. *Fantasia* was a tugboat weighing perhaps 100 tons compared to our ten. Our cleats had to be strong enough to handle the weight of both vessels.

Then came the long motor to the other locks at Gatun. The asbestos wrapping on the exhaust scared me, but it was nothing but a little unpleasant odor-wise. I slowed down the RPM from 1600 to 1400 and it stopped.

After the locks at Pedro Miguel, we came to Culebra Cut (now Gillard Cut), the nine-mile channel dug through the mountains at the Continental Divide. This excavation bedeviled and threatened completion because the sides kept caving in and filling it up with dirt. The French initially thought 19 million cubic yards would have to be excavated. Eventually, it took 96 million cubic yards and hundreds of lives. More dirt was removed from Culebra than the French estimated it would take to build an entire sea level canal.

After passing through Gillard Cut, we motored through Lake Gatun, the man-made lake in between the seas that allows ships that have been lifted up by the locks at one end to cross to the other side. Replenished by rainwater and surrounded by jungle that had been left untouched to discourage attacks, we made our way to the locks at the other end that would lower us down to sea level. Out came the food and beer as we marveled at the scenery. Was the weather and environment that oppressive to us? Absolutely not. The climate was not noticeably different from Puntarenas. We had ice. We had insect repellant. We had electricity. We knew the cure for yellow fever and malaria.

Went the short cut and waited on a buoy for down locking. We go first on these, and they are a piece of cake. As we left the last lock, we entered a windy Caribbean Sea for the Panamá Yacht Club in Cristóbal. Luckily, Customs screwed up and we got in, rather than having to anchor out in the flats overnight. Had filet for dinner.

Once we were tied up to the dock our crew was able to take the train back home instead of spending the night on board. Plus, we could easily sneak Ralph on shore, much to his relief. We knew we were fudging protocol, but we had become major league Central American bullshit artists, claiming ignorance convincingly.

A day later, Henry and I caught the train back across the Isthmus and were mates for *Sirius* on their passage – a boat ride where I could sit back and enjoy, taking in the sights much more at ease.

9

THE SAN BLAS

HELEN SR. AND HENRY still with us after passing from one great ocean to another, our next adventure was going to be sailing to the San Blas Islands where they would catch a flight out – the first of several connections to get back home. One major consideration with guests is that they have limited time – thank goodness, since H & H were sleeping in our bed – so it was imperative to do as much touring as was humanly possible during the visit. This is the reason we took off for the San Blas Islands on a day we normally would have stayed in port.

5/14/77
We got off on a gray, windy day around 10:00 and motored through the breakwater opening. It was rough and nasty. We had to motor to windward with staysail and double reefed main. Our main mast supports show signs of fatigue so we will have to keep an eye on them.

We arrived at Porto Bello around 3:00 with two blue fin tuna and a barracuda. Henry instructed us, and we managed, with his expertise, to make a good milk chowder.

That evening Helen and I rowed Ralph to shore and walked through the fort now in ruins. I need to know more about its history.

After getting banged around in the rain for five hours, we motored into the protected bay at Porto Bello in a light drizzle with gray skies accentuating the overwhelming tropical, deep-green jungle vegetation. The surface of the bay was covered with small green leaves that parted as we slowly made our way through the dark water underneath. Tossing the lead line, we snuggled up as close to the old fort as we could. Comfortable and calm after rough seas, alone in the anchorage, we saw no people or houses.

Our clearest historical picture of Panamá and Porto Bello was drawn from an extraordinary collection of *Fiction, Fact & Fancy concerning the Buccaneers & Marooners of the Spanish Main: From the Writing & Pictures of Howard Pyle*. Published in 1903, it had been a Christmas gift to Helen Sr. from her father in 1925, which she graciously passed on to us. From Chapter I:

> Just above the northwestern shore of the old island of Hispaniola – the Santo Domingo of our day – and separated from it only by a narrow channel of some five or six miles in width, lies a queer little hunch of an island, known, because of a distant resemblance to that animal, as the Tortuga de Mar, or sea turtle. It is not more than twenty miles in length by perhaps seven or eight in breadth; it is only a little spot of land, and as you look upon the map a pin's head would almost cover it; yet from that spot, as from a center of inflammation, a burning fire of human

wickedness and ruthlessness and lust overran the world, and spread terror and death throughout the Spanish West Indies, from St. Augustine to the island of Trinidad, and from Panamá to the coasts of Peru.

The original *boucaniers* were native inhabitants who had developed a method of preserving meat by roasting it on a barbecue and curing it with smoke. Their fire pit and grating were called *boucan* and the finished strips of meat were also known as *boucan*. In time, this motley collection of international refugees, escaped slaves, transported criminals and indentured servants who roamed along the coasts of the islands became known as buccaneers (bacon eaters) and the term came to describe an unscrupulous adventurer.

In the shallows of Porto Bello, where the beach slopes into the bay were hundreds of pieces of terra cotta tiles smoothed by the sand and wave action. I keep a small piece on my desk with the almost certain knowledge that it had been underfoot or at least in close proximity to the vile pirate, Morgan. We would learn a lot more about him after sailing to Providencia, Colombia, the staging ground for Morgan's 1668 raid on both Porto Bello and Panamá. Except for the lack of human beings, the harbor was much the same as it was when found by Christopher Columbus on November 2, 1502, 475 years before us. It was officially named "Puerto Bello," or beautiful port, by Diego de Nicuesas in 1509 when he sailed here and lost a few of his men – killed by natives.

As Helen and I walked through the remains of the fortifications scattered beneath our bare feet on that overcast afternoon, there was a sense of what had taken place – it stirred the imagination, as ruins tend to do.

5/15/78
Making two trips, we all rowed in early to look at the tile lying around on the beach. Pulled the anchor around 10:00. It has been a long week. H & H need constant attention. If one needs a nap, the other takes over – long visit.

We looked for a few anchorages before going on up to Isla Grande. Three hours of rough weather. Glad it was a short trip.

5/16/78
Off again early for the San Blas Islands. The weather was awful with rain, heavy seas and wind the entire time. Our worst weather in a while.

Arrived at Provenir about 5:00.

5/17/78
Henry was up at 5:00 this morning saying that the Kuna Indians were coming. Later, Helen took Ralph to shore and cleared us in. The check-in fee was $3.00.

We had entered a time warp.

The Kunas are a Native American tribe that moved to the islands from the mainland in the mid-1800s, and they are the most primitive tribe in existence in Centroamérica to this day. Women wear gold rings in their nose and colorful hand sewn mola blouses for which they have become famous. Before the Spanish invasion, both men and women went mostly naked. The men covered themselves with dye while the women covered themselves with intricate body paint. Eventually, the tribe was confronted, as were all of the indigenous people in New Spain, by Christian missionaries who told them that the Lord Jesus and the Virgin Mary didn't like nudity and that it was sinful to go about their daily lives without any clothes on. With thread, needles, scissors and fabric imported from Europe, trying to please the missionaries, the women began making clothing that resembled the colorful body paint they had formerly worn. These "molas," became a staple of Kuna trade and a source of revenue allowing them to buy outboard motors for their dugout wood canoes called "ulus" (the "u" is pronounced like it is in t<u>u</u>be).

Even though the San Blas Islands are technically part of Panamá, they remain autonomous to the point that we had to clear Customs with the Kuna authorities when we arrived. Fiercely fighting off conquering forces for hundreds of years, they have retained their sovereignty.

5/18/78
We got Helen Sr. and Henry to shore for some breakfast, then to their plane. In a matter of minutes they were gone. It was a good but long visit.

We soon learned that after marriage the Kuna groom is required to move in with and contribute to the bride's family, a cultural custom that I might have had a hard time with.

One of the oddities of sailing is that the line used to tie a dinghy to a dock or another boat is called a "painter," and it is secured to the small boat by a "painter ring." Our painter and painter ring were fine, but when visiting another boat, I made the mistake of letting someone other than me tie off the painter. Helen and I had been cross with each other, so I went alone to *Convivial* to see if they had a bottle of rum they would sell. They didn't but offered me a drink so I climbed onboard. After a few I excused myself and was going to row back to *La Dulce*, but our wonderful, tough dinghy that Helen had built in our yard in Santa Ana, had floated away along with our hand carved mahogany oars. It was a terrible loss as we depended on it daily. The only back up we had was an inflatable Avon that doubled as our life raft. It rowed horribly. Our only hope was that with the wind blowing onshore, it should have floated toward land as opposed to drifting out to sea.

We were both upset, especially me, but sometimes negative things turn out to be positives. Dealing with unexpected situations like this took us down some paths we otherwise would have missed.

5/21/78
Helen and I took our boat out looking. We first went to Carti and thought a man was saying he had it. He came on board but apparently we did not understand. He piloted us in and we went looking without any luck.

We asked everyone. Going from island to island, we asked for help in finding it. We returned depressed.

We spent a rough night.

The next morning we discussed our situation and decided that I should take the plane to Panamá City and buy materials to make another dinghy as we couldn't get along with the rubber one. It was almost impossible to row into the wind. But just as I was about get into the small plane, we got news from Mauricio that our ulu had been found and that he would take us to it the following day.

5/23/78

Mauricio arrived 7:00 and we took off for Soledad Mandango, an island not on the chart. First, we took Mauricio's friend to another island where we eased up to their small dock. He disembarked with the help of the entire male population.

About two miles over on another island was our ulu. The village was neat and clean with all women in traditional garb or bare breasted. It was raining so we went into one of the huts to negotiate. Twenty dollars for the dinghy with a mola thrown in.

We had been to the nude beaches of California, but we had never been to a regular village where people went about their daily lives with their breasts exposed without hoopla. For Soledad Mandango with a population of about thirty-five, our arrival was obviously a big event. Unlike Porvenir and the two nearby islands, these people had little contact with outside visitors. Later, when reliving the moment, we could only imagine what had gone on in the town meeting that surely preceded our arrival. It must have been serious as they had to decide how much to ransom the boat for.

"But, look," I reasoned, "If you had lost your ulu, and I found it, I would gladly return it to you without charge." The problem with my logic, the head negotiator pointed out, was that they hadn't lost their ulu. I had. They all smiled and nodded in agreement – men and women – everyone, young and old – Kunas one; Harrisons zero.

"Okay, $20, but would you add some molas into the bargain?"

Spanish was the common language we were using, but we couldn't understand their native dialect, meaning they could consult with each other during the negotiations. Still, it was fairly obvious that one side was against any compromise, and the other compassionate side was saying, "What the heck, throw in one of little value." The compassionate side won. I gave them a twenty-dollar bill, and they gave us a so-so mola. Our ulu, which was sitting off the ground, had been thoroughly cleaned, oarlocks in place with the oars neatly laid across the seats. It was ours once again.

Everyone was happy as the nearly naked townsfolk all waved to us from the shore. We two gringos and Mauricio, who had stayed clear of the haggling, rowed back to *La Dulce Mujer* and Ralph, who was anxiously awaiting our return and the return of his ulu, *Dulcita*. Sometimes dinghies are named, usually they're not, but one of the best was the tender for *Viento*, or wind. Their ulu was *Pedo*, or fart.

We returned, and I took Mauricio over to the Hotel Anai, both of us in foul weather gear – bought him a beer and gave him a finder's fee.

For us, one of the great mysteries of the Kuna Indians was what they did with their money. Anchored in between Porvenir and a Cay with a small hotel, we had a good view of the comings and goings. It was obvious that the outboard-powered ulus went to more remote Cays to buy molas that they would sell to tourists who rarely ventured far from Porvenir, the main island. Weekends were the busiest, selling a lot of them for cash money – no traveler's checks, and no credit cards. But come Monday, you couldn't get change for a $20 bill. There were no banks nearby. No way would they trust a Panamá or Colón bank.

Helen and I speculated that maybe they somehow converted the money into gold and hoarded it. The women do wear gold rings in their noses so gold would be the logical valuable to change the greenbacks into. The Kunas, also known as Cunas, don't spend much – outboard motors and gas seemed to be the big-ticket items. Food is primarily from the ocean, and they make their own liquor, which they are required to get drunk on during the celebration of a woman's first menstrual cycle and weddings.

All ceremonies are super secret and strictly off limits to outsiders. A flag is flown to alert people that they should stay away until further notice.

With our dinghy back in its davits, we sailed to various unpopulated San Blas islands of which there are supposedly 365 or more, generally taking it easy, catching fish and eating conch. When cleaning conch, there is a tough slime we had to scrub off our hands with sand, but man did they taste good cooked in a chowder or raw with lime juice.

After three weeks, we felt it was time to go back to Cristobál and Colón to prepare for our trip north to Providencia, a stopping off point on our way to Roatán, Honduras. Still trying to figure out the damn sextant, we guessed we were ready to make our first real trip where I would have to navigate. It would have been hard to get lost in the waters we had been sailing in up to this point, but that was about to change. No matter how much I read, the sextant continued to befuddle me. On our Zonie friend's advice, we bought a used Radio Direction Finder (RDF). Not very exact, but by homing in on one of the "omni" stations used by aircraft, it would be better than nothing.

10

PROVIDENCIA

HOWARD PYLE'S PHENOMENAL BOOK begins with the following observation:

> Why is it that a little spice of deviltry lends not an unpleasant titillating twang to the great mass of respectable flour that goes to make up the pudding of our modern civilization? And pertinent to this question another – Why is it that the pirate has had, a certain lurid glamour of the heroical enveloping him round about? Is there, deep under the accumulated debris of culture, a hidden groundwork of the old time savage? Is there even in these well-regulated times an unsubdued nature in the respectable mental household of every one of us that still kicks against the pricks of law and order? To make my meaning more clear, would not every boy, for instance – that is every boy of any account – rather be a pirate captain than a Member of Parliament?

Our last taste of Panamá was the bar at the Canal Zone Panamá Yacht Club adjacent to the City of Colón. So harried were our preparations that on the day we wanted to leave, we were simply too tired. All we could do was rest, buy some last minute groceries, top off water, add a last bag of ice and have a few at the Yacht Club horseshoe bar. It was open 24 hours a day. The drinks were cheap, the barstools comfortable and the air conditioning freezing.

The next morning we left Panamá, making good headway until nightfall when rain, thunder and lightning hit us hard. After my watch, from the shelter of the cabin, I could see Helen at the helm silhouetted intermittently by bolts of lightning accompanied by crashing thunder as *La Dulce* knifed her way north in the middle of a sloppy, hostile ocean. We had the right amount of sail up as I had put in two reefs and taken down the jib leaving the staysail as our only headsail. We were moving along at a good clip, salt water pouring over the deck then running to the scuppers where it drained back into the sea. Helen was quite a sight, with her yellow foul weather jacket, hair plastered against her head from the driving rain, wearing her safety harness. Though I didn't want to leave her, I had to catch a little sleep and be ready for my watch.

Our position and progress were confirmed when, off our port side, we saw the glow of San Andreas' city lights, an island not too far south of Providencia.

Just before dawn, the rain let up and that's when I began to notice a westward drift, which made us keep pointing up more and more into the wind until we finally sighted the mountains of Providencia jutting out of the sea and turned on the motor. It was the RDF that let us know how fast an unexpected current was carrying us to the west. Had we been carried west to the treacherous, sparsely populated Mosquito Coast along the eastern part of Nicaragua, we could have been sucked up by the shallow waters and shifting sand that could swallow a grounded boat and her crew. Having struggled too long with both the mechanics of taking an astrological sight and the math to turn it into a line of position, I knew it really was time to figure out how to use the perplexing sextant.

But we didn't die on the Mosquito Coast. We eventually came upon the lee of Providencia and the tricky narrow entrance through the coral reef that led us into a protected bay that the real buccaneer, Captain Morgan, knew well. Entering the harbor, we slowly approached the mouth, making our way just as they had in the early 1500s – by reading the color of the water and using our lead line (with one not so small advantage – a motor). Without one, because the prevailing wind is from the east and is blocked by the mountains, early sailors probably had to put two longboats with oarsmen in the water. If they were unable to tow the larger boat, one would have been used to keep the ship from drifting onto the reef while the other carried an anchor as far forward as they could. The men on the windless would then pull the ship up to the anchor and the process would be repeated until it was dropped for the final time in the relative safety of the harbor. Sparsely populated, it would have been perfect for buccaneers. A lookout on top of the cliffs could easily see any approaching ships by day, giving ample warning time to prepare to defend themselves with cannon they had placed high on a bluff. At night, entry through the reef would have been impossible. Close by the cannon was "Morgan Head," a natural rock formation that bore an eerie resemblance to a human head that was said to be that of Captain Morgan himself. It was from the safety of Providencia, where we were anchored, that he set off on his boldest adventure.

And now it was determined that the plunder harvest was ripe at Porto Bello, and the city's doom was sealed. The town was defended by two strong castles thoroughly manned, and officered by as gallant a soldier as ever carried Toledo steel at his side. But strong castles and gallant soldiers weighed not a barleycorn with the buccaneers when their blood was stirred by the lust of gold.

Located only 250 miles south-south east of Providencia, with a strong prevailing easterly trade wind, it was a broad reach that could be made easily in two or three days.

Landing at Puerto Naso, a town some ten leagues westward of Porto Bello, they marched to the latter town, and coming before the castle, boldly demanded its surrender. It was refused, whereupon Morgan threatened that no quarter should be given.

The castle was attacked and, after a bitter struggle was captured. Morgan was good as his word: every man in the castle was shut in the guard room, the match was set to the powder magazine, and soldiers, castle and all were blown into the air, while through all the smoke and the dust the buccaneers poured into the town.

From our cockpit, the cannon overlooking the Providencia harbor were still visible on the cliffs above the port that was now occupied by a small flotilla of two sailboats and four sailors – Paul and Marilyn (on *Phoebe*) and Helen and I. We would soon be joined by a third when Clark and Yvette arrived on *Sirius*. Our first time ashore, seated at a two-table cantina in the small town, feeling bold ourselves, we drank to those who had gone before us.

6/18/78

Helen took Ralph in while I read some Path Between the Seas. *As she rowed back she yelled to me that a sailboat was coming. Clark and Yvette with Matilda. We rowed over to greet them. After the hook was down, Alberto, the port captain, said they could go ashore or to our boats and could check in later.*

We all went to Fresh Water Bay where we had beer, sausage and crackers.

Then, we went back to Phoebe. *I played and we all had a good evening.*

There was one paved road around the island where infrequent pick-up trucks, with wood benches along each side of the bed, served as public transportation. If the truck didn't come, you just walked in the middle of the road, which is what we did for a couple of miles to an unpainted wood house with tables outside. Between the house and the beach facing the reef, the water was every shade of indigo one could imagine. The black women proprietors cooked some spicy conch that, along with their hospitality, was special, at least to us who had arrived the same way Buccaneer Captain Henry Morgan had – through rain and lightning.

> But let's just say you get there
> To some island off somewhere
> Cold beer and life taste amazingly good
> You took your chances, this time you sailed and won
> Feel pretty good about yourself and proved that you're
> still young.

> - "Short On Underwear" by Ben Harrison

6/20/78

We got up to a nasty day. I went early with Clark to get fuel after being up much of the night watching the weather. It was wet and neither of us was in a great mood, but I loaded 20 gal. and Clark 12 gal.

I got some new radio beacon numbers from Paul.

In the afternoon we all headed in for Fresh Water Bay and the barbeque chicken. I played hoarsely to a loud group but all seemed to enjoy it. Alma and husband requested an old country song: "Tell the man to turn the juke box way down low, and you can tell your friend there with you he'll have to go."

Sang on truck back home – all dinghies O.K.

Read about Capt. Morgan's even more outrageous plunder of Panamá.

And now Captain Morgan determined to undertake another venture, the likes of which had never been equaled in all of the annals of buccaneering. This was nothing less than the descent upon and the capture of Panamá, which was, next to Cartagena, perhaps, the most powerful and the most strongly fortified city in the West Indies.

From Old Providence, once again he sailed south. After the capture of the Castle of Chagres at the mouth of the river with the same name that feeds Lake Gatun and the Panamá Canal, they canoed as far up river as they could, and then:

Ten days they struggled through this bitter privation, doggedly forging their way onward, faint with hunger and haggard with weakness and fever. Then, from the high hill and over the tops of forest trees, they saw the steeples of Panamá, and nothing remained between them and their goal but the fighting of four Spaniards to every one of them – a simple thing which they had done over and over again.

Down they poured on Panamá, and out came the Spaniards to meet them; four hundred horses, two thousand five hundred foot soldiers, and two thousand wild bulls which had been herded together to be driven over the buccaneers so that their ranks might be disordered and broken. The buccaneers were only eight hundred strong ... but in the space of two hours the Spaniards were flying madly over the plain, minus six hundred who lie dead or dying behind them.

Then they marched toward the city. Three hours more of fighting and they were in the streets, howling, yelling, plundering, gorging, dram-drinking, and giving full vent to all of the vile and nameless lusts that burned in their hearts like a hell of fire.

For three weeks Morgan and his men abode in this dreadful place; and they marched away with one hundred and seventy-five beasts of burden loaded with treasures of gold and silver and jewels, besides great quantities of merchandise, and six hundred prisoners held for ransom.

Whatever became of all that vast wealth, and what it amounted to, no man but Morgan ever knew, for when division was made it was found that there was only two hundred pieces of eight to each man.

For Helen and me just being in Providencia and interacting with the offspring of former slaves and pirates and combinations of the two, was mystical. Except for a few trucks and diesel-powered generators, it was almost the same as it was in 1670. Adding to our good fortune and the good time we were having, we happened to be there for the annual carnival, which takes place the last week of June.

Here comes the carnival

The carnival is wonderful
Palm trees on old pick-up trucks
No one falls out
It's mostly luck
Here comes the queen
She's dressed in white
Her dark skin shines
Reflects the night
Here comes the carnival
The carnival is wonderful

- "Here Comes The Carnival" by Ben Harrison

It was a wonderful farewell.

We, along with the other two boats took off the next morning for Swan Island, not far from the Bay Islands.

I was still struggling with the sextant. The sights I took from the anchorage at Provedencia, even though we were in calm water and knew our position, were not even close. I had to be doing something fundamentally wrong as they were not even in the same ocean. Though we could make the trip with dead reckoning and the RDF, we sure did like the idea of safety in numbers with seasoned sailors who actually could navigate by the sun and stars.

6/25/78

Alberto piloted us out and brought over a walkie-talkie from Clark so we could stay in touch.

With all three boats in communication, Phoebe *had to motor a bit to keep up but amazingly we all stayed close to each other, especially* Sirius *and us.*

We took sights and conferred on our position in this rather dangerous passage. We passed Quito Sueño in the late evening avoiding Punta Gorda.

My sights, though improving somewhat, were still not very close to our actual position according to Clark and Paul's sights – a fact I kept to myself. Even so, I was learning that the biggest problem with using only the sun and moon is that you don't get intersecting lines of position. Eventually, using three heavenly bodies accompanied by a little luck from the mathematical Gods, we could get three lines of position, forming a triangle that the boat theoretically should be inside.

Just to make the math more difficult, a calculator couldn't be used as we were dealing with 360 degrees that each had 60 minutes and 60 seconds. It wouldn't be long before special calculators were made for navigation, but they were short lived as the GPS became affordable. As hard as I'd been studying and trying to work through the computations, the biggest culprit turned out to be the forms I was using. They were overly complicated by trying to fit all types of sights onto one worksheet. The spiral book that finally let me in the door had a series of forms – one for sun sights, another for noon sights, along with separate forms for star, planet and moon sights. Each form had only the calculations necessary for that heavenly body. From darkness to light, suddenly it began to make sense.

With the sextant as our main navigation device, the only technological advance we had over the early explorers was accurate time, which is crucial. We were able to receive Greenwich Mean Time (GMT) over our Zenith

Transoceanic radio. Before Marconi and the wireless, navigators had to depend on a mechanical chronometer, one of their most precious and essential devices. What the sextant does is measure the angle of a heavenly body from the horizon at a specific moment in time.

This is especially important as you only have a short time between civil and nautical twilight when the star and the horizon are both visible. At first you need a star-finder to figure out which one's what. Once you know the heavens better, this isn't as complicated as it sounds. Betelguese, or Beetlejuice as we called it, the brightest star in the easily identifiable constellation Orion, was one of our favorites as was the planet, Jupiter, which was usually the first celestial body to become visible as darkness set in.

This is when the actual sight is taken. When we were ready, we would start a stopwatch at the top of the minute. When the star is brought down by the sextant's mirrors, the very moment it kisses the horizon, the person taking the sight says "mark," and the watch is stopped. Now you know the hour, minutes and seconds the sight was taken. The function of the sextant is to measure the angle at that very moment.

The Nautical Almanac gives the body's data for each hour of every day, with extra pages where you can find minutes and seconds. With the Local Hour Angle (found by correcting the body's Greenwich Hour Angle from the Almanac for your assumed longitude), your assumed latitude and the body's declination (from the Almanac), you can find the height of the body if you are where you assumed yourself to be. With Sight Reduction Tables, which are large bound books filled with numbers that require interpolation, the navigator can find the calculated altitude. Comparing the observed altitude with the calculated altitude from the tables the navigator can decide whether you are closer or further away from the calculated altitude. From this you plot a line of position (LOP). Lastly, be sure to add in the feet the sextant is from the ocean at the time of the sight.

True, once you get the hang of it many of the steps are automatic using a worksheet – the devil is getting the hang of it, and even when you do, the sight has to be taken while the boat and the navigator are battling the elements. It's not easy – Amelia Earhart's navigator had to rely on a sextant to determine their position as they flew over the Pacific Ocean. The altimeters of the day, relying on barometric pressure, were not very accurate and the sight had to be taken from a vibrating piston driven airplane.

11

SWAN SONG

6/26/78

Nighttime went well. We had rice and bluefin tuna for dinner snacking throughout the night. The other boats self-steered beautifully with their Aries wind vanes, while we had to stay at the helm continuously. Needless to say we were jealous.

Helen and I were going to go straight for Roatán, but Clark talked us into coming to Swan Island as Roatán meant another night out.

THE ONLY THING ON SWAN ISLAND was a now defunct U.S. weather station. Every vessel within hundreds of miles turned on their radios for the daily 1:05 pm report, which was the only way to get a marine forecast in English. Without it, we and countless others would have been as clueless as Columbus. Our boxy, bulky Zenith Transoceanic with nine D-cell batteries, a great radio, picked it up loud and clear. We would later learn that it could too be used as an RDF.

The weathermen stationed at this lonely outpost generously invited us to celebrate the July 4th, Independence Day, with them. On our first day there, a lobster boat from Guanaja, the easternmost of the Bay

Islands, gave us buckets full of lobster antenna. Though hard on the hands, they tasted just as good as the tail.

7/2/78
I did the dishes, then Helen and I worked on navigation. Things weren't coming out right so I quit around 4:00 pm disgusted.

Went in and got some shrimp from Spencer who has a few shrimpers in addition to his cattle and job as engineer at the weather station.

7/4/78 4th of July
We went in around 10:30 am for the big baseball game. Helen and I were on opposite teams and had a great time.

Hamburgers and beer all afternoon and dancing in the evening to Saturday Night Fever *by the Bee Gees.*

Spencer killed a cow the next morning on the cement pier – skinned and butchered it as it hung from a hook. Later that evening Tony almost drowned.

7/5/78
We put off leaving for another day as Paul showed signs of changing plans. We joined the July 4th clean up party, which was as good as the real party. We ate steak and shrimp and later drove around the island.

Later, folks wanted me to play the guitar so Tony, the chief, drove me in a truck to the anchorage. Together we rowed to the boat where he proceeded to fall in the water and swamp the dinghy. After an attempt at hauling him up in the boswain chair, he told me he feared a heart attack. He could barely hold on to the bumpers. I gave him a life jacket to hold and swam him into the beach in the old life saving carry. Scared me and him.

Scared is an understatement. He was overweight, but not outright fat. Still, I thought he could climb from the dinghy to *La Dulce*. When he couldn't and fell in, we were both thrashing around trying to keep his head above water. That's when he told me he couldn't swim. The beach wasn't far away and salt water is buoyant, but as panicked as he was, anything could have happened. It could have been tragic. Despite my attempts to calm him, he was hyperventilating as I swam the side-stroke. Boy, was he glad to get his feet on land. Had he drowned or had a heart attack, I don't know what we would have done. We probably would have had to stay until someone from the States came down to investigate and take his body back. Emotionally, it certainly would have affected us, his fellow workers and relatives.

Out of supplies, and having done everything there was to do there, we were anxious to make the last leg of our trip. Clark and Yvette were heading back to Texas. Paul and Marilyn decided they were ready to get back to the States too, so we waved goodbye to them as we pulled anchor. On a clear breezy morning, they rounded the point on their way north, and we steered southwest toward the Bay Islands.

7/6/78
We headed out at 6:30 for Roatán. The day was beautiful and we sailed under main alone as the wind

was at our backs. I took numerous sights of the sun and a couple of Venus. A shark hit and robbed our lure, but that was the only action fishing. A little cockpit sex to pass the time.

The night like the day was free of squalls much to our relief as we could see lightning all around. Steered 240 degrees the whole way.

Not long after daybreak we sighted the mountains of Bonaca, which the locals call Guanaja.

We could tell by our progress that we were going to have a hard time getting all the way to Coxen's Hole before dark to clear Customs, so we decided to slip into Port Royal through an opening in the coral reef alongside Fort Cay and spend the night illegally. Not only are the Bay Islands implausibly picturesque, we were sailing over and anchoring on hallowed sea bottom. Among many others, the sailing ships of Christopher Columbus, Conquistador Hernando Cortéz and later Captain Henry Morgan had all sailed and anchored right where we were. They navigated by the same stars and saw the same mountains coming out of the clearest water one could imagine. These small anchorages were a refuge for the explorers, conquistadores and buccaneers – places where sailors could restock provisions, gather produce and slaughter wild pigs.

When Christopher Columbus discovered the Bay Islands on July 30, 1502, they were populated by Paya or Pech Indians, depending on the source, that were related to the Maya. Though no grand temples or sophisticated stelae were built like the ones in the great cities of Copán, the ceramic artifacts of Roatán, called "yabba ding dings," suggest cultural ties. Throughout the tumultuous years of alternating Spanish and British occupation, both sides left sunken ships, rum bottles, cannon, cannon balls, swords and other litter scattered among the yabba ding dings. There were still historical pieces in the brush, on the beaches, and under water when we got there.

The Spanish ruled the Bay Islands from the time Columbus found them noting that the natives, "lived on a white grain from which they make a fine bread and the most perfect beer."[4]

Other than a few houses on the hill overlooking Port Royal and the dock in the corner being built by Rusty (who would soon be hacked to death with a machete by a pissed off worker), the topography wouldn't have looked much different than it had hundreds of years ago, although there was probably a lot more action back then – campfires on the beach, drunken sailors, pigs roasting and un-Christian behavior. We rowed Royal Irish Ralph in where he was happy to be running along the shore where so much had taken place.

---

[4] William V. Davidson, <u>Historical Geography of the Bay Islands, Honduras, 1999.</u>

12

THE BAY ISLANDS

7/8/78

Up before 5:00 am and underway about 5:30 as we waited out a squall then motor-sailed for Coxen Hole to check in. We observed French Harbour and Oak Ridge from about four miles out before dropping hook at 10:00 am.

We were hailed to a dock where six soldiers stomped aboard for some fifteen minutes. We then went to the Port Captain's office and watched him put stamps on our visas, then to the ship's agent with whom I was required to deal. The harbor officials didn't overcharge, but they made us hire an agent who overcharged and then slipped them part of the "fee," which amounted to:

$4 per passport

$20 for entrance papers and cruising permit

$10 for salida

$38 total

of which I paid $28 and $3 to two guys to tie us up at the dock.

WE DIDN'T LIKE THE SOLDIERS in military boots rummaging through our personal belongings. There was no way to keep an eye on them all as they swarmed, but there wasn't a damned thing we could do about it other than complain in the journal. In their defense, nothing was ever taken even though they didn't appear very well off – youngsters, really.

Having been out of communication with civilization for weeks, the first thing we needed to do was let our families know that we were alive and had arrived safely. The only place on the island capable of making an international call was a run-down, one-room adobe shack that was *the* telephone company located on the highest hill in the middle of town.

On our first attempt we were told to wait until after 1:30 in the afternoon as the reception was better. In the Bay Islands, there were very few business phones and fewer private lines – no pay phones. All in all there weren't but about 25 lines on the entire 37-mile-long island, and they all had to go through the house on the hill. Residents generally used VHF radios for local calls and single side band radio for international communication. The only way to get there was to climb up a steep dirt path that always left us a little winded when we reached the top.

Once inside we discovered that *the* Roatán telephone company was a vintage 1920s termite infested switchboard that was staffed by one female operator. On the desk part, that was approximately two-and-a-half feet wide, there were male jacks attached to wires that could be pulled out and plugged into female sockets. A hand crank on the right side generated the electricity necessary to ring the phone on the other end of the line. Our calls were always "por cobrar" (collect).

"La Cieba! La Cieba! La Cieba!" the lady shouted into the horn shaped transmitter that was set on the desk so she could talk while she cranked, "Conteste! Conteste! Conteste!" Answer! Answer! Answer!

Sometimes it worked and sometimes it didn't. If we could get hold of La Cieba, 30 miles away on the mainland, the call would be routed through Tegucigalpa and then on to Texas and Missouri. The calls never went through quickly. More often than not, it took hours, but there was always a pleasant breeze and a panoramic view of Coxen's Hole as we read worn paperbacks that had been passed around or wrote letters. Throughout Central America mail was reliable and relatively fast as long as it was sent first class. Writing to friends and relatives had become a major source of entertainment for us. Our parents had especially enjoyed our lengthy correspondence from the time our journey began.

There were several reasons why we decided to come to the Bay Islands. Foremost, surrounded by the second largest barrier reef, we'd been told how spectacular they are. Complementing the physical beauty was a large contingent of colorful English speaking blacks and whites whose fathers and mothers had been on the islands since the early days of buccaneering and slave trading. The mix also included the Spanish-speaking sector creating an interesting blend. We would soon learn that typically, whites weren't good at Spanish and the Spaniards, as they were called, were not good at English. Most blacks were bilingual. All who spoke English had a lilting accent that pronounced the letter "v" like "we." If you were wery, wery bad you might get WeD.

Not only were the Bay Islands remote and enchanting, there was talk within the ex-pat sailing grapevine of gringo opportunity. Rumor had it that Caribbean Sailing Yachts, CSY, was soon going to open a large charter operation and that they needed experienced nautical personnel to maintain and supply their incoming fleet.

There really weren't that many of us sailing around Central America. When we arrived in the Bay Islands, there were maybe four or five sailboats passing through. It varied, but even if cruising people hadn't met us personally, they most likely had heard about a couple who built their boat in Costa Rica. This is the reason Tim Short, an English yachtsman who was in charge of this new corporate undertaking that was to have a luxury hotel and dozens of forty-four foot charter sailboats, was aware of and took interest in our arrival.

Ran aground getting away from the dock, which I'm sure cleaned the barnacles from the keel. Went to a dock Tim had secured for us.

We looked around and had a beer as the telephone reception wouldn't be good until later in the afternoon.

After repeated failures, the hand crank rang La Cieba who called Tegucigalpa who contacted the overseas operator.

The whole place including the switchboard had been worked over by termites. Helen talked to Jane and Tom, and I talked to Mom and Bill who want to come down around the first of August. I will check things out and call in a week.

Returned and talked with Tim for a while as he looked over our boat. Then had a beer with his wife and got the lowdown on CSY. They would be great to work for, and they need me. I hope we get together.

That evening Tim took us to Brick Bay, the future home of CSY, and then to French Harbour for dinner overlooking the water at the Buccaneer Inn, owned by Guido, a loony Italian Nazi. German WWII memorabilia decorated a wall near the entrance.

Feeling us out, Tim asked us about our experiences and what our future plans might be. He hinted that I might fit in when the project was a little farther along. We were excited, especially since he paid for dinner. But before we did anything business wise, we needed to explore French Harbour and Oak Ridge, the other main towns.

Oak Ridge had a population of about 500. There was one road coming into town that dead-ended at the shrimp processing plant, pretty much the economic center of town where I bought five pounds of broken jumbos for $7.50. The town itself is built around a horseshoe shaped estuary, and the only way people got from one place to another was by boat or by walking on the path that went all the way around, about half a mile. Most homes were built on stilts with piers extending into the deeper water so shrimp boats could tie up when they weren't at sea.

Having been told that Harvey and Bunnie, two expatriates who had a house overlooking the entrance, often allowed boaters who were passing through to tie up to their dock, we anchored and rowed over to introduce ourselves. They invited us to stay, which made things much easier for Ralph. Fresh water was in short supply so when we went to the bathroom in their house we were told, "In the land of fun and sun, we don't flush for number one."

After a couple of days, we cast off and sailed to French Harbour for the first time.

7/17/78
Cash on hand:

Traveler's checks	*$400.00*	
Cash Ł15 (lempira)	*7.50*	
Fuel and ice Ł33	*-16.50*	
	Total $391.00	

This was, for us, a relatively healthy amount, and we would later brag that we arrived with $400 and left a year later with that same amount.

After taking time to learn our way around, we got our first paying job working for Ed and Sally who owned the *Cajun Queen*, a customized shrimp boat with large cabins and a walk around engine room that had both a washer and a dryer. On *La Dulce* we washed our clothes in a bucket using a toilet plunger (exclusively for clothes) to agitate the salt water and soap. Then, after rinsing with fresh water they were hung out to dry on our lifelines.

Ed, a bear of a man with a big belly and shaved head, was a hustler who had made his money in Louisiana. Sally, petite and mild-mannered with a deliberate way of speaking, was a sweetheart most of the time. The *Queen* was tied up to Seth Arch's dock in French Harbour next to the haul-out and needed some sanding, caulking and painting, which we were eager to do. For the next month, as we got to know people, we settled into a moderate working schedule.

8/19/78
Got going and worked two hours on the Queen's *starboard side. Took the cayuga they have on board from the San Blas (chief's ulu) to the store on the other side. On the way back a bit of water came in. We had no bailer. Soon some more water came in, and I jumped overboard to try to keep Helen from going over but she did and so did the groceries. John came out and gave me a bailer and took Helen and the soggy groceries back.*

Helen wasn't wearing a bra, and I could see that all eyes were on her soaking wet T-shirt revealing in detail two very pretty breasts that she selfishly, and unsuccessfully, did her best to cover as she returned in the Whaler motorboat.

8/22/78
We worked on the transom until it rained. We retired to our boat for the afternoon. Played long at the patio with Bob and his harmonica and then ate jambalaya on the Queen. *Their barge sunk.*

Up until Ralph's loss of appetite, he had been having a good time in Roatán where everyone liked him. Actually, he was still having fun but losing weight. Seth had let us tie up to the dock on First Cay so Ralph was able to gallivant around, swim and sleep in the cool shade underneath a hauled out shrimper. We were worried that he wasn't eating enough. This had happened before when he had parasites so Helen took a stool sample and flew to La Cieba on the daily DC-3 flight. She returned with medicine that we thought would take care of it. When it didn't, we sailed to Oak Ridge to meet with a retired U.S. physician who had a small clinic that he opened on Wednesdays.

8/23/78
Took Ralph to Dr. Duster. He said in so many words that Ralph was done for and had heartworms. I said he would go to the U.S., and he said it was a waste of time.

Two of the doctor's dogs had died from heartworms and he had dissected them afterwards graphically describing what he had found. Naturally, we were terribly upset as Ralph was our surrogate child who had been with us through so much over the past eight years. He was famous and everyone was upset when they heard the news.

We immediately made our way back to Coxen's Hole where Helen called her parents. They checked with a vet who said there was a slight chance he could save him but treatment would have to start immediately.

The very next day:

8/24/78
Built Ralph a cage to go on the airline.

8/25/78
Up at 4:00 so we could visit more before she left. Got her on the plane at 8:00 am, and I was sad to see them go.

This could have been the last time I would see Ralph, our wonderful red dog.

8/26/78
Got hold of Helen on the ham radio and found she had made it safely with Ralph. They had been to the vet and Ralph had hook and heartworms. The heartworms are serious and the cure dangerous, so we will have to keep our fingers crossed. Also, it takes a full six weeks so she will have to leave him there for a while if he lives.

8/28/78
Finally got through to Helen by phone, and she told me Ralph's most dangerous days would be from now until Wednesday but from there it is a long three week recovery period and that she must stay for it. Then he must remain another three weeks but not so heavy. Talk about depressed. Another bad night's sleep.

8/30/78
Our sixth wedding anniversary. I was really lonesome and wanted Helen with me. Worked all day on the Queen *after moving boat back and forth.*

We got Helen on the ham and found Ralph was still alive and hopefully over the worst. Read and retired depressed. Fixed a special dinner – two pieces of bread, one pear, one can cold beans.

In Roatán avocados are called pears.

9/8/78
Happy Birthday Ben! – 33. I walked most of the way to Coxen's Hole to eat lunch and call Helen. Arrived

around 11:00 and went to the post office to pick up my mail. In the little café overlooking the harbor, had a beer and beefsteak while reading Helen's letters and looking at the photographs. They were great. We are in different worlds and definitely eating different steaks – hers would be a thick, rare tenderloin and mine about 1/4 of an inch thick something or other cooked well and smothered in onions. It took me 2 1/2 hours to get through on the phone, but luckily she was home. Ralph's doing better and other than being apart things are okay.

A week later I heard about the approaching storm from the weather station on Swan Island.

9/15/78
Cleaned boat. It looks as though hurricane Greta is headed this way and I am nervous. Tomorrow will tell. The night was very calm which is not reassuring.

The Cajun Queen *and* Lascar *were the only other foreign boats in French Harbour, and we got together to talk survival strategy on the* Queen.

9/16/78
Woke up around 6:00 and found the entire harbor filled with shrimpers, which left an empty feeling in my stomach. I went over to the Queen *to see what was going on as I still cannot find the spare batteries for the radio. It looks as though it is coming down our alley. Aboard the* Queen *Tiny, Bill, Seth and I talked it over. Seth said he would take me to a place that was as safe as there was so I will go with him.*

I finished up the work on the Queen *and moved my tools back aboard* La Dulce.

I was going to go over for lunch at Dino's but saw Lascar VII *coming around. I knew I should go when they did, so I cranked her up and started to follow running at a high RPM to keep up. It was spooky as seven shrimpers had simultaneously left minutes before. It was a spectacle to see over half of the boats in French Harbour pulling out in unison. We motored past Dino's and old French Harbour for several miles to a small entrance leading to a protected bight.* Lascar *cleared but I ran aground, too far to the starboard. I moved to port and cleared the entrance.*

It was a beautiful night with a full moon.

9/17/78

At dawn getting ready. Put foresails below. Dave came by and behind him were shrimpers, eleven of them trying to get in. I was tense after working like hell, am tied up to four shrimpers. I rowed out the 35- and the 45-pound CQR anchors. It is heading directly for us. The shrimpers are tied to the mangroves, and I am in the center of them all – a rather terrifying place to be.

Took down the boom and lashed it to the cabin. Lashed down top, everything and all lines are out after marrying them all together.

Rowed over and got three lbs. of shrimp they wouldn't let me pay for. Sunk the dinghy and tied her off so she wouldn't hit the hull.

At least I'm well provisioned. My last meal had been canned corn mixed with canned tomato paste, heated and poured over bread. I had bought enough beer, ice and rum to last the storm.

I could receive transmissions over our Zenith Transoceanic radio so I was able to pick up the weather report at the 1:05 pm broadcast from Swan Island. I just had no way of transmitting over the walkie-talkie Bill had loaned me as the batteries were dead, and mine weren't the right size. All of the stores are sold out.

When I first arrived at the secluded bight, *Lascar*, a steel motor yacht, and I were the only ones there. We had tied ourselves off to the mangroves until a parade of eleven shrimpers came steaming in making us re-do everything. I was selfishly a little annoyed, but there wasn't anything I could do about it. How could I tell them they couldn't use the shelter of their own bight with a storm bearing down on us? A second good reason for keeping my mouth shut was no one in their right mind *tells* a shrimper to do anything.

9/18/78

Just received a weather report from Lascar *and it is 55 miles ESE of Granaja at 16.2 degrees latitude and 85.1 degrees longitude. It appears certain it will pass directly over us. The worst around noon. It is moving slowly at 10 knots and winds are expected to be 110 to 140 as it is increasing in strength. If we can hang on today we should be all right. In 2 or 3 hrs. it is expected to be at 16.5 N 86.0 W and as far as I am concerned that is here! The tide is up about 2 to 3 feet and the surf on the tiny section I can see through the bight opening is crashing and blowing 50 feet in the air at times. These islands are going to be blown apart or sunk.*

This was not a rational conclusion – *I* was in danger of being blown apart or sunk, not the islands.

8:30 *The barometer is dropping like crazy 29.5 to 29.1 in about 2 minutes. Wind up to 50 or so – table shakes as I write. The whole boat shudders, and it isn't even here yet. I am tied to the shrimpers and they to the mangroves so our fate is held by those rooty trees.*

The shrimp boats were two-by-two in a semi-circle around me. One would power into the mangroves and another would tie up alongside.

Just heard 60 knot wind – Barometer 28.95 at 8:40 – we seem to be holding, but we will have to hold in twice as bad. I can almost see the barometer move 28.92 at 8:45 –.03 every 5 min. Just had biggest gust.
9:00 Debris everywhere, stern is being picked up and my heart is thumping. Adding comments nervously – one line is so tight it is absolutely straight – must be 80 knots, barometer at 28.8. I honestly don't know if we can stand 6 hrs. of this. The other sailboat is holding. I hope I am in the right spot. I was able to see dinghy when we rolled and it seems to be O.K. The wind is unbelievable.
9:07 Winds of perhaps 100 now. Water blowing through cracks in companionway door.

9:15 – 28.7 and falling. Lascar *stern against shrimper. Made a hot rum. All rather unbelievable. I hope the cleats hold.*

9:35 Wind may be changing. Leaves (quite a few) on boat from surrounding trees. I can open companionway for air and the roar is amazingly loud.

9:45 Wind shifted from NE to SW so here she comes again. Holding on anchor to starboard but have 2 lines to shrimpers also. Lascar *now lashed against shrimper. Anchors must have drug. The time is going very slowly. I wonder what Helen is thinking now. I hope this is over by Thursday. Eye may have passed wouldn't say for sure.*

9:55 Barometer starting to rise.

10:07 Holding on CQR 35 with chain. 28.65 was the bottom on this barometer. Heard two shrimpers talking about Lascar *banging one of the shrimper's hull on the Citizen's Band.*

Swan Island Weather Station – 125 top wind.

Right over Roatán

Weakening under influence of land

16.5 W 86.4 N confirmed on radio

That's where I am!

There is bound to be destruction, and Helen, I am sure is worried absolutely to death. I wish I could tell her I am all right as is the boat.

11:15 Winds may still be 100 and seem to be increasing I hope not for too long. Gusts just take up patches of sea and lift them up.

3:30 Things have really calmed down so I bailed out the dinghy.

6:30 I rowed to Lascar VII. *I went aboard and had a glass of ice tea and said how I would like to tell Helen the boat and I had survived. He said I could on his Single Sideband so we just called her right up.*

I was okay and Ralph would live, but he had to stay in Jefferson City for more treatment. Helen Sr. and Henry agreed to keep him allowing Helen to come back to Roatán. We could get him back with us somehow, but in the meantime he would have to be content riding around with Henry in a golf cart and generally having his way on 1112 Vineyard Square, a dead end street. Helen would soon be coming home.

9/21/78

Cleaned boat one more time and bought five lbs. of shrimp. Earlier I had to move over to First Key on the inside of Lascar. *I scrubbed down the waterline and straightened up. About 11:00 I rowed over to Seth's and started walking to Coxen Hole until a bus came along. I checked mail, which was closed, so I went back to the outdoor place. Drank a beer, had beefsteak and talked to a couple of Texans.*

Helen finally arrived about 5:00 and looked as good as I knew she would. We were happy to see each other in a big way. We came back to the boat and loved and unpacked. Drank wine.

9/22/78

I got up early and went through things while Helen slept. She was really tired. Later I rowed in to buy eggs to go with the canned bacon she had brought. There were none in town so I returned. We cooked the bacon anyway and cleaned up some.

We were so glad to be back together it was sappy.

13

THREE MEN IN A TUB

THERE WAS SOMETHING about the nature of the business of Caribbean Sailing Yachts, my prospective employer, that didn't sit well with those of us who had sailed to Roatán the old-fashioned way. The Bay Islands were hard to get to – up until this point in time. Key West is the closest point of departure from the United States. Though a sailboat would most likely be running with the wind from there before changing to a southerly course after rounding the western tip of Cuba, the Gulf Stream roars through the Florida and Yucatan Straits at up to five knots in the opposite direction. A sailboat could easily be sailing westward and actually be going backward, which had happened to us at Punta Mala on the Pacific side of the canal. The old square rigged galleons had a rough time navigating these relatively narrow passages, and that's why Key West was once the richest per capita town in the United States – the people living on the island looted ships that foundered on the reef. If business was slow, lights were changed to confuse the captain and shouts of, "Wreck ashore" would once again signal a race of shallow draft schooners manned by "wreckers" toward the disabled vessel to salvage the cargo. Many a delicately detailed dress worn by a local girl was originally destined for someone else and more than one silver service was inscribed with initials of a family other than the one using it. A boatload of pianos was said to have greatly enriched Key West's music appreciation when the wrecker gave them away to local families.

Coming from Panamá, as we had, was a lot easier because we were going with the current, on a beam reach, but then again to come from Panamá you had to get there in the first place. The northerly current from Central America is so strong and predictable that one could pull out of Colón in a heavy displacement vessel like a sailboat, close the hatch and go to sleep and in a few days you'd be north of Swan Island. Another two or three days and you would be abreast of Cozumél, and eventually without having to do anything, the boat would float past the Keys and Miami on its way up to New York.

Now, as planned by CSY, anyone with the money could hop on a plane and within a day be anchored next to us wearing Hawaiian shirts and khaki shorts held up with a belt displaying nautical flags, dining on a boat provisioned with lobster and steak. It just didn't seem right. It was too easy, and all of their boats looked exactly alike – cookie cutter sameness with maroon trim.

The name of the first charter boat to arrive was *Insidious*, and that pretty much summed the whole thing up. With very mixed feelings I reluctantly joined the travesty for money.

9/23/78
Tim came by around 11:00 am, and we talked about the job. I said $1,000 per month and accepted $800 with

plane tickets for us both to the States and medical insurance.

And so it began and not unpleasantly as our first task was for four of us to take a cruise to Utila on one of their boats to check out the westernmost island and draw a navigational chart to help CSY yachtsmen find their way into the harbor, avoiding a big unmarked coral head. After an uneventful, picture-perfect sail, we arrived around 1:00 in the afternoon. While the others wandered off in different directions, I watched a local baseball game and then headed to the Bucket of Blood Bar where I had a beer with a good-sized woman who had just smacked her husband upside the head hard with her fist. I was afraid to be anything other than sympathetic to her and, after hearing the story with a little spittle thrown in, was persuaded that even though she had been drinking, he deserved what he got.

Back at Brick Bay, my next assignment was to work with a crew to get the first boats ready for their inaugural charter. Helen, the photographer and artist, was commissioned to make a large plywood map that would be used to brief the incoming sailors before sending them off on their own.

The first foreboding hint of the dark side of the beast I had gotten myself involved with came when I told Tim that it would be a good move to hire Bob, a carpenter I knew who lived in French Harbour, to help us meet our schedule as we were falling behind. Tim agreed and said he could afford $400 per month. As directed, I personally offered Bob the job for that amount, and he accepted.

10/27/78

Got everyone working on provisioning Insidious *and getting it cleaned up. Bob had come by and had begun work when Tim, the commander and chief, arrived. He talked to Bob and pulled a real cheap shot by chinching him down from $400 to $300 per month – the former figure was the one we had previously agreed upon. When I found out I threw a fit and called CSY the cheapest bastards and threatened to quit if Bob didn't get the $400. Tim said he would give him a choice of $300 with health insurance or $400 without and then scared him into the lower figure. Tim comes on with this CSY is employing you like it is doing some great favor.*

I hadn't a clue what health insurance he was talking about. There wasn't a hospital on Roatán or any other healthcare facility other than Dr. Duster on Wednesday afternoons. There must have been some practitioners of some sort on the islands, but we didn't know about them. On the mainland, healthcare was free for citizens and cheap for residents.

10/30/78

The dinghies and a good part of the goods arrived from the Hyber Star *on a dump truck. Tim and I visited Seth and talked to him about making more ladders.*

CSY, in order to save money on shipping, sent the dinghies from the States stacked one on top of another without seats. The good news was that, due to my knowledge of fiberglass, I was about to become a "jefe" again. My job was to build the molds, lay up the fiberglass seats and install them in each dinghy.

Nobody likes to be around fiberglass, so Romeo, Bob and I were left alone in the small shop where we began working. We, who would soon call ourselves "three men in a tub," tried to make the job as entertaining as possible by listening to soap operas on Radio Roatán and joking around in general. From the outside, it sounded as though we were having too much fun inside the cramped little building, and this became a point of contention between Tim and me.

This is how our name came about. When I first started working for CSY we anchored in Brick Bay, but it wasn't nearly as nice as French Harbour where Romeo and Bob lived so I joined them going back and forth to work in one of CSY's dinghies. With the three of us sitting on milk crates putt-putting, the unfinished hull did resemble a tub. Here again our good-naturedness was not welcome. Tim just didn't think we were serious enough about this most serious business. But even he couldn't dispute that we were making good progress in the fiberglass department. The dinghies would be ready ahead of time for the first wave of charters.

11/19/78

Waiting to be picked up by Bob and Romeo. They were late because Lou had locked up the motor. When we got there, Romeo and I varnished the Daphine II, *which was still a mess, but we got it varnished and somehow it looked good. Barely beat the rain to Louis's where we had several bottles of beer.*

Helen was anxious for me to return to the boat to hear the news. Ralph is OK with no more heartworms and only has to take the preventative medicine for the rest of his life.

What a tremendous relief.

The cloud over Ralph's life had lifted, but soon real clouds began gathering. I had never experienced rains in biblical proportions like those that came from the skies the same afternoon we received the good news about our dog. For fourteen days the sun never did break through the low, dark clouds. The work areas and the dirt area where the hotel would someday be were nothing but red mud. There was too much moisture in the air to do glass work so we salaried employees were laid off until it finally let up two weeks later. In the meantime, everything was damp. Rowing over to French Harbour from First Key in our foul weather jackets to get supplies, our shorts still got wet. We would have to wring them out and hang them down below near one of the kerosene lamps where they never completely dried.

When the sun did break through, everyone came out of their houses with smiles on their faces as they hung out laundry. It was truly a time for Thanksgiving, which was just a few days away.

11/22/78

Romeo returned, and we went for a turkey – we got one, a U.S. 15 pounder. I was amazed. There will be a big party on our boat tomorrow!

We ate out at the Buccaneer and saw Tim with a friend and his wife who loves martinis that she calls drunk olives. He was a little standoffish, but I didn't think much of it.

11/24/78
Thanksgiving! I helped clean and do some things in preparation for the party. At 12:30 the turkey went in, and it cooked beautifully in our Paul E. Luke oven. We rowed to Jackson's for ice and to the store where we talked to the Sandpipers and sort of invited them. They still feel sick from the dengue fever.

We returned and several of us were relaxing with a drink in the cockpit when Tim surprised me. He came up in one of my dinghies. I asked him aboard which he refused and then told me that he had some bad news. He handed me my check and a week's severance pay. He said (and I let him spit it out) that we just had different philosophies and that neither was right or wrong. He just felt it wasn't working. He said he hated dragging things out and that I could think about it and come hit him Monday or we could talk it over. I told him I had been planning to quit in order to work on Skookum, a wood Alden Schooner, and that I appreciated his frankness. We agreed I had made some positive contributions before he powered off into the sunset.

It made Helen mad that I hadn't quit first, but I didn't care as long as I was free. John Brady, Harold, Romeo, Giovanni, Reid, Molly and Bob – we all had a big time and the turkey was unbelievably good. I played a little.

11/24/78

Motored over to French Key and John's. They came by our boat later, and we went to Dino's for a couple. I saw Reid and he had talked to the people in Houston. We're hired at $6 an hour, up to $320 per week.

Working for CSY was now a thing of the past, but it was not forgotten. I would eventually write two songs based on the experience:

> Just got fired and I'm proud of it
> Get fired again, no doubt about it
> The boss and I sometimes we don't see eye to eye
> I was working in that awful fiberglass
> When the molds were finished they fired my ass
> CSY and I we didn't see eye to eye
> They fired me on Thanksgiving Day
> Said we were going our separate ways....
>
>   - "Just Got Fired"

And:

> Ben, why you workin' so hard?
> Workin' while I'm singing a song
> Workin's always going be here
> Someday you're going to be gone

The latter, was inspired by Compa, the CSY dump truck driver. He was playing his guitar waiting for his next assignment when he asked me, "Ben, why you workin' so hard?" On the Island of Roatán, Compa was a legend among men and a no-good-for-nothing among women, who flirted with him anyhow. His wife, though attractive, was seriously bitter about his work habits. After a heated argument over his lack of ambition, he calmly said he needed to go to the store to buy some cigarettes. He didn't come back for over a year. Escaping to New Orleans, he played the guitar there until he became homesick for island breezes, clear water and the coconut trees.

His wife she keeps plenty of cigarettes
She's still just as mean as can be

- "Ben, Why You Workin' So Hard"

Romeo would be the next to leave CSY followed by Bob, but it would not be the last that Tim would hear from the Three Men in a Tub. Romeo's next venture was to open a small restaurant in an unused room with an adjacent covered patio at the lumberyard where we would hang out in the shade overlooking the water and shrimp boat dock. Rowing from First Key to French Harbour, about 150 yards across the channel that cuts through the reef, we always tied up at the lumberyard dock as larger boats rarely tied up there. Romeo, always the businessman, moved in a stove, refrigerator, some tables and chairs and opened up for business a week after he quit CSY. From then on, every Thursday and Saturday night Bob and I were the band and would become French Harbour stars.

12/1/78
It was a big night at The Patio as Romeo took it over. We all had shish kabobs and it was a fun evening. Romeo, who has a glass eye he takes out every now and then as a

joke, was at his absolute best, and I think he will make a go of it.

Skookum was a 70-foot wooden Alden schooner needing major work that Reid Christian and his girlfriend, Molly, had flown in from Texas to do. Working for Reid, a curly haired redhead who, in addition to being skilled, had a wicked sense of humor, as opposed to CSY was the difference between night and day. He and I would become close friends. The work was going to be challenging.

We started by building a workbench on the dock, as it would save time in the long run. But, before any serious construction could begin, Helen and I flew to the States for the first time in three and a half years to see Mom and her new husband, Bill, and to go to Missouri to get good ol' Ralph. As we were passing through Customs in New Orleans, the agent asked how long we had been out of the country. When we told him over three years, all he did was pat the outside of our bags with his hand and say, "Welcome back to the United States."

Ralph was beside himself with joy when he met us at the Jefferson City airport. When it was time to return to Roatán, he uncharacteristically rushed into his homemade crate. We'd missed him, too. Traveling by air with a big bird dog (in a homemade crate) and multiple suitcases loaded with new tools and clothes was a circus. We greatly appreciated the charity, forgiveness and helpfulness from both airline employees and others travelers. Always curious, they were fascinated by our chaos. On the jet headed for Honduras, everyone would look at us when we heard Ralph occasionally bark in the hold below. In the

DC-3, they put the crate right behind our seats in the back of the plane.

The family was whole again with our happy, healthy dog roaming around the Key, fishing or sleeping in the shade. We had a great arrangement with Seth Arch who didn't mind us tying up to the dock for free, using his electricity to do work on other boats because we were doing "yacht" work that he didn't want to do. There were no cars or roads on First Key, only the big shrimp boat haul-out and the generator, which they ran during work hours. Most of the shrimp boats at that time were wood, and we witnessed some major repairs including the replacement of an eighty-foot wood keel approximately twelve inches wide and eighteen inches tall running the length of the boat. These guys were good at shaping them with hand tools including an adz.

We were on the inside of the dock. *Skookum* was on the other so that's where we spent many an hour putting her back together. She'd been through some rough times.

We worked hard daily, but on Thursdays and Saturday nights *stand back* because half of Roatán would converge on Romeo's Patio for music by me and Bobby, who played a mean harmonica, and whoever else would show up. Joe Joe, who would sing bits of Jimmy Rogers' songs while he drank too much, was always one of the first to arrive. His dad had been shot dead in front of him when he was nine-years-old, and he hadn't been right since.

One night, unable to sleep with thoughts of him rattling around in my brain, I got up and wrote my first real song, a ballad:

He's fifty and he looks like seventy
When he was nine I was told
Someone shot his daddy in front of him
From then on he was old, he was old ....

    - "Joe Joe"

I was afraid to play it at first, not wanting to offend him or his friends and family. Roatán approved when I eventually did.

12/28/78
Had a big night at Romeo's back at midnight. Earlier we had worked on Skookum.

12/29/78
Rough day although I managed to work through it. I had to row over for ice with Ralph, and it was so hot I put some in a rag and sucked on it while Ralph licked on a clump I gave him.
A welcome sunset and early to bed evening.

12/30/78
We rowed Molly and Reid over and were having a beer in preparation for Saturday night's festivities when we heard someone say, "It's Ralph. He's swimming across the channel!" We couldn't believe it. There were too many in the dinghy so we had left him behind.

Ralph, who loved the action at the Patio and French Harbour, wasn't about to be left out of the fun. The one being left out was Tim, who couldn't bring himself to join the Three Men in a Tub, and it surely gnawed on him. I was such a big Roatán star, the icehouse refused to take my money and insisted that I take all the ice I wanted for free. The music sessions were the talk of the island and Romeo was raking in enough to begin building a new and nicer restaurant overlooking the water.

In the summer of 2005, when we returned to Roatán to reminisce, I had to revisit Brick Bay, once the home of the now defunct CSY operation. Perhaps it was wrong to feel good about the fact that the venture had failed, but I did. The hotel they had built was run down and the docks were falling apart. On the other hand Romeo and his restaurant are still alive and well. Bob Reiman has a contracting business and continues to record and perform his Roatán music all over the island. Tim would eventually lose his job with CSY and come to Key West for a visit. He found me playing at Two Friends and heard me play, "Just Got Fired" about the French Harbour Thanksgiving Day Massacre. He took it well enough, and we talked about old times for a while before I got on my bike, guitar in hand, and pedaled home to *La Dulce Mujer*.

14

RÍO DULCE AND
THE RUINS

ABOUT EIGHT MONTHS after we arrived in Roatán, after the work on *Skookum* was finally "finished" (if work on an old wood boat is ever finished), Helen and I decided to sail to Guatemala. We had heard a lot about the Río Dulce and wanted to see the ruins of Copán just across the Honduran border.

1/17/79
Sailed back to Oak Ridge from Port Royal and, after looking at a sailboat that had problems, sailed to French Harbour. Rainy morning, beautiful afternoon.

1/21/79
We had a good session playing – the hit of the night was the "Roatán, Utilla, Bicho-Blotch, Bonacca Blues" written by Reid – best line was, "Watch Romeo and your dinero."

This musical parody of the Bay Islands was hilarious. A "bicho" is a sand flea, and they are treacherous almost invisible little things. Worse than mosquitoes, the bite leaves a red blotch that doesn't go away in 15 minutes. The best defense was and still is the circular green coils that sit atop a small metal holder and burn for about an hour. Bichos weren't bad during the day, but come evening they were a fact of life on Roatán.

By this time in our wanderings, we had, through experience, become tougher, bolder, braver and more competent sailors. *La Dulce* was in good working order and had done well against the forces of nature. Equally important, she was comfortable. The fans over our bed and the galley worked as well as we had hoped. Cooking with propane was done on the best stainless steel marine stove made. Our double berth was cozy and surrounded with varnished teak. From our pillows we could look up at the stars through the open forward hatch that funneled the evening breezes. She carried a lot of water and a good amount of fuel. Shaded during the day by our Bimini top, the vinyl covered foam cushions in the cockpit where we sometimes slept were a pleasant three inches thick. In our main cabin there was a table that could seat five and the equivalent of a couch on the other side. An oriental rug added color – a smaller one next to our berth did the same. Kerosene lamps in each cabin gave the teak an amber radiance.

Navigation wise, I was finally up to speed. After some advanced instruction on celestial navigation by another sailor, I learned to take star shots that enabled us to determine our position within approximately a mile by triangulating position lines.

There was no doubt in either of our minds that we liked ports more than oceans, but this was our way of seeing new ports and new places. If anything, the passages in our self-contained, cruising home made the destinations even more special.

The sail to Livingston, Guatemala, was an easy one-nighter with a full moon and the glow on the horizon of Puerto Cortés to the south, making navigation so simple I didn't even need to take sights. The only hassle was going dead downwind which caused a lot of motion. Tired of the roll, we broad reached away from the shore and back again to make the sail more comfortable if a little longer.

3/11/79

We got on a broad reach again. The meals we had were super and breakfast was a good one.

Caught a 15-20 pound tuna. I reeled it in and Helen gaffed it perfectly. It has been so long. I cleaned it and we had fish for lunch.

Decided to anchor in Oxtail Bight rather than try to make Livingston because of the hour and the day. We anchored in three fathoms. I snuck Ralph in. We ate fish and retired early.

The next morning, after bumping across the sandbar at the entrance of the 30-mile long river, we hauled up our Q-flag and launched the dinghy to row to the dock. Customs was on top of a cliff that we climbed and cleared without any hassle for $27. Livingston is a strange little place, more like Jamaica than Guatemala. The population, mostly black Garifuna with their own culture and language, are descendants of slaves that escaped from Puerto Barrio, Belize and other banana plantations.

Accessible only by boat, the town is at the entrance to the Río Dulce, a river that winds its way to Lago Isabál, the lake at the head of the river.

3/12/79
Arrived Livingston at 11:00 in heavy rain that let up for our entrance. The Port Captain was super, and we had absolutely no problems. Bought a case of beer and headed for the RÍO DULCE. The river is beautiful and did not disappoint us in the least.

We motored upriver to the Catamaran Inn, not far from where the river meets the lake. Owned by a gringo couple, it was the only place we could safely leave the boat, allowing us to travel inland. The pirates of old were long gone, but thievery in Central America was something all cruising sailboats had to deal with.

What would make this trip qualify as an all-out adventure would be the arrival of Henry and Helen Sr., who were en route to join us once again. Henry, especially, is quite a presence. When it's, "Up, up and away with HPA (Henry P. Andrae)" look out because it is not going to be dull.

3/14/79
We had cleaned up the boat before going to the hotel bar. Having been assured H & H could not possibly get to the Catamaran on the day they arrived, they did just after we rowed to shore.

The road from Guatemala City ends at a gravel parking lot on the other side of the river. From the hotel we saw them pull up, so we went to the edge of the shore and sent one of the larger dugout canoes across the water to gather and load their gear, including the many things they had brought for us. Looking extremely Anglo and gringo, they made the trip across the span of river to our side where we helped them to the Inn and got them situated in their room.

Our first excursion with them was a trip down and then back up the jungle lined Río Dulce, through the towering canyons and lush vegetation. There is one winding part of the river where you "box" your compass, i.e. it goes around a full 360 degrees.

3/15/79
Started early for Livingston on a rainy morning. Arriving around 11:00, we tied up to the dock.

Helen bought groceries, and we started down the hill for the boat. Henry and I then went a few doors over, across the small haul-out, to see if we could buy some fish. It was then that the day lost its composure. After we bought a snook at $1.10 a pound, Henry cut about 1" out of his head on a low hanging barbed wire so when we walked up to the boat – the wind was picking up as a squall was coming through – blood was everywhere. A patrol boat pulled up that I thought was going to raft up without fenders so we hurriedly cast off and anchored out while I rowed in a chop to get the fish and ice. I didn't bother telling Helen Sr. that there wasn't anyone to give him stitches even if he needed them. My Helen fixed him up with butterfly bandages after shaving a little hair. It wasn't as bad as it looked.

We got back late and ate in the hotel dining room where Henry invited seven people to the boat for lunch the next day. He always pushed it. After the drama in Livingston and a full day of trying to keep things in check, Helen and I were exhausted.

Our next excursion was a road trip to the ancient ruins of Copán. Early, after locking the boat and loading Helen, Helen Sr., Henry, Ralph, me and our suitcases into a big dugout canoe, we crossed the river to where the rental car was parked.

Henry and Helen Sr. have always enjoyed dressing well and, even in the Guatemalan heat, there was no reason why they shouldn't look their best. Henry, wearing a blue striped seersucker sports jacket, beige slacks and casual shoes, was at his dapper best when we water taxied to the other side. But by the time we had the bags in the trunk, Henry had worked up a pretty good sweat and decided at the last minute to take off his sports jacket. He folded it neatly and laid it on the top of the suitcases before closing the trunk. We all piled into the little un-air conditioned Toyota, Henry at the wheel, Helen Sr. riding shotgun, my Helen was in the right rear, and myself in the left rear with Ralph sitting on my lap. Then Henry started looking for the car keys – high and low, on the ground, in the pockets – everywhere until he realized that the only set of keys to the car were in the pocket of the jacket he had just locked in the trunk.

There were no locksmiths. There wasn't even a town nearby, only the Catamaran Inn at the end of the road on the other side of the river. One amused on-looker, who was enjoying us gringos, couldn't contain his curiosity and asked what the problem was. I explained the predicament, and he told me that, "Sí," we had a problem all right.

The question at this point was just how hard, time consuming and expensive the solution was going to be. The worst would be to have to call Guatemala City and find someone who could locate another key and have it driven to us. Based on our experiences in Central America, if this were even possible, it would not be easy or cheap.

The only other alternative was to somehow break into the trunk. With considerable effort I pulled out the back seat and luckily there was only a thick cardboard barrier between the jacket and me. Carefully, sweat pouring down my face, not wanting to mess up the car too much, I pulled down a corner reached in and pulled the jacket out through the small opening. Then after pushing the cardboard back and putting the seat back in, we unlocked the trunk and again placed the jacket carefully over the top of the suitcases.

The first stretch was over a dirt road that would connect with a paved highway that runs from Punta Barrios to Guatemala City. The car was small, the load was heavy, it was hot and the road was rough to the point that every time we hit a pothole Helen Sr. would let out a grunt. Ralph was panting and his bony ass was grinding into my lap as he vigilantly kept watch – the wind coming through the open window blowing his ear into my face.

We were all in better spirits when we reached the paved part of the highway, but after about 20 kilometers of smooth sailing, we had to take a rutted, rougher dirt road to get where we were going. Copán is in Honduras, so about an hour after turning off of the blacktop we came upon a dusty, open-air hut that was manned by two Honduran Customs agents. We had little difficulty getting through and eventually, after a lot of grunting and groaning, hot and dusty, we arrived at the fabled site of one of the largest of the Mayan cities that had gone to ruin centuries earlier.

We checked into a little 12-room hotel on the town square, making a brief visit to the ruins before evening cocktails and dinner at a small restaurant next to the hotel. The town was hopping as it was fiesta weekend so we were probably lucky that there were two rooms available when I'd called the day before for reservations.

Vendor's grills lined the square selling tortillas filled with chicken, goat and beef. Carts selling sweets attracted bees that buzzed around the sugar nonchalantly. There were soaring spirits and lots of drinking as the festival got underway with fireworks and festivities that would go on well past midnight. This was all taking place outside our hotel window that we had to leave open to keep from sweltering.

Henry and I had philosophical differences, and we could argue about any number of things, especially with a snoot full. Drinking was something we both did well. That night, liquored up, we argued at the dinner table about which religion was crueler – Catholic or Mayan. It was pointless. Was it better to burn someone at the stake or cut out their hearts? He was drinking Scotch, and I was chasing tequila with beer. Both Helens were exasperated, bored and wished we would just shut up.

Early to bed, the carnival was still going strong when I woke up around 1:30 am with a bad case of cottonmouth. Needing relief, I put a glass underneath the faucet of the sink – nothing came out. Not a drop. My head hurt and my throat was so dry I could barely swallow. The fiesta wouldn't be over for hours, so I dressed, went out and bought two ice-cold club sodas on the street to wash down some aspirin. We were told the next day that due to leaky faucets the water was always cut off from 1:00 am until 6:00 am. Henry, who claimed he didn't get hangovers, somehow managed to suffer through it without liquids. In the morning we returned for a tour of the grand monuments of the Mayan civilization.

The historical mystery is that, unlike the Aztecs whose civilization was intact when the Spanish arrived, the Mayan cities had already been abandoned. No one seems to know exactly why. Their great cities were already growing over with tropical vegetation some 500 years before Cortez set foot on what would be called New Spain.

It is a mystifying thing that man, creator of all the beautiful and majestic cultural products of his world, should at the same time be the most brutal destroyer. Let a people create palaces of beauty, cities of delight, a cultural world, which would seem to be the supreme objective of human effort, and another people must do its fiendish best to blast it from the earth. Let life become tranquil, happy, abundant in all that is desirable in existence, man rises up to crush it into poverty and utter annihilation.

- Anthropologist,
Edgar L. Hewett

Had Henry and I been more intellectually sober in our discussions of mankind, there are fascinating human traits that we could have delved into that become tweaked by the imagination when viewing a lost civilization like the ancient Mayan. The art, architecture, geometry and engineering that went into these monumental stone structures showed man's ability to create elegance, beauty and majesty – the mathematical and astrological acumen dramatically illustrated by Copan's Hieroglyphic Stairway, their stairway to heaven.

In addition to the artisans who built these temples and carved the hieroglyphic stelae, there were merchants, bureaucrats, politicians, thieves, chieftains, warriors, slaves, manufacturers, farmers, butchers, transporters of goods, musicians, cooks, cleaners, clothiers, entertainers, athletes and ball games ... and of course, heavily in the mix was sex and religion. The Mayans had horrific sacrificial rituals mutilating themselves and others for the glory of God in anticipation of the paradise that awaited them in the afterlife – that or their desire to enlist the deity to favor them in an upcoming military campaign. In addition to slicing people open (women and children included), leaders would cut and pierce their penises and in some cases string their collective dicks together with the help and urging of priests. Women would pierce their tongues, catching the blood on tree bark, which they burned as an offering. These rituals, with the rhythm of intercourse in the background, were complicated by love, lust, attraction, revenge, beauty, money, unfaithfulness, power and procreation. What goes on with the God given equipment between our legs is something religion has shown a great deal of interest in throughout the ages – restraint and sacrifice, in one form or another, being a common theme. Historians generally concur that Mayan priests embraced celibacy, some more successfully than others.

At the height of Mayan glory, there was elaborate costumed pageantry. The spacing of the buildings of the fairground areas inside the perimeters made it easy to envision leaders colorfully dressed in dyed, ornamented clothing wearing headdresses of exotic bird feathers majestically standing above the crowds as throngs performed choreographed ceremonies below.

On our final morning, after spending a last couple of hours at the ruins, it was again time to go, "Up, up and away with H.P.A." None of us had slept well either night with the fiesta going on. Tired and testy, the bags were a little harder to stuff in the trunk as the sun rose. Based on the way Henry and I were being treated by the Helens, there was no doubt they were more than a little tired of listening to us. Henry, undaunted, even after we were all seated inside the warm car, said, "Wait," and raised his right arm and hand the way he always did when inspiration came upon him. He opened the door, got out of the car and went back inside the little hotel while we sweated and waited. About ten minutes later, walking back to the car with a big grin on his face, Henry had two beers in his hands, both for him. The day was just beginning.

The sandy dirt road from Copán back to the blacktop had ruts so deep the bottom of the car often hit, again aggravating Helen Sr.'s back and again making her involuntarily grunt like a female tennis player. I, who had taken over as driver, wasn't going very fast, either. Ralph was now in Helen's lap in the back seat next to her mother who judging from the look on her face wasn't enamored with me, her husband or Ralph.

After what seemed like an eternity, we passed through the Customs outpost and were almost to the paved highway when Henry, riding shotgun, saw a panorama that he simply had to photograph. I pulled the car off to the side of the road as he reached underneath the seat to get our camera. "Must be under here somewhere," he opened the door and got down on one knee to look. We opened the trunk and went through everything – until we finally figured out that Henry had gone into the bar at the hotel with it hanging from his shoulder. Concentrating on the cold beers, he must have left it on the counter. We were going to have to go back and get it.

Having just passed a little restaurante that looked okay even though there were a couple of pigs (clean pigs) outside, we decided that the Helens and Ralph could wait there while Henry and I made the drive back to the hotel. It was about an hour each way.

When we got to the border guards, trying to get out of paying the fee for the crossing, I went inside Customs and told them that my dumb father-in-law had left our camera at Copán and that all we were going to do was go get it and come back. In-laws are a universal problem. The guards laughed as they let us through without paying or stamping our passports. Henry, who knew I was using his name in vain, was amused.

Miracles of miracles, it was behind the bar. The bartender, to Henry's chagrin, told me all about how he had come in for the beers, started talking (no one spoke English so they had no idea what he said) and how he had left the camera on the bar and that it wasn't until we left that he realized it was ours. Happy that we had found it, Henry had one for the road and we were off again. Smiling, Customs waved us through when we showed them the camera.

We'd had a big day, and night, and day, by the time we got to Guatemala City after dark.

3/20/79

No one believed we would ever arrive, but we did. Got a room at the El Dorado and cleaned up. We had a good dinner at the hotel before Kathy and Rob came by. Later we went to their place after saying goodbye to Helen's folks.

A mutual friend had introduced us to Kathy and Rob, and they were extra hospitable, letting us stay in their guest room. After being shown around town and dining out that evening, we were ready to get back to the boat.

3/24/79

Up at 4:45 am to catch a ride with Silvia Segovia, the spaghetti manufacturer in Guatemala. He had a huge jam-packed Chevrolet station wagon, which meant Ralph had to ride the whole way on the floor, awake naturally and irritated he couldn't look out of the window.

Back home, we napped and read all afternoon.

3/25/79

Picked up the bones and split. T-bones that is for Ralph after T-bone night at the Catamaran Inn. We motored about a mile and anchored at Fort San Felipe before taking Ralph in for a good run and some bones. We brought soap with us, knowing he'd be greasy afterwards.

Constructed early in the 16th century to guard and defend Lake Izabal and the warehouses that had been built to store goods entering from or leaving for Spain, Castillo San Felipe de Lara is a stone fortress with terra cotta tiled floors and roofs situated on a man-made island. A small bridge spanning the mote separates it from the mainland. Its mission was to defend against constant attacks by pirates operating in the Gulf of Mexico. Despite the fort's location and imposing architecture, it was not a military success.

It was overrun for the first time in 1595, and as a result, King Philip II of Spain built Sande Tower and added 12 artillery pieces and 12 soldiers. When that tower was destroyed in 1604, Captain Don Pedro de Bustamante built Bustamante Tower. Even with the added fortifications, pirates, including Diego the Mulatto, "Pegleg," Anthony Shirly (the "Adventurous Gentleman"), Careful and William Jackson (who had their base on Roatán), sacked it almost at will. In 1651 it was rebuilt for a third time only to be greatly damaged by buccaneers during the years from 1660 to 1666. Then, in 1672 the ramparts were raised just in time for the 1679 raid by Dutch pirate Jan Zaques, who stole munitions and artillery before setting fire to it. In time it became obsolete and became a part of history. Restored in 1955, only the lone groundskeeper, our red setter, Helen, and I were there to enjoy it at our leisure in 1979.

Anchored out, sitting in the varnished teak cockpit in the shade of the Bimini, we had a terrific panorama of the fort and the coast. On shore we had a wonderful view of *La Dulce* in the same place pirate ships had had to pass to get by the fort's artillery.

It was a very exotic experience for us to be in places like this – on a boat that we cut every single piece of wood to make. Fixing dinner, one of us would be in the galley and the other seated on the top step of the companionway helping prepare whatever we had at the time. Unless it was raining, we ate in the cockpit by the light of our kerosene "anchor light" made of brass with a clear lens. The cabin would be a little hot from the stove by the time we were ready to take our plates outside under the stars.

Helen and I have always enjoyed each other's company and this whole endeavor wouldn't have worked had we not. There were times when we got cabin fever, but at Fort San Felipe, after Helen's parent's visit, we were content to be off by ourselves with our dog. We went over charts, and made some decisions about our future while we were anchored there. The big one was that we weren't ready for the States yet.

15

GOODBYE

AND HELLO

LEAVING GUATEMALA'S RÍO DULCE, after bumping back over the sandbar at the entrance, we took a northerly course to Belize, a truly delightful sail with the eastern trades driving us up a passage protected from the ocean swells by an ancient living reef. We were headed under full sail for the small town of Placencia, south of Belize City.

A pleasant surprise awaited us – a co-operative that sold fresh seafood brought in daily from commercial fishermen. At bargain prices we could get shrimp, lobster and several varieties of fish. Because Placencia is on sand that's so soft it's difficult to walk, narrow cement walkways connected the buildings in the small town without roads.

The seafood co-op wasn't the only thing unexpected. There were a lot of British soldiers that manned bunkers with WW II artillery hidden under camouflaged awnings, protecting the formerly British colony from attack by their neighbor, Guatemala, with whom there was a long running boundary dispute. Where there are soldiers, there are bars, so Helen and I and the folks from two other gringo boats in the harbor had a big first night out.

After a relaxing week in Belize, we followed another boat through fields of large coral heads to the ocean.

4/17/79
Followed Sea Laurel *through reef and headed for Turniff Island. They fell off and it didn't take us long to know they had decided to go to Florida. Started beating to clear Glover Reef at 1:00 pm, heading back to Roatán.*
Rough night with water all over the deck.

4/18/79
Celestial sights told us we had dropped down and needed to tack. It was apparent we had a long way to go. The chop was awful. We had to motor to make headway against the wind and current.
In the afternoon we sighted Roatán.

We really didn't want to spend another night out waiting for sun-up, but Coxen's Hole turned the electricity off at 11:00 pm. Without the town lights it would be impossible to see anything. We were familiar with the channel and felt reasonably certain we could make it if we pressed.

It was white knuckles until we dropped the hook close to a half-sunk rusted freighter in the harbour. Five minutes later everything in town went black except our cabin lights.

Relieved to be back at French Harbour after clearing Customs and making the short sail eastward, Ralph was happily splashing around in the shallows chasing fish when we heard him scream – literally. Holding up one front paw, he was running for us howling in pain. We had no clue what the heck had happened until we found a hole about the size of a 50-cent piece in the armpit of his front leg. It had to have been a stingray's tail that lashed him when he accidentally stepped on it. A doctor from another boat passing through sewed it up.

As idyllic as the Bay Islands appeared, they were not without unexpected danger, heartbreak, intrigue and even murder. The whole island was caught off-guard when "Tiny," a huge man we knew who owned and operated a barge with a crane that could put in pilings for docks, was on his way back from Oak Ridge when the boom came loose and fell on him, "killing him dead." Rusty, with whom I had stayed up late one night playing the guitar, and who seemed like a good guy, was confronted by one of his workers who was drunk and mad at him. With a machete he "chopped him," making his wife a widow in that blood drenched corner of Port Royal that was supposed to be their retirement home.

We almost hit the sunken fuselage of a Cessna airplane as we anchored in Port Royal one afternoon. Two days earlier it had crashed killing both the pilot and the girl he was trying to impress. After taking off from the coral airstrip at Fort Key, saying goodbye to friends, they were hot-dogging with a fly-over when one of the wheels hit the water. Both were dead by the time anyone could get to the wreck that was in about 12 feet of water. We looked down from *La Dulce* at the ghostly aircraft clearly visible with a wing near the surface. Without Tiny, it was going to be hard to raise it from its sunken grave.

In the late 1970s, the Sandinistas were causing trouble in Nicaragua that was deemed a threat to our national and economic interests. Government men from the Central Intelligence Agency were clandestinely in the area and reportedly had even mined some Nicaraguan ports. One U.S. operative, while a husband was away, became "involved" with his wife at their home on Cayos Cochinos (Hog Cay). The cuckold is a savage, mean bird, and it can make a man do things he otherwise wouldn't. The story was all over the islands that the jilted husband came after the CIA agent who almost got himself killed by a super pissed off, humiliated non-Communist. File that one under "D" for divorce with two kids terrified by the way Mommy and Daddy were acting.

Though we had become a part of Roatán, accepted and fairly well-known throughout, as much as we loved it there, we sensed that it was once again time to move on. Romeo's new restaurant was an instant success. Of course, we played for the grand opening, but it was a lot bigger place and harder to work without amplification. It was not going to be the same as the little outdoor patio.

We had spent many a pleasant afternoon and evening at the old place jawing with the captains and crew of the fishing fleet. It had been the scene of the great debate I started one afternoon as we drank Salva Vida, "Life Saver," beers. There are two types of hulls. One is a displacement hull like a full keel sailboat, and the other is a shallow draft hull that gets on top of the water like a speedboat. What I put forth was that there is a hull speed for displacement boats and no matter how much horsepower it has, it physically cannot go faster. That is why a freighter hitting 30 knots cannot tow a sailboat. As it approaches hull speed, a large bow wave and stern wave form a trough that the hull sinks into until the boat goes under and/or the line parts. Most thought my theory couldn't possibly be right. Their argument was: common sense says if you could put a million horsepower in the boat, it would have to go faster. To my delight, three days later it was still a hot topic. Being able to cause that kind of ruckus in under a half hour was something to be proud of.

On July 5, 1979, we cast off on a beautiful sunny morning and watched the mountains we had come to know so well slowly disappear, leaving us surrounded by a deep blue ocean with small white caps that would get bigger as the sun went down and the wind picked up. We were headed north to Cozumel, México.

7/6/79

Another shitty day. A lot of foredeck work. I got a noon shot out of lack of other possibilities. Also took a couple of sun shots. RDF won't work. No stars at all in the evening.

7/7/79

We turned on the motor in the night to make time. We were under staysail and triple reefed main. I got a star sight early that put us east of Cozumel so we headed west and hit Cozumel around 1:00 after a terrific squall that would later be part of a hurricane in the Gulf.

Motored around the island and moored next to Skookum *at the city marina. We also ran into the* Cajun Queen *and a few minutes later* Tauramina *came sailing in. Customs let us wait until Monday to clear so we all went into town for beer.*

Back at the boat we met Mark, who played a good guitar.

Before we made the 90-degree course change to Cozumel, just before the sun's light would obliterate the stars from the heavens, there was a slight break so I quickly took a sight without knowing which star it was. I had become sophisticated enough with celestial that I knew mathematically, using our Nautical Almanac, how to figure out which star it was and draw a line of position that told me it was time to take a left and head west.

Ed and Sally had sold the *Cajun Queen,* but wanted us to do a little touch up work on her before the new owner took over. *Tauramina,* a big, wide beam seventy-foot charter sailboat that had a double-planked mahogany hull and a cockpit large enough to seat twelve, had been rafted up to us in Roatán for a while. This would be the last time we would see her. In the near future, she would be lost off the coast of Honduras after being hit with gale force winds during a severe squall. Blown aground when the engine failed due to bad fuel, Joe was lucky to be rescued by helicopter. All he had left was the wet shirt and pants he was wearing and his cat. When weather permitted, he went back to try to find her and couldn't. She had vanished without a trace, probably sucked into the soft sand of the Mosquito Coast.

7/10/79

We went into town and later had a really nice evening on Joe's Taramina. We played some subdued songs with Mark.

*While at the marina, I shackled our 45-pound CQR to
200 feet of 5/16 BBB galvanized chain I had bought for
next to nothing in Roatán. It changed our lives for the
better as it greatly reduced the chances the anchor would
drag. The first time we used it was off of the pier directly
in front of town in water so crystal clear, it was more like
a swimming pool than the ocean. We could see the anchor
20 feet below even at night if there was a moon.*

*Close to the beach, we could easily row in, pull up the
dinghy, walk across the street and eat at El Portal, an
outdoor place that had the best chicken tostadas covered
with freshly made green hot sauce.*

7/27/79

*Sweated out another weather report and rowed into
town. On the beach we saw a fisherman who had caught
a shark. It was huge and the guy gave us a piece of shark
meat that we made fish gumbo from.*

*A heavy squall hit in the night and we were almost hit
by* Skookum *who had all kinds of trouble. I was up from
1:00 to 4:00 am.*

We were worried about hurricanes as we should have
been in July. Cozumel was not a good place to ride one
out.

Bird dog and a bird.

Helen doing laundry under sail.

Our Cassens & Plath sextant, made in Bremerhaven, Germany, sitting on top of its protective case.

With Helen in Missouri caring for our sick dog, I tied up to shrimpers in anticipation of Hurricane Greta that would pass directly over Roatán.

Helen using a sailmaker's palm to tie off the end of some
line that would be used as a reef point on the mainsail.

Our dinghy, *Dulcita,* really was our car. The oars were hand
carved mahogany and the photo was taken in French Harbour,
Honduras.

Me and my Martin D-28 guitar.

16

FIVE YEARS GONE

WE LEFT ISLA MUJERES, which is north of Cozumel and Cancun, on a splendid hazy morning, with Reid from *Skookum* on board to help us with the passage. After being outdoors much of the time for several years, all of us, Helen included, had a deep tan from the waist up and from the bottom of our shorts down. Our brown hair was bleached blond.

7/30/79
I cleared Mexican Customs – a super pain – while Helen and Reid ran errands. We got off around 10:00 and spent an hour and a half rounding the point. We did get to sail for an hour or so but had to motor the rest of the time. The weather looks good.

A Cuban boat gave us a large snapper, which made a great dinner thanks to Helen.

It was a steel hulled fishing boat from which one of the crewmembers motioned for us to approach them. When we came alongside, he held up a big red snapper that he wouldn't let us pay for. We didn't know much about Cuba other than we weren't supposed to go there. Had we been more aware of the shortages of goods, there were other things we could have given them in addition to hats and t-shirts. All said and done, it was gratifyingly naughty behavior on both our parts as we were surely doing something internationally wrong. They were giving a communist fish to capitalist Americans who readily accepted it and in so doing surely broke some serious laws involving the U.S. embargo that had already been in effect for 19 years in 1979.

8/1/79

Stopped motor to hear weather. Restarted, she would not go into gear. Somehow the transmission had pulled out. We started to break it down and decided against it. We could sail it in. The only problem would be dodging the freighters.

We had to shut the engine off for weather reports because, for some reason, it interfered with radio reception and since August is an active month for hurricanes, this was not a good time for the transmission to crap out. As the boat rolled around becalmed, I went below to see if it was something I could fix. The cables were fine and the lever that should have engaged the transmission was moving the way it should, but no matter what I did the motor wouldn't turn the prop. Contorted, with a flashlight, I came across a crack on the underside of the transmission housing. It wasn't something we could repair as the transmission oil had drained into the bilge. Even if I did get it turning it would burn out quickly. Realistically, the only thing we could do was make the rest of the trip under sail, which was not that big of a deal since we had worked hard at becoming good sailors. We were used to being self-reliant, it's how we thought. That's why we had taught ourselves to do virtually everything, including docking and anchoring, under sail. It would have been impossible to return to México against the current with only light winds. Though the motor wouldn't go into gear, it still ran, enabling us to keep the batteries charged and our running and cabin lights on.

The biggest danger was our ability to maneuver in light air. Sailing pretty slow at about two knots, if a freighter appeared on collision course at night, could we get out of their way fast enough? Reid is a really good guy, and a competent sailor who we were comfortable with when he was alone at the helm.

When we turned the corner from a northerly course to an easterly course into easterly winds, we had to tack back and forth in the Straits, but the current was pushing us along in the right direction as fast or faster than we were sailing so even with light to moderate air, we were making progress.

Coaxing *La Dulce* along, eating fresh fish, it was a pleasant sail. With three of us aboard, we had the luxury of a full four hours off in between two-hour watches. Ralph, the helmsman's constant companion, had adjusted to life a on the boat as much as he ever would. It was comforting, especially at night, to have a good dog to keep us company.

8/2/79
Sailed all day and came up on the light we were looking for. I took a bunch of sun sights.

That night we dodged ships and tacked. We could see Key West on the horizon.

Alone in the cockpit that last night, there was a lot to think about as I rubbed Ralph's ears. Did we even belong in the States, the land of plenty? The rhetorical question my ex-boss had asked me on the way to Puntarenas before our ill-fated sailing adventure with the bitches, was, "So now you're a Costa Rican?"

Soon, with paper towels and plastic grocery bags available everywhere, we wouldn't need our molded egg container that we took to the store with our canvas "tote goat" to carry food in. Five years earlier, Helen and I had left safety for uncertainty and now, were we coming "home"? Having been away for as long as we had, it was impossible not to examine the life we were now returning to – a place where everyone had a car, everyone had shoes, a place where there weren't many colorfully painted houses. There wouldn't be a blue and pink grocery store, or turquoise-painted apartment houses with yellow trim and lots of flowers. I wondered what lay in store for us now that our Costa Rican Adventure was almost over, and we found ourselves in the land of color television.

I was experiencing a total reversal of the apprehension we had at the border crossing from the United States to México at Nogales. I remembered how we felt when we returned from the other side of the border to the Motel 6 where we could see the night manager through the window wearing a neatly pressed pale blue shirt and dark blue tie doing paperwork – how there was a feeling of order inside our room with its bright, white sheet-rock walls and cling-wrapped Styrofoam drinking cups – how, in English, at the side of the entrance to our room, there was a plan detailing how we should exit the building in case of fire – how the price of the room and consumer protection laws were neatly posted behind Plexiglas screwed into the metal door.

Now these had become exactly the things I was afraid of – homogenized chain stores, chain restaurants and fast food. Helen and I had been meandering for years – singing, sailing, doing manual labor, drinking cheap liquor. We had become accustomed to the smell of central markets. We were used to foreign tap water and liked hole-in-the-wall bars and restaurants.

We could always go back I reassured myself as I decided it was time to make a tack from a northeasterly course to a southeasterly course. The evening celestial sights had been good so we knew our position, but our charts lacked detail close to shore. We needed to stay far enough out in the Straits of Florida so as to not even get close to the reef that lay just below the surface running along the Florida Keys.

I felt bad that Reid, who was sleeping in the main cabin below, would have to move because the low side would soon be the high side, but he was tired enough to go back to sleep easily. Helen, in our double berth, wouldn't have to reposition, just adjust.

On August 3, 1979, after being out at sea for five days and nights, we made several close tacks to position ourselves so we could sail north, up the channel. Without more detailed charts, this was the only way we knew for sure we could get to Key West without running aground. That morning, drinking the last of our Tecate beers, it was impossible not to get a little tight in the throat, sailing on a beam reach heeled over nicely as the town got closer and closer.

Passing the Australian pines and red brick Fort Zachary Taylor, we sailed by the old Navy base and Custom House before coming up on a cluster of boats anchored out from the Pier House Resort. Making one pass around that made those on other boats visibly nervous when they realized we were coming in without power, we jibed, passed in between two boats and then dropped off with the current before coming about so we could sail back toward the spot we had chosen. We were a small boat, yet we were a big small boat weighing over 20,000 pounds. The next time around, we started letting the sails out as we slowed to a stop over the place we had decided to drop the anchor. Pushed back by the current, the anchor held us in an open spot not far from the main channel.

As we were dropping our sails, bagging the genoa, tying down and putting on the mainsail cover, the owner of one of the nearby boats rowed over. He told us the holding ground wasn't very good where we were so he and Reid dove down and tied another line to a submerged engine block that was not far from where our anchor had caught.

Then Ralph and I rowed in to get change for a dollar for the pay phone to call Customs. It came as a great relief that I was able to clear so easily, telling only one white lie. When asked where our point of departure had been I said, "New Orleans." Technically, that was true, but it was in a commercial airplane returning with Ralph to our boat that was still in Roatán, Honduras, which had never before been in the United States. The whole saga would have been too complicated to explain, and surely would have caused problems for everyone involved, including potential import duties that might have stirred things up even more. I felt I was doing us all a favor by *not* going into how we had built this 38-foot sailboat in the mountains of Costa Rica, just the two of us.

THE END

Taken from up the mast in Key West, Florida.

EPILOGUE

THE DAY AFTER WE SAILED into the Key West harbor, I was hired to perform at Two Friends, a bar and restaurant, located close to where we were anchored. That first gig led to a sixteen year run as a relatively successful professional musician. The best was a nine-year stint at the Bull and Whistle on Caroline and Duval Street where, in addition to tips and tape sales, my pay was 15% of the register. I wrote and recorded a lot of music while playing there.

Still living on *La Dulce Mujer*, we had our first son, Benjamin Andrae Harrison, who lived aboard for his first five years. During that time we sailed the Bahamas and up the East Coast twice. In 1986 we bought our house and gallery and had our second son, Cole Harrison, in 1990. We still lived aboard while we rehabbed the house, but the day eventually came when we moved to dry land, which was the beginning of the end of our relationship with *La Dulce Mujer*. Though our initial idea was to periodically rent the house and stay on the boat, it simply didn't work out that way.

At the time, the only affordable place to tie up had become the city marina at Garrison Bight and still it was over three hundred dollars a month. Taking her out sailing became less frequent in large part due to the amount of time it took us to get to blue water. From Garrison Bight we had to first round Fleming Key. It would take us almost an hour to get to the point where we could sail to Sand Key and the reef, which took another two hours.

Fishing in the Gulf Stream had become one of our favorite pastimes and our dock slip location was making it much more difficult. We liked to troll along weed lines under sail until we got a mahi mahi on the hook. Then we would back wind the main, leave that fish in the water, and cast for others in the school. On a good day we could bring home fifteen to twenty pounds of fresh fish. Now that we were further away, it took the entire day to do what we had previously been able to do in an afternoon.

With two children it was clear that we couldn't afford her nor were we using her as much as she needed to be used. She wanted our attention, and we were drifting apart. As hard as it would be, we knew we would have to sell her. But before we could do that I needed to do a massive deck repair. I wrote a musical, *Undying Love*, about the true story of Count von Cosel's bizarre love for the terminally ill Elena Hoyos, while I did the work on her. That lead to the book *Undying Love*, which was optioned for a movie that has yet to be made.

Eventually, we found a buyer for *La Dulce Mujer*.

The deal was thirty-five thousand dollars and I would completely redo the bottom as it had had trouble with blisters. That turned into a massive job, too.

People say the happiest two days of your life are when you buy your boat and when you sell it. That was not at all true for us. We cried, feeling somewhat the same way we had felt when we left our little house in Santa Ana where we did most of the construction. We had made the boat. At the same time, it had made us.

As of the year 2014, Harrison Gallery has survived for twenty-eight years for two reasons: first we bought at a good time, but much more importantly, Helen, using the skills she learned working with wood, has made magnificent sculptures.

I'm still playing music, writing and fixing things.

In 2005, a full thirty-one years after we began the drive from California through México and America Centrál on our way to Costa Rica, Helen and I along with our youngest son, Cole, took off on a trek to revisit our past.

In Costa Rica, much to our amazement, the little plywood house in Santa Ana was still there looking as it had when we left. A pretty Tica with her young son graciously let us roam the yard where, once upon a time, *La Dulce Mujer* majestically sat in her cradle patiently waiting for us to get to work each morning. The same mango tree dropped its fruit in the same places and the orange trees still blossomed. The other amazing thing was that the factory where the Cabo Rico 38' originated was still there as was our friend, Dañiel Jiménez, and they were still making sailboats.

Puntarenas looked much the same. So did the Gulfo de Nicoya as we very slowly sailed on an automobile ferry to the spot where the Hacienda Nicoyana aka Joe Hills had once been. Cole couldn't understand why we would spend an entire day to briefly look at a now overgrown inlet, but there were so many memories. From there we were taken about a half mile in a small motorboat to visit our old friends Cece and Dave who had been so gracious while we were in Puntarenas. Their house was close by, and we had some delicious ceviche as we reminisced. Calypso Cruises, which they own and operate, had thrived, coming a long way from when we were there in the 70s.

Leaving from San José, five plane changes and we were back in Roatán, Honduras, staying in a cottage on Half Moon Bay. Many of those we'd known were still there including, Eric and Terry Anderson, who, back when, had befriended us and entertained us at their home in Port Royal.

Three plane changes later we were back home in Key West.

Below deck.

Our double berth.

La Dulce Mujer tied up in Key West behind Turtle Kraals.

Tied up at Dolphin Pier at the Garrison Bight Marina.

Tied up at the old submarine pens at the Truman Annex after it had been abandoned by the Navy.

Acknowledgements

SAN FRANCISCO, CALIFORNIA, where Helen and I moved after we were married, was a wonderful place to live, explore, love and dream of things like building our own sailboat. There's no place like it. It was Helga Walthers who helped us get settled when we arrived.

South of San Francisco, near Los Angeles, lived marine architect, W.I.B. Crealock, who designed the midship cockpit Tiburon 36' that was to be built in Costa Rica and sketched out the 38-foot aft-cockpit version extending the hull by two feet. Our sailboat turned out to be the prototype for a boat that would be named the Cabo Rico 38'. What he had designed proved to be a great sailboat, but perhaps more importantly, when we visited to discuss our planned modifications, he didn't look at us as though we were fools for taking on such an enormous project. He understood.

One of the big instigators in our quest, with whom we became close friends, was San Francisco yacht broker and entrepreneur, Jim Ryley, and his wonderful partner, Donna. They played a leading role in egging us along. Eventually, we followed them down to Costa Rica where they would produce this new blue-water cruiser.

We were not alone building our boat in Costa Rica. We are indebted to "Don" Johnny Schofield, the owner of the factory in San José, where our hull was built and where I would eventually work. He was one of the people who helped us immensely, often behind the scenes.

Jim Ryley's brother, Rick, and Frank Day, the other partners in TransAm Marine were in on it, too, as was Scottie Clark, the shipwright who moved to Costa Rica from California, to oversee the making of the mold and production. He patiently answered our incessant questions about how to do virtually everything as we worked on the design and began the building of *La Dulce Mujer*.

At the factory Dañiel Jimenez, who moved over to the boat factory from the automobile manufacturing side, was a tolerant, smart and benevolent boss. The seventy something workers at the factory were the best. From the beginning Helen and I had total access to the factory, and they soon accepted us as equals. When I was hired by TransAm and FibroTécnica, it was a pleasure to work with them as we navigated the problems of construction. Flying by the seat of our pants, we were all trying to make a really good sailboat, and I think we succeeded.

Later, Dennis Garrett, who took over from me at the factory, and I worked together in designing the Cabo Rico 38'. We became good friends, and he helped us tremendously before and after those frantic days leading up to the launch. Everyone did.

Writing a book is a long process, at least it is for me. First, there is the actual getting it down on paper—then comes the hard labor—editing. Mark Howell, Susan Mesker, Arnold Hermelin, Bud Navero, Woody Allen, Alisha Anisko, and the ever tenacious, Helen, made this a better book.

Thanks to Tom Corcoran, Ketch & Yawl Press and publisher of the trade paperback version of *Undying Love*, for whimsically coming up with the name, *Sailing Down the Mountain, A Costa Rican Adventure*. He's a crime fiction writer with a good eye and ear for how to go about this rather crazy author business.

Guy Clark generously gave us permission to use lyrics from his great song, "Boats to Build," which, I think, helps explain why we set out to do what we did.

Thanks also to my publisher, Shirrel Rhoades, creator of Absolutely Amazing eBooks and The New Atlantian Library. He and his crew do a fantastic job in the evolving book market.

Finally, although chagrined at our idea, Aleen, my mom, and Bill Caudill, her husband really gave us a helping hand while we were building the boat as did Helen's parents, Helen and Henry Andrae. Unfortunately, my dad, Frank Harrison, was not alive to see the completed sailboat, but I'm sure he would have approved of the final product.

La Dulce Mujer under sail.

Still on our shelves today, these books traveled with us long before the Age of the Internet:

Boatbuilding by Howard I. Chapelle
The Circumnavigators by Donald Holm
Voyaging Under Sail by Eric C. Hiscock
Sou'west in Wanderer IV by Eric C. Hiscock
Atlantic Cruise in Wanderer III by Eric C. Hiscock
Cruising Under Sail by Eric C. Hiscock
Self-Steering for Sailing Craft by John S. Letcher, Jr.
Cruising in Seraffyn by Lin and Larry Pardey
Seraffyn's European Adventure by Lin and Larry Pardey
Boatbuilding Manual by Robert M. Steward
The Ocean Sailing Yacht by Donald Street
Fiberglass Kit Boats by Jack Wiley
The Merck Manual of Diagnosis and Therapy,
   the medical bible that tells all about illnesses and cures.

For more of our photos that we couldn't fit in the book, go to www.benharrisonkeywest.com

OTHER WORKS BY BEN HARRISON

Ben's website is benharrisonkeywest.com and he can be reached by email at benharrisonkw@gmail.com.

The website for HARRISON GALLERY is harrison-gallery.com, which is located at 825 White Street, Key West, FL 33040.

Books:

CHARLIE JONES - From California to Corpus Christi, Texas, and Mexico, this fast-paced generational novel follows different characters as they navigate parenting, sex, art and money. Often funny and at times emotional, it's a racy and entertaining ride through their lives. Absolutely Amazing eBooks/The New Atlantian Library

UNDYING LOVE – A darkly humorous non-fiction book about the bizarre Count Carl von Cosel and his unearthly love for the beautiful, but terminally ill, Maria Elena Hoyos. It takes place during the 1930s in Key West. Absolutely Amazing eBooks & Ketch and Yawl Publishing (trade paperback)

OFFICIAL VISIT - A book about college and professional baseball recruiting, which Ben and his son went through. Author House (trade paperback)

Ben's books can be purchased on *Amazon.*

Music:

KEY WEST, A MUSICAL TOUR ABOUT TOWN - Chronicles the foibles of the characters, past and present, of the quirky island of Key West.

DUVAL YEARS - A three CD collection of music written and recorded during Ben's years as a regular performer on Key West's famed Duval Street.

ERIN ELKINS and BEN HARRISON - Ben shares the vocals on these original country/jazzy compositions with Erin Elkins, a Key West girl currently performing in New York City.

AIR SUNSHINE - A musical journey back to the time in Key West when "there were five digit phone numbers, dogs without leashes, bars without TVs, and silver airplanes in the clear blue sky." Included is a song about Bettie Page, who lived in Key West for two years.

Ben's music can be purchased on *Amazon, iTunes,* and *CD Baby.*

Musicals:

KEY WEST, A MUSICAL TOUR ABOUT TOWN

UNDYING LOVE (book and music by Ben Harrison)

CLOUDS OVER THE SUNSHINE INN - About a fictional chain of hotels that cater to the health-conscious traveler– a comedic parable about getting your just desserts. (book by Ben Harrison and Richard Grusin, music by Ben Harrison)

Thank you for reading.

Please review this book. Reviews help others find Absolutely Amazing Ebooks and inspires us to keep providing these marvelous tales.

If you would like to be put on our email list to receive updates on new releases, contests, and promotions, please go to AbsolutelyAmazingEbooks.com and sign up.